Stories That Heal

Dr. Alexander Loyd

And Contributing Authors

Cover Design by Ravastra Design Studio

Book Project Management by Ed Ernsting

Published and Printed in The United States of America

CONTENTS

INTRODUCTION

All of life revolves around stories. You might say all of life *is* a story. Think about it, you meet someone new and after the pleasantries, the first thing you want to know is, "What's your story?" At the end of the day you come home and hear, "Hi, Honey, how was your day?" And you tell the story. Almost every book, movie, song, or poem you could name tells a story. Every aspect of our lives revolves around them.

Why is that? I think one reason is because the spiritual heart–what psychology calls the subconscious mind–is more than a million times more powerful than your conscious mind. If they are in conflict, the unconscious wins every time. The language of the spiritual heart and unconscious mind is images, usually moving images from our memories. We call these stories.

Stories can heal like magic. Or maybe I should say, the right story can heal like magic. Ancient manuscripts say that when Jesus taught, he always taught using stories, or parables, as he called them. It even emphasizes that by saying he never taught without them. Why? Because stories go directly to the heart.

In those same manuscripts, King Solomon said something which was a turning point in my life, "Guard your heart above everything else, for from it flow all the issues of life." The heart is the story place, the moving picture place. What Solomon is saying–and I've confirmed this with scholars and theologians in the language that Solomon used–is that any and every problem you could ever have in your life comes from the spiritual heart. If you heal it there, you are truly healing it at the source.

About three-thousand years later, Dr. Eric Nessler, a chairman at Southwestern University Medical School and Medical Center, said in an interview that he had finally found the source of all life's problems–the source of illness, disease, depression, and anxiety, the source of unhappiness, the source of health problems, whatever. He calls this source, "cellular memories." That's another way of saying the stories in your heart from your own life, even the parts you can't remember, even down through your ancestry in stories and memories from before your lifetime.

For more than thirty years now I've been trying to help people through counseling, therapy, and energy medicine. Before I stepped away from traditional counseling and therapy, one of the most effective ways I found to help people was called Narrative Therapy. Narrative Therapy is a hidden gem of psychology that few people know exists, but I found it to be the most powerful area of psychology. It simply involves hearing the right story for your problem with an open mind and heart.

Our mind works by association. If I say, "Christmas," or "birthday," what do you think of? If I ask about the wonderful foods or smells of your life, what do you think of? We could do this all day. My question is, are you trying, with your willpower, to think of Christmas trees and birthday cakes and your mother's famous recipe? No, of course not. You can't keep from thinking those things. That's because your mind works by association.

It works that way whether the memory is good or painful. If you say, "first love," or "best vacation," you will start smiling without even realizing you are doing it. If I say negative things like "worst day," or "the person who hurt you the most," it's the same thing in reverse. Your face will tense up, you will start feeling a heaviness in your chest. If you think about it long enough you may get a headache, or even feel a little sick.

Dr. Daniel Amen says that when we remember these stories, the same chemical reactions happen in our brain as when they originally occurred. It's as if they are happening right now. That's because your unconscious mind does not differentiate between what is real and what is imagined. It also doesn't differentiate between past, present, or future. It's directly connected to your survival instinct, treating everything as present-tense reality, 360-degree, raw, surround-sound experience.

The language of the spiritual heart and unconscious mind basically is stories. So the right story will heal.

I remember when the love of my life, my wife Hope, spent twelve years in depression. It was the most painful thing I've ever been through, although it was much more painful for her. The most helpful thing she ever found was a story, written by Catherine Marshall about one of the most painful times of her life. Out of all the counseling, the therapy, the medications, I believe that story helped more than everything else put together.

For years, I've been wanting to put together a book on self-narrative therapy. That's what this book is: stories that almost no one has ever heard before. They're not from celebrities, but from normal, every-day people, including me. We are sharing the stories of our lives in the hope that it will help you heal. I believe it will.

Let me give you a few suggestions before we start. Firstly, I would encourage you to read everything, because we've assembled stories that are very different, trying to make sure that anyone and everyone who reads this book will find at least one or two that will impact them. Don't expect every story to be a home-run healing experience for you, but hold out for the one or two. That's what we were going for.

My second suggestion is that before you read a story, you say a simple little prayer that you will be able to put all of your preconceived notions, beliefs, hopes, and fears aside. Open your mind. Open your heart. Even open the cells of your body to receive the good that this story can do in your spiritual heart and mind and body. For light, for love, for healing, for joy, for peace, for forgiveness, for trust, pray that whatever associations you need from these stories will go straight to your heart, without your fears or anxieties getting in the way. Pray that nothing negative will happen, but only the good, only the positive, only the transformative and healing.

Understand that there is significant pain in a lot of these stories. That's part of life! If there wasn't pain, it would be hard to come up with a single story. What we're looking for is the victory out of pain, the love out of pain, the life that comes from going to a higher place, despite pain and sometimes because of it. Certainly, the story of my wife and I was filled with pain.

Please read and enjoy. Saturate. Don't try to make anything happen, just get out of the way and allow these stories to do their work in you. I believe revelations will come to you, "Oh, wow! That made me think about this, it made me feel that. It made me see this in a different light." Those things can be absolutely miraculous.

I pray for you. I wish God's blessing on you. I wish for light and love and happiness and health, for you and your family. Have a wonderful, blessed day.

CHAPTER 1

LOVE ALWAYS

Dr. Alex Loyd

You never know what's going to happen in advance. How would it have changed my life if I did? Would that thing even still happen?

I woke up on a beautiful Sunday morning in 1993, not having a clue that what was going to happen that day would change my life forever. I was thinking about all the normal things—what am I going to have for breakfast? What am I going to wear today? What's my schedule—how trivial it all seemed at the end of that life-changing day.

At that time Hope and I lived in Chattanooga, Tennessee, where I was working full-time for a non-profit group, working with teenagers and their parents and families. Adolescence is one of the most chaotic times of their life, and also one of their last chances to change before they are out on their own and pretty much programmed for the way they are going to live the rest of their life. That's what excited me about working with them. It's what I'd been doing for the previous seven years, and it's the only thing I had done since graduating from college in 1983.

There were about 150 teenagers in my group. We did all sorts of things together, some fun and some serious. We went on retreats and trips. We camped. We had meetings every week. We talked about life and love and God and school and parents. During the week I met with individual teenagers to work with them one-on-one. It was a wonderful group of kids going through one of the hardest times of life, discovering who they were and what life was all about. I loved working with them.

At the time, we had our own drama group. That was about twenty of the teenagers who would meet weekly and work on little skits that had life lessons. Then we would go to schools, churches and community groups where they would perform. They would do a number of little three-to-six minute skits, all with life lessons, but more fun than a lecture from some boring guy like me. They would perform for other teenage groups, retirement and old-folks' homes, anyone and everyone, really. Of course, the skits about life lessons were always the most impactful to the members of the drama group itself, much more so than to any of their audiences.

This particular group had been together for about a year. It was almost like an extended family, with inside jokes and nicknames and all that sort of thing.

Sundays like this one were different from a weekday. I was spending time with my family and friends and attending a morning church service there in Chattanooga. After lunch, I started making plans to pick up my group and travel about an hour away for the performance that evening.

Mary woke up that same Sunday with all the normal thoughts of a fourteen year-old girl, talking on the phone, enjoying time off from school work, and looking forward to getting with our drama group. She was an integral member, looking forward to an adventure for the day, spending time with us, her close friends, and getting back home late.

As we were going through our day, both Mary and I had an unidentifiable sense that something was different about this day. I found out after the fact that Mary had been acting out-of-character all day. One of the biggest examples was that without being prompted in the least, she cleaned her room up from its normal can't-find-the-floor-with-a-map, teenage girl room until it was immaculate. Both of her parents were shocked. They could not remember a time she had done anything like that.

When she left home to meet the drama group, Mary had gone to each one of her family members, told them that she loved them, and then left. Every one of her family members said they could not remember another time in Mary's life when she had done that. Her typical thing was "I'm out of here. See you later." But not on this day.

The day goes on. The drama group meets in the parking lot. We pile into the bus and head out. Everyone is having a wonderful time. Some people have cokes or tea or coffee or water. Some don't. There is music playing. For the entire hour there are the wonderful, joyful sounds of teenagers having fun. We had several adults with us on that trip, and looking back, I don't think it was an accident that we had two emergency-room nurses along for the ride. It was not unusual for us to have one, but just as often we had no medical personnel of any kind, and I cannot remember another time when we had two. But we did on this trip.

The group we were performing for had a reception where we all got to know each other, then we transitioned to the auditorium for the performance. My group was excited, joyful. They loved doing this. Every time they performed they would chatter all the way home about how the performance had gone, lines that were missed, lines that were improvised, and stumbles over carpets and cords and duct tape. Things like that were all part of the fun, all part of trying to help others and help themselves as well.

But this performance would be different than any performance we'd ever had, and any performance I witnessed in the twenty-four years since.

The curtain rises. The spotlight is on. In fact, I was in the audience holding one of the spotlights as the curtain comes up and the first skit starts.

Mary is the centerpiece of the first skit. As it starts another girl named Janie comes out on stage first and says her line, then it's Mary's turn. She comes out and says her first line. On any other night, the skit proceeds from there for the next six minutes… but not on this night. On this night Mary came out, and said her line perfectly, and then fell over.

Stumbles on stage happen pretty frequently, so it took a few seconds for all of us to realize that something was terribly wrong. Immediately, our two emergency-room nurses were on the stage with Mary, trying to do whatever needed to be done. They quickly assessed that something was seriously wrong. One of the nurses shouted to me to clear the room. We did that, numbly. Our host was apologizing to the audience. Everyone was in shock as they quietly, calmly, prayerfully, filed out of the room. I took our group of teenagers, the drama group, and myself to another room that our host showed us. The two nurses were all over the situation. There was nothing I could do to help.

In less than a minute 9-1-1 had been called. The host group was standing by, waiting to help, but other than that the nurses were alone with Mary. Most of the audience was in the parking lot, praying, talking, upset, alarmed, or literally in shock. In our drama group the effect was much worse. Boys and girls were crying, not "I didn't get my way about something" or "somebody hurt my feelings" crying, but real hysteria, as if their own lives were in danger.

Some of the teenagers were physically unable to speak. Some were asking a million questions. Most just stared at nothing with glassy eyes.

We tried to pass the time together by talking. We prayed. We held hands. We sang songs. We did anything we could think of to help and comfort the members of our group who were almost to the point of hysteria. But we were off our playbook, just trying to pass the minutes, wondering what we should be doing. In one sense the minutes seemed to drag on forever as we waited for news, but in another way it was like they were passing too fast. What we really wanted was to reverse time, to go back to when everything was okay, to just pack up and go home and leave while everyone was still okay. Of course, we knew we couldn't do that.

About an hour later one of the emergency room nurses called me out of the room. She was crying and trying to hide it, probably not wanting to alarm us even worse. She informed me that Mary had died. A beautiful fourteen year-old lady who smiled all the time, who never had a negative word to say, who encouraged everyone, cared about everyone, loved everyone, and tried to help everyone. A daughter.

When I got that news I was not only devastated and out of my element–I felt like I was out of my body, watching myself from somewhere else. I've never had that feeling before or since. I also knew that I had to go back into that room and tell Mary's twenty closest friends that she had died. It was unthinkable, unspeakable, and I was still in shock myself. But it was my job, there was no one else.

I said a little prayer and went back into the room. I have no idea what I said, but over a few minutes I tried as lovingly, as gently, as calmly as possible to share with the other students what had just happened.

The room exploded. People were screaming or crying hysterically. An ambulance had taken Mary to the hospital, so our two nurses were back with us, trying to help me counsel and love those other nineteen teenagers who were now dealing with what, for most of them, has remained the biggest trauma of their entire lives to this day.

We probably stayed another hour to hour and a half. Almost like we thought things might go back to normal if we waited there long enough. We couldn't even put into words what we felt, but we didn't want to leave. Maybe we felt that would be closing the door on an irreparable situation.

But of course, we had to leave. I wept as I drove us home. It was the most silent bus ride in all the ten years I worked with teenagers. Yes, we talked some. We prayed some. We did everything we thought might help, but it felt like we were dying all the way home.

When we arrived in the parking lot, we found that word of Mary's death had spread like lightning through the phone lines. As soon as we parked the bus and opened that door on the Bluebird school bus, we were met by hundreds of parents, counselors, preachers, friends, and neighbors gathered together as if going to a sporting event, but in total, dead silence, without a smile anywhere.

When we stepped off the bus, the crowd enveloped us, hugging us, crying with us, and saying nothing.

Over the next three days came the chore of making arrangements, talking with Mary's parents and family, who were beyond devastation, and in a lot of ways have never recovered. That makes sense to me. The death of a child is probably the most tragic thing that can happen to a parent.

We had the visitation and viewing at the funeral home. I'm told there were more people there than any funeral in living memory. There were people lined up way out the door into the parking lot, waiting to come in and honor the family and their wonderful daughter.

I'd been asked to say a few words at the funeral, and while I was honored to do that, I also really wished that lot could have fallen to someone else. I did not feel in any condition to speak, and couldn't think of anything to say that would really help. But I did get through it. Then we buried her.

A number of important things happened in the aftermath of the burial. The first was a conversation with Mary's best friend, Amy. She came by my office one day not too long after the funeral, and we talked and cried together. I don't remember what we talked about, probably how we both felt numb and like we didn't even want to go on ourselves.

Then Amy shared something that both shocked me and delighted me. She said that when the drama group gathered in the other room after Mary collapsed, She had left the room. She didn't feel like she could stand still, she had to get away and let her emotions out. So she walked out into the parking lot alone. In that parking lot, she recounted, Mary came to her from the sky in non-physical form. Amy shared with me how Mary's living but non-physical form stopped in the air a few feet from her and smiled, how she had been her joyful, fun-loving self, and how she told Amy that she loved her, that she was better than she had ever been, and that she wanted Amy to live her life to the fullest.

That visitation in the parking lot is what allowed Amy to move on from that point in her life. Many people in those kinds of situation get stuck on the trauma and never recover.

That visitation switched this trauma from being life-altering to life-encouraging. Of course, before Amy told her story, she said, "You're going to think I'm absolutely crazy. You're going to think I was having a hallucination. You're going to think this is just the trauma speaking. All I can tell you is it really happened. She really talked to me. She was really there. I saw her. She looked different but also in some ways the same." That was Mary's only visitation. Amy knew Mary had somehow insisted on appearing out of love for her friend, knowing how much pain and trauma her death would cause.

As she told her story, I looked into Amy's eyes, and I was totally convinced that whether she had truly experienced a visitation or not, Amy was not lying. I had gotten pretty good at telling when a teenager was lying. It was my business, you might say. Amy was not lying. She was telling the truth as she experienced it.

I was stuck, in a way. Mary didn't visit me, and while her visitation of Amy was encouraging, I wondered if it had all been in her mind. The mind is unbelievably powerful, especially in situations like this. So I started searching for answers, something that would somehow make some degree of sense of this senseless situation. Somehow, I got the idea to start interviewing people who had near-death experiences. It was absolutely life-changing to me. I've wondered at times whether my research into near-death experiences was the reason I had been a part of that situation? I don't think I ever would have gone there without Mary's tragic death.

What I found was person after person all over the world who had either been legally declared dead, or come close to it. These people had experiences that defied not only the laws of nature, not only logic, but in many cases defied imagination—stuff you couldn't dream up if you tried.

One was from a medical doctor in Chattanooga, a surgeon. He had a gentleman on his table who had been in a terrible accident and died. The trauma team was trying to revive the person, and succeeded a number of times. Here's the interesting part: Every time this person was revived, he would tell the doctor, "Please don't let me die. Every time I die, I go to hell." Obviously, this shocked the doctor. He had heard about people with the more common experience of seeing a bright light and a tunnel, but this person was experiencing the opposite. "Every time I die I go to hell. Don't let me die!"

As it happened, the doctor obeyed that order and saved the gentleman's life. But why did this change my life? Every single person I could find who had a near-death experience totally changed their life. Most of the time, it was 180-degree change. Their friends and family would say, "What has happened to you? You're like a completely different person. You're like someone took you away and put someone else in your body."

In a number of cases the family would struggle to find their equilibrium because the change was so dramatic. But in every case I could find, the change was a positive one, so much so that I wrote a thesis on it a few years later. People who used to be stingy suddenly weren't stingy anymore. In fact, they were not only generous, but overly generous. People who were mean and irritable and hard to get along with became warm and kind and loving. People who were all about money didn't care about money anymore. People who had addictions were suddenly free and clear without even any withdrawal symptoms. It was absolutely remarkable.

There were several take-aways for me. Number one, you never know what is coming. That applies to good, bad, and everything else. You rarely have warning when the critical times in your life come. The only solution to that is to always be ready, to always be in a place where you can say, "I am living the life I believe is right, good, loving, and truthful. I'm living the life I was born to live." Be ready all the time.

Secondly, things that you cannot change will change automatically when confronted with the life after this life. I've counseled with people for more than thirty years, and one of the main things I've learned, which is common knowledge in the field, is that people seldom change. It just doesn't happen. They may make little changes, but they can't make big ones. I wish I had a nickel for every client who's asked me during a session, "Why do I keep repeating the same patterns? Why do I keep doing what I don't want to do and not doing what I do want to do? Every so often I'll have a resolution to change, and I either won't change at all, or it will last for a short time and then change right back. Why can't I live the life that I am meant to live?"

Some of the latest research in biology, chemistry, and physics indicates that we have no free will to significantly change our life. About 99% of people are literally in a brain state where our free will has been taken away. I believe the only way we get it back is when a trauma like Amy's, or a near-death experience causes us to give up on safe or gradual change. It changes people to a place where they don't care what the end result is going to be. They say, "I'm going to walk out on a broken limb. I realize I may fall and kill myself, but I'm not continuing to live this same life over again. That time, for me, could come at any moment, and for better or worse I'm going to live my life in love, joy, peace, humility, generosity, and gratitude.

It's the Scrooge story that Charles Dickens captured in *A Christmas Carol*.

The lesson I took away is that I need to have a near-death experience without actually having a near-death experience. I need to have a near-death experience without real, physical danger. So in my consulting work from then until now, I've always kept that in the back of my mind, that most people cannot make choices that are dramatically different from the choices that they had been making their whole life. But those things can change if something dramatic happens which places my fear of change in perspective against that of living anything less than the best life I can live.

To that end, I developed a technique which I used in counseling some with, for the most part, excellent results. I'm not suggesting you do this, and if you do, please check with a licensed health-care provider first. The idea was to have the client imagine and meditate about their life continuing to go the way it was already going, especially in light of the negative things in their life that they wish they had been able to change. I had them meditate on that never changing, and getting to the end of their life knowing that they lived a compromised life rather than the one they most wanted to live.

I would have my clients focus on that and meditate on it until it made them physically ill–sick at their stomach, headache, a few threw up, etc. The interesting thing to me is that afterward, my clients would frequently be able to make dramatic changes in their lives that they had never been able to make before.

Here's why I think that happens. I had a friend, actually a friend of my wife's. This woman's father had been a three-pack-a-day smoker for fifty years. He had tried to quit probably thirty times in fifty years, experimenting with counseling, hypnosis, patches, everything. Nothing worked. Much later, as a grandfather, he started feeling bad. He went into the hospital and after a few tests, they told him that his lungs were basically black. "You have six months or less to live," they said, "Get your affairs in order." The gentleman went home and did what he had done sixty times a day for the past fifty years. He went out on the back porch and lit up a cigarette to smoke, only this time as soon as he put the cigarette to his lips he threw up, as if the cigarette was rat poison. He tried again a little bit later. Still nauseous, can't smoke. Tries later. End of the story, he physically can't smoke anymore.

Interestingly, he experienced no physical withdrawal from nicotine whatsoever, after three packs a day for fifty years. That's supposed to be impossible.

He goes back to the doctor for the next checkup and to talk about treatments, but finds something unexpected. The doctors are apologizing on top of themselves over and over again. It seems the results of his test were somehow wrong, his lungs haven't got even a speck of cancer. The doctor said, "If you've not gotten anything by now, you probably never will. I guess you can go back home and keep smoking. You're one of those rare people who it doesn't affect." He's overjoyed. Not because of the smoking, but because he's going to be around for his children and grandchildren. He goes home to his back porch, thinking, "Now I can smoke without guilt or fear." He lights up, puts it to his lips, and throws up, convulsing. He tries again later. Same thing.

The end of it is he can no longer smoke. His mind, heart, and spirit have flipped a switch internally, so not only did he not have withdrawal from nicotine, but he physically could not smoke anymore. This story proves that the spirit, mind, and heart, what you might call the subconscious, have unbelievable, life-changing control over every part of our lives.

I believe a miniature version of this story is what happened when I had my clients meditate on continuing their own self-destructive behaviors, allowing them to change in much the same way.

I have two big takeaways from all this. Firstly, you never know how long you have, so you have to be ready all the time. You have to live your life now. Secondly, most people can't change, even if they try. Something dramatic has to happen to cause a shift from living based on end results, based on seeking pleasure and avoiding pain, to living based on love for the people in their life. This is exactly what happened with my friend when he was told he had six months to live, he was thinking about his grandchildren, his children, his life, all the people he loved and cared about. The love from that overcame the fear, the addiction, the withdrawal. It gave him back his free will. This is the power of choosing love without reservations, of saying, "Bring on the pain if it means pain, but I'm totally focused on people that I care about, and living a life of honor and love and joy and peace."

This is the only thing that will trump our inability to have free will.

I try to evaluate that every day now. Am I living by end results, by seeking pleasure and avoiding pain, or am I living life of radical love, regardless of the end results? This is what I'm completely committed to, not sticking my toe in the water. I'm all in no matter what.

If you can ever reach that point, the hypothalamus flips a switch in your brain. You are given your free will back and are able to significantly change your life for the first time.

The year before her death, Mary used to write me little notes all the time. The teenagers and I were always writing little notes to each other. Mary had written me fourteen notes in the year before she died. Every one of them was signed, "Love, Mary," or "I love you, Mary," or something like that.

She wrote me a note right before she died that was different from the other fourteen. This one she signed, "Love always!" That has been my banner, my filter, my North, for the twenty-four years since Mary went on to another place.

I can't wait to see her again. I know that she will hug me with that big, beautiful smile on her face. One of the things I'm going to tell her is how her death gave me life. And not just me, but many of those teenagers who are now adults.

That would be my question as you are reading this. Do some things in your life need to die in order for you to live your best life? If they do, you have a fight ahead of you. These things don't die easily.

I would pray. I would meditate. See if any of this helps you, causes you to think of something about your life, about your situation.

You may be in a place right now where you don't even have the free will to significantly change your life. In my experience this will only change if you commit wholeheartedly to a life of radical love. That must be priorities one, two, and three.

Love always!

About The Author

Dr. Alexander Loyd, best-selling author and founder of the revolutionary Love Code and Healing Codes techniques, helps people live their happiest, healthiest and most successful lives. With a PhD in psychology and ND in naturopathic medicine, Dr. Alex combines proven psychology, medical science, energy medicine, and spiritual principles to help you reduce stress, identify and heal the root causes of emotional and physical problems, and remove negative beliefs and barriers that hold you back from happiness and success. His techniques and practices have helped people all over the world experience whole life healing in their relationships, jobs, bodies, minds and spirits.

Dr. Alex has appeared on ABC, NBC, CBS, FOX and PBS, and his methods have been featured in outlets such as People, Time, USA Today and Oprah.com. Prior to discovering The Healing Codes, he had a private practice as a therapist. He has clients in all 50 states and in 163 countries.

Dr. Alex is passionate about helping people heal and live their happiest and most successful lives. His genuine and accessible communication style helps make complex scientific principles easy to understand and apply, and his methods and tools are easily self-taught and practiced. With a holistic approach to healing the mind, body and spirit, Dr. Alex empowers people to live whole, happy, and healthy lives in peace and love.

CHAPTER 2

GETTING TO KNOW YOU
Hope-Tracey Loyd

Life is hard ... and then you die. This was how I felt all day, every day during a period of deep depression many years ago. I said it so often my sweet husband would cringe when he heard it. Life was too much, too overwhelming, too…too everything. I felt like I couldn't deal with daily life. I just wanted to crawl into bed and cover my head with the quilt.

Reading M. Scott Peck's book, *The Road Less Traveled* was when I really began to understand what is meant by the phrase, "Life is hard." I'd heard the phrase before, but in my mind I was always adding words to it. Life is hard… for those that make poor decisions. Life is hard ... if you don't get a college education. Life is hard ... if you marry someone not well-suited to you. I picked up the book because I didn't understand why my life had become hard. I did things "right," so why-oh-why did life feel so hard? I got my college degree, I married a wonderful guy, so why was I struggling with everything in life? Now, finally, I got the message. Life is hard for everyone in different ways, even when you are a "good" girl, even when you marry a great guy, and even when you get a college degree.

How in the world had I totally failed to understand this for so long? Could it have anything to do with the fact that I felt like a twelve year old girl trapped in a twenty-two year old's body, or that I didn't have the knowledge or life skills to grasp adulthood with both hands and ride the roller coaster of life?

I suspected something was up with me after the birth of our son. Seven years into our marriage and after enduring three miscarriages, we were finally blessed with the most incredible baby boy. I was flying high. I felt like a princess. I couldn't get enough of him. But when our sweet cherub turned the tender age of six months old, my husband lost his job. Hard reality choked its way into my rosy little world. It wasn't out of the blue. Tension had been building for some time. I think the powers that be hated to fire someone expecting their first child, so they waited and gave us some cushion time before the hammer dropped. Before it happened, my husband and I had even been talking about how he might want to go back to school and get his masters in counseling. Maybe this was perfect timing, since we didn't want him working full time and going to school round the clock and missing our child's early formative years.

After my husband was released from his duties, we decided to temporarily move into my hubby's childhood home and live with my widowed father-in-law. We thought we would stay just until we could find somewhere else to live. This way Hubby could immediately start school full time, and I could live my dream of staying home and caring for baby bumpkin. Perfect plan, right? Well, somehow in the next few months, I found myself crying all the time, hiding from my father-in-law, and not wanting to leave the house. I lived in sweats, not cute sweats but old, ugly sweats, and I was so very sad. Finding another place to live on our own never quite seemed to happen. There was never enough time or energy or money. The few times I did venture out to a friend's house, I usually whined to them the entire time about how hard my life was and how it wasn't supposed to be like this. Why did getting out of bed, dressing myself and feeding my son breakfast exhaust me? My friends, bless their sweet hearts, tried to help me, pray with me, and give me advice. Honestly, I'm sure they were sick of my whining and were happy to send me on my way.

I saw psychologists, psychiatrists, counselors, doctors and chiropractors. I took walks, spent time in the sun, and gobbled so many supplements that I was rarely hungry for food. I read the Bible, along with every self-help book I could get my hands on. I prayed and journaled in notebook after notebook. I cared for our son, but when he was napping or playing with his dad, I was wiped out in the recliner. I was so exhausted that even when I had time to sleep, I couldn't. I knew becoming a mother was a difficult transition, but my friends didn't seem to be struggling quite as much as I was.

During the process of trying as many mediums for anti-depression as possible, I took a simple personality test in a book my husband was using in his master degree training as a counselor. Using *The Feeling Good Book,* by Dr. David D. Burns, I took the test and—wait for it—scored in the suicidal range. Now, I didn't think about killing myself all the time, but I did often wish I would die. I didn't wish for a terrible disease, but a quick death, a tragic car crash maybe.

Our main road was very narrow, with lots of large vehicles going too fast. It could happen. It wouldn't take much for a big truck to veer over into my lane (please?) and take me out head on. But usually if I was out and about, my dear son was with me, and I didn't want him to lose his sweet life too. A quick aneurysm, maybe? It wasn't unheard of for a twenty-eight-year-old to have a stroke or heart attack, was it? I knew, *knew* in my heart, that my family would be much better off without me holding them back. I would get sweet relief from all the hard things I was enduring, my husband could remarry a much perkier, happy, fun wife who would be a much better mom to my son, because I didn't have fun like my husband did. Fun to me was a quiet day alone with a book and a cup of tea, or a long walk in the woods alone with my thoughts and prayers. Now that was a fun day I would sign up for! But play dates and amusement parks and terrible animated movies and throwing any kind of ball was work for me. And then I would feel guilty for not enjoying my life and for wishing away my existence.

That test in *The Feeling Good Book* pinpointed much that I knew about myself, but had never been able to put into words. All those crazy ways of thinking perfectly described my inner life — and I hadn't even known how unhealthy they were! Finally, my husband was able to understand what was going through my head! It explained *so* much. I'm not saying I checked the boxes, got my results and was suddenly on the road to recovery. It took much more than that. There were years of unlearning and relearning and feeling at war with my brain. There were so many times when I felt like I had two people in my head talking. Not in the split personality kind of way, more like the angel and devil that sit on opposite shoulders. Two conflicting voices. Only I was just meeting the angel, and I'd been friends with the devil my whole life.

I was raised in a religious home and always loved church and the Bible stories that taught me right and wrong living. I love my Christian heritage even though I misinterpreted many of the teachings. I knew the Bible said that we would have trials in this life. Look at David, killing Goliath as a boy, and with a sling shot no less! Such faith! But why in the world did he think it was a good idea to invite the lonely, beautiful, and very married Bathsheba over for dinner when her husband was off at war? What a mess we are. We all struggle with conflicting thoughts and difficult decisions. But somewhere along the way, I developed a belief that if I did my best to be a very, very, very good girl, the hardest parts of life would not visit upon me. Ha! How sweetly naive.

When I am in need of information, I read. I love to read and research, and once I had discovered *The Feeling Good Book*, which helped me so profoundly, I made it my mission to track down another book and another, and another. Just seeing something in print that I already knew in my heart validated me so much, and gave me the words to understand and explain who I was.

Soon after the cloud of depression began to lift, my husband and I took the Myers Briggs test. It was the next "Aha!" moment in my life. Hello, I'm ISFJ. I learned I was Introverted, which explained why my extroverted friends seemed to enjoy being out and about, scheduling playdates and going to the park and getting together for dinner. It sounded terribly exhausting to me, but for the first time, that was suddenly okay.

I had a dear friend who often brought her son over for play dates. One day she mentioned that she could not stand to be home alone with the children for more than two days a week. She actually had to force herself to stay home, to clean, and do laundry for those two days a week. She made sure to keep the schedule full for the other five days, and panicked if she saw empty space on her calendar. I, on the other hand, panicked if I had to leave the house more than two or three days a week. I needed time at home with my family.

Armed with my new knowledge of introversion, this introvert decided that while her hubby *says* he is an introvert, he is really on the extroverted side of the scale. You can't pigeon hole people quite as easily as you would like. After living with this man for many years, my understanding is that if he and I are both introverted, he would be much closer to the extroverted tipping point, where I would be on the deep end of the introversion scale.

The Myers Briggs also told me I was an "S" for sensing (I focus on the present and concrete) and a "J" for judging (I like a planned and organized approach to life). Guess what my dear husband was? He was an "N" for intuition (focuses on the future and possibilities) and "P" for perceiving (likes a flexible and spontaneous approach to life). Surely that couldn't be a reason for our marital difficulties. If he makes some extra money and starts talking about vacations we can take or new technology we can buy, I think, "Well, after tithe and taxes its only X amount of money that we can actually spend, and Dave Ramsey says we really need an emergency fund in case the car breaks down or the water heater explodes." We were learning so much about each other, and what used to be heated arguments became discussions of how we were knit together differently.

I believe that not understanding who I was before adding the commitment of marriage and parenting really set me up for my trip into depression. Not having the skills to effectively communicate my needs made certain that I would fall flat on my face. The many varied personality tests I took gave me the information on myself and my husband that I needed to make necessary changes.

One thing I did as a recovering depressed mom was join a Cooking Club with eight of my girlfriends from church. We were all mothers with young children who needed and deserved a night out once a month. We took turns hosting and trying new recipes, even though it was less about cooking and more about encouraging. Now, the Introvert in me *rarely* wanted to go, even though I loved and respected these women. But I learned that if I made myself go, even when I didn't want to go, I was always glad I did.

One evening, someone brought up the different personalities represented in Winnie the Pooh. I think someone had read *The Tao of Pooh,* and as young moms we all were *very* familiar with the characters. We went around the table and guessed what the other girls were, and then each would reveal her true Pooh Identity. It was such a fun and enlightening evening, even though I had known these women for years, I was constantly surprised by what they revealed. One of my dearest friends was a reader, a deep thinker, and a poet. I was sure she was an Owl, but she confessed she was truly a Piglet, with great fear that often held her back. Some thought I was a Pooh, who went along with things and made the best of it, when in reality I was a Rabbit, who had definite ideas about the *right* way to do everything and was desperately trying to help everyone else by keeping them in line. It was such a fun evening! When I got home I shared our discussion with my hubby. He and I talked more about the Pooh Theory of personalities, and concluded that I'm Rabbit with a touch of Eeyore, and he is Owl with a large dollop of Tigger.

After a long battle, my depression has been healed through the work my husband does in alternative energy healing. I tried anti-depressants with all their unpleasant side effects, supplements, exercise, prayer, journaling, and counseling. While it all helped a little, there was no complete relief until The Healing Codes.

But depression was only one of the great struggles of my life. One of the other biggies was and is my marriage. During our early years, there was a time when we separated and seriously considered divorce. After a few weeks apart we began some marital counseling and started reading books together on how to have a healthy marriage. One of the first books we read was Gary Chapman's *The Five Love Languages.* So much wonderful, eye-opening information! My love language is "Acts of Service." So I would get my husband's car washed, run errands for him, cook a favorite meal or dessert. He was always buying me gifts that I was supposed to be excited about, but I wasn't. Guess what. His love language was "Gifts."

I should've been excited about the gifts. It was sweet, "it's the thought that counts" and all. But my practical nature was irked when he spent money on something I didn't want, and can you believe he rarely even noticed when I went out of my way to clean his car or bake his favorite cake? I felt like I was always saying "Hey you! Look at the time and hard work I put in to express my love for you!" Can you imagine how exciting it was to learn how we were speaking past one another, only expressing our love in our own languages? For the love of all that is blessed, empty and reload the dishwasher and I'm yours! Wash and vacuum my car? I'm in heaven! For Alex, I learned that a memento of a trip, concert tickets, some little thing he never expected you to remember that he mentioned he liked— these were the things that made him feel loved.

For too long we were trying to love each other with the language that was meaningful to ourselves instead of each other. Remember the verse, "Do unto others as you would have them do unto you?" This was doing unto him so that he might do unto me. I don't have to be like Alex. He doesn't have to be like me. But we do need to honor our differences, which is harder than it sounds when the dishes are piling in the sink and he's still holed up in his office working or watching a movie.

Another helpful book in our early marriage bumps was Gary Smalley's book, *Making Love Last Forever.* It had a wonderful personality test in it relating to animals. The Otter makes everything fun, the Beaver gets things done, the Golden Retriever is a loyal friend, and the Lion is a Strong Leader.

Here was yet another example of how Alex and I were cut from a different cloth. He is the Otter who thinks, "Let's have fun and make the work fun!" I'm a Beaver who thinks, "Let's see how much we can get done! Busy, busy, busy!" When my husband helped with the dishes, he needed loud rock music to make the chore fun, but often by the time he got the music set up, I was done with the dishes and frustrated that he didn't really help. Understanding the differences in how we go about tasks was so helpful.

In *Created to Be His Help Meet,* Debi Pearl identifies three types of men who represent different aspects of God: Mr. Visionary, Mr. Steady, and Mr. Commander. As soon as I read it, I knew I had found something to help me better understand my husband.

I literally ran to the den and said "I HAVE to read you something." I read the description of Mr. Visionary to him, and when I looked up he had tears in his eyes. He said that he had never before heard how he was created so clearly put into words. It was also helpful to further read and understand that I was raised by a Mr. Steady. Yet another high-wattage light bulb went off, and I understood that for too many years I had been expecting a man who was designed to be a Mr. Visionary to behave like a Mr. Steady, because that's what I was used to. Alex couldn't live up to my expectation because he wasn't put together that way.

This understanding of how we were beautifully and purposefully different was life changing for us both.

One of the toughest tests to take was the one my own husband designed when he graduated with his PhD in psychology, *The Healing Code Heart Issues Test*. This is an intense one to take because it shows not only your strengths, but also where you're breaking down in life, where you need to get down to the nitty-gritty and do some hard work.

According to this test, there are two inhibitors to life as you want it. One is Unforgiveness versus Forgiveness. I discovered some Forgiveness Issues I needed to work on that I thought were dealt with, but evidently were not. The other inhibitor is Harmful Actions versus Healthy Self Control. I did better on this one (remember the very, very good girl). But even though I don't go for some of the hardcore harmful actions, I can definitely go overboard on chocolate, caffeine and TV binge watching.

The next section of the Heart Issues tests deals with wrong beliefs. As a recovering depressed person, I still struggled with Joy versus Sadness. No big surprise there. Sometime I really want to smack those Polly Anna types, they can't really be that up! With Peace versus Anxiety, my depressive personality reared its ugly head. I once saw a cartoon on Facebook of a girl with a cape on and a huge "A" on her chest. The blurb said, "Anxiety Girl, able to leap to the worst possible conclusion in a single bound." Yep. Preach.

Alex and I recently celebrated thirty years of marriage. I have no idea how we got to that number so quickly, but we did. Taking several different personality tests and understanding how we are designed was a huge contribution to our personal and marital growth.

You don't know this about me, but I'm an Academy-Award-winning Actress. Well, that's what I tell my family. I haven't officially received the award from the Academy, but if they could see me perform I know they'd be impressed. When we host a party, my friends and family are amazed at how much I enjoy myself. Well, yes and no. I've learned there are times when you must dig deep and find that small, extroverted part of yourself, and not only release her, but fan the flame and let her grow.

I've been known to say I keep all my extroversion in my pinky toe. But I can now pull off a Super Bowl Party of fifty, or an End of the School Year party of about a hundred for my son's Home-school Tutorial. I've learned that I can do this to make memories, after lots of planning, and by taking lots of quiet time for myself before and after. My family knows that I'm willing to host parties (ick) for them, because I love my family and try to honor who they are. My youngest is the most extroverted in the family and loves to have groups over, but he knows I need a heads-up before he arrives with his band or basketball team. My oldest loves to have small, close groups of friends over that stay up all night talking and playing games. But both boys know to keep quiet after I go to bed, because you really don't want to release the monster that shows up when mom doesn't get much sleep.

My family knows that right before a big party, I'm probably going to be in a tizzy no matter how much advance planning I have done, and that my favorite words are, "What can I do to help?" They also know that when the last person leaves, I'm crashing alone with a book or HGTV and a cup of tea. I'm now in recovery mode, do *not* ask one thing of me until I resurface.

Anytime there is conflict I have to stop and breathe. If I take a moment to reflect, I often realize that I'm expecting someone to behave just like me, which would totally be boring since I'm such a homebody who prefers a book and a cup of tea to social interaction. But when we have expectations of others, we are often setting ourselves up for a mighty fall, which may or may not look like a grown woman having a temper tantrum. The minute I think about how something *should* go or how someone *should* respond, I've set up an unacceptable goal where the results will definitely fall short of what I imagined. My hubby calls these, "Joy Killers."

I still have to pause sometimes, and remember that my purpose in life is very different from my husband's purpose. I continue to read books that affirm my special traits. Recently I read the book, *Quiet* by Susan Cain. I cried tears of joy as I read page after page of information perfectly describing me! It felt so good to know I'm not the only introvert out there, and that it is okay to be an introvert in a world that lauds and encourages extroverts.

I'm not a writer and I didn't really want to write a chapter for this book, but my husband encouraged me, insisting that I did have something to say that could be helpful. Sometimes I feel like my journey is my own, and not something to share, considering that I seem to be taking the not-so-scenic route.

The other day, my husband talked to a college friend who had recently discovered the Gary Smalley book with the animal personality inventory, and had a similarly positive experience to ours. When Alex mentioned that we had discovered that book almost thirty years ago, our friends were amazed. They thought it was a new book!

After having this conversation with Alex, I realized that we all need to share what we have learned along the way with those on a similar journey because we don't *know* where they are on that journey. What I've already learned might keep them from getting stuck in the mud trying to do things completely on their own.

Learning more and more about yourself and others, understanding others, especially your family and those you deal with daily is so beneficial to a full life. Growing and learning never ends ... until you die.

About The Author

Hope-Tracey Loyd lives happily in the country hillside of Franklin, Tennessee with her husband, Alex, and sons, Harry and George.

CHAPTER 3

UPON WHICH I STAND
Gabriele Rotter

Vicious, painful and piercing bites ripped through my wrist again and again as blood gushed out. I held on to the twisting, contorting and raging cat as long as I could, but it was a futile effort. I had to let go. The attempt to rescue Snowflake, my husband's runaway cat, had failed. Within 24 hours, my severe wounds landed me in the hospital battling life threatening infection and receiving the first of five rabies shots. I lay there replaying the rather challenging first months of a new marriage.

During recovery at home, my husband, Bill, approached me as I lay resting on a sofa. Staring intently at my dangling bare legs, he looked down and loudly asked, "Why do you have such big feet?" My Cinderella fantasies of a romantic husband comforting me vanished, and my heart sank with Bill's quizzical comment about the size of my feet! Strange as it may seem, his question would prove to be quite profound.

My near fatal attempt at rescuing Snowflake, and Bill's curiously profound question occurred only four months into our marriage. Something happened the moment Bill asked me, "Why do you have such big feet?" As I stood up to answer, it was as though someone spoke *through* me and *to* me. "God knew that I was going to have some heavy loads to bear, so He made sure to bless me with these big feet!" I was stunned by my own answer. Where did those words come from? It was an epiphany that launched me on an amazing journey of transformation, change and healing.

Shattered Fantasies

I got more than I bargained for when I said "yes" to Bill. Living on a ranch with 27 acres meant work, and lots of it! In all fairness, Bill had no idea how much work was involved when he bought the place. Mowing, gardening, weeding, clearing trees, chopping wood, hauling rock, and fence repairs were endless jobs. Adding to the long list of daily routines was the care of two Saint Bernards. Aspen, a giant and most gentle female, was battling bone cancer. Hans, an ever active and uncontrollable male puppy was in desperate need of training. Then there was Snowflake, Bill's sly and sinister Himalayan cat with bad attitude. Care for the ranch and animals fell mostly on my shoulders, as Bill's near miraculous recovery from congestive heart failure two years prior, left him with low energy and some physical limitations. I had lived in the country for years, so it was a natural for me to take on the tasks. Springing into action, I dove into my new life with enthusiasm!

Almost immediately, one misfortune after another began to happen. Aspen's cancer took a turn for the worse as she started losing control of her bodily functions. Bill grew despondent over her rapid decline. Hans became more than we could handle. I had managed to house train him, but his conduct proved to be quite the challenge. Three trainers later, we were still unsuccessful. Between Aspen's loss of control, and Hans' flying hair covering furniture and floors, the house was a constant mess. Working full time and keeping up with mounting daily care and routines was getting hard.

As if I didn't have enough on my plate, only weeks before our wedding, the sum of all my fears arrived at my doorstep–my mother! She and my stepfather, Otto, had moved from out of state to be close to me so I could help them with *their* needs and care. Mom was diabetic and wheelchair bound. My stepfather suffered from a multitude of health issues. I had promised them years earlier that when the time came, I would take care of them. Well, it came all right, as did everything else, all at once!

Suddenly, I was taking care of two households, three adults, three animals, and working full time. It quickly became evident that I couldn't handle the demands of my job *and* tend to the ranch and everyone's needs. So, I voluntarily left my career behind. Within a matter of months, I went from living life as a joyful, independent and successful full time Realtor, to becoming an anxious and stressed newlywed thrust into roles for which I was totally and utterly ill prepared. It was like going from Disney World straight to the nursing home.

A Time Capsule

With Mom and Otto living close by, I felt like I had gone back in time. My mind was constantly reliving the past.

Although filled with some wonderful memories, my childhood years were also filled with drama and trauma. I was completely and utterly terrified of Mom. As a dominant head of the house, she could be anything from glamorous to explosive, and was a master of criticism who ruled with an iron fist. From as early as I can remember, arguments between my parents were intense and occurred frequently. I lived in constant fear of emotional upsets, wishing only for everything to stay peaceful. I dared never say no to anything asked of me, and tried my best in giggly and entertaining ways to bring about laughter and happiness. It was quite the mission for a little girl.

When I was about 10 years old, my Mom put a gun to her head and walked out the front door threatening to kill herself. I remember the scene as vividly today as when it happened years ago. Standing on the front porch screaming at the top of my lungs, I yelled, "Mommy, please, please come back, Mommy please don't go!", as I watched her drive away in the car. I never screamed so hard in my life, nor cried such tears of desperation. The fear I felt was unimaginable, leaving a deep emotional wound, escalating my anxiety.

I leaned heavily on my belief in God and Jesus to give me comfort. In my bedroom was a beautiful wood carved statue of Mother Mary that hung on the wall over the bed. I can't tell you how many times I stood on the side of my bed, leaning in as close as possible to Mother Mary, praying to her, asking for help in my times of need. It gave me great comfort and hope.

Mom had controlled everything and anything I did. I was told what to say, do, think, feel, eat and wear. Never encouraged to express my own thoughts and opinions or make my own personal choices led to me feeling insecure and inadequate. I had a sense of guilt about anything and everything as well. No matter what went wrong, or when tempers flared, I wondered if I might be the cause, or could have done something to prevent it from happening.

So you can imagine what a shock it was to my Mom when, as a senior in college, I fell in love, became engaged and eloped! I felt I had no choice. My engagement and plans for marriage caused Mom to come to the University with the intention of yanking me out of school to bring me back home. Under no circumstance was she going to let me marry this man. My elopement caused a huge crack in our relationship. For years, whenever Mom wrote, she addressed me by maiden name only. After my first son was born, things settled down a bit, and by the time my family expanded with another boy, I felt that perhaps we were on a road to recovery. But Mom's meddling and involvement, coupled with my inability to communicate properly with my husband, led to the demise of my first marriage. Becoming a single Mom and trying to build a life on my own was not what Mom had in mind for me, so I got no emotional support from her. It was the distance in miles separating us that became the saving grace of our relationship. I lived in Kansas, and she lived in Florida, where I grew up.

Sixteen years passed. Mom's occasional visits and phone calls always left me feeling drained of spirit, and laden with guilt in some form or fashion. Living on acreage in the beautiful Kansas countryside made me feel so free and untethered from Mom's control. I thrived on having space around me. Spending time in nature was fuel for my spirit. Each breath of the fresh country air rejuvenated my heart and soul. I had built a successful business in residential real estate, specializing in none other than land, ranches, and country estates. My passion and love for the countryside served me, and others, well.

Again Comes Love, Marriage and Geriatric Care

Then along came Bill, a marriage proposal and the Kansas arrival of meddling Mom and Otto! During our first months together, Mom tried to be her charming best. Otto was basically reclusive and non-social. Bill did anything and everything he could to accommodate Mom and Otto, and I worked overtime trying to be Wonder Woman taking care of everyone's needs. All that space around me didn't seem anywhere near enough. I felt restricted, trapped and stuck. The atmosphere at home changed when Aspen lost her battle with cancer. Bill became somber, having taken her death really hard. Hans, our ever active and increasingly giant puppy helped to mitigate some of Bill's grief. Hans' constant activity and uncontrollable nature created unrest and irritation for both of us.

Suddenly, the "honeymoon" was over. My daily care trips over to Moms morphed from being greeted with hugs and kisses, to the addition of criticism and discontent. No sooner than I walked into her house, I could tell by the look in Mom's eyes that drama was about to begin. If she disapproved of my appearance, there was no hesitation in telling me that she didn't like my hair. Or Mom mentioned my clothes, or that the pants I had on made me look fat, or maybe my lipstick wasn't the right color, or I looked tired.

The list could go on and on. Criticism had never been something I took lightly. Disapproval, condemnation and blame flowed in excess on a daily basis. They remained like daggers in my heart. With more being thrown at me again, feelings of heaviness came to my chest, as anxiety and panic tried to overcome me.

After returning home from daily visits with Mom, if it was a particularly stressful day, I would speak to Bill about what I considered to be Mom's hostile takeover. Yet Bill brushed it off, finding it all rather amusing. I clearly saw that dealing with Mom was going to be *my* battle alone. I had no choice but to deal with it and face it head on. Mom liked Bill, and he knew it, taking delight in her admiration of him. But that delight began to wear off as an emotional tug of war developed between Mom and Bill for my time and attention. Bill became resentful of time spent away from home, feeling neglected. Mom, on the other hand, cried each and every time I got ready to leave her house, wishing that I would spend all day, every day, with her. I was caught in between, feeling guilty and torn about both issues. I became a nervous wreck, as emotional tension kept mounting.

A Turning Point

Then, it happened, Snowflake's brutal and vicious attack. I had rushed myself to the doctor early the morning after the incident, ending up in the emergency room. No one knew about it except Bill. As I lay in the hospital bed alone on Christmas Eve with life-saving medicine flowing through my veins, I finally called Mom. She was worried, wondering why I had not already been in touch with her that day. I was supposed to be home preparing the family dinner! As soon as I heard Mom's voice, I burst into tears, telling her all that had happened. We both cried.

A momentous shift occurred as Mom stepped into a self-designated role as Queen Mother. Furious about what had occurred, she sternly made Bill promise that if ever found again, the malicious cat was to be put away immediately! She took over all preparations for Christmas, and dove into creating a feast fit for Kings, while waiting for her daughter to come home. We celebrated not only Christmas, but also the gift of life. Here was Mom, the one who needed help and care, coming to my rescue and caring for me. I was so grateful that she was close by in my time of need.

Finding Grace

My spiritual life had spiraled to an all-time low during those first strenuous months of my marriage to Bill. Recovery from blood poisoning, having to undergo the series of rabies shots and developing further complications from massive antibiotic therapy made me feel pretty sorry for myself. Struggling emotionally with everything that was happening in my life, I dwelled on frustration, resentment and felt overwhelmed.

What a time for Bill to ask me why I had such big feet! But ask me he did. The impact was sudden and profound. I felt like I was on autopilot with someone else doing the talking *for* me when I answered that God had given me big feet knowing that I was going to have some heavy loads to bear.

Like a roll of thunder and bolt of lightning, the power of my divinely inspired words made an immediate impact.

Bill stopped and asked, "What was that you said again? I need to write that down!" My words brought focus and attention back to what had seen me through some pretty rough times in my life–my faith. It had been sorely lacking, and I needed to do something about it to save myself from drowning in my sea of self-pity. God had given me big feet. It was time for me to truly stand on them.

Mom felt lonely and forlorn sitting by herself with no one to talk to whenever I wasn't around since Otto preferred to sleep most of the day away. Time alone gave her ever scheming and critical mind fuel for depressing and woeful thoughts. So, I decided to take her on special outings with me. A passion we shared was cooking and canning. As the seasons arrived, we visited local U-Pick farms, harvesting vegetables, fruits and berries to our hearts content. Trips were a huge hit, and wonderful relief from the daily stresses of caregiving obligations.

On one particular outing, I had to push Mom on a long gravel road to reach our destination. The gravel was of medium size, making it easy for me to push the wheelchair. I had gotten really good at transporting Mom across just about any terrain, so I built up some speed and was going at a fair pace when all of a sudden, one wheel hit a larger rock. The wheelchair stopped, but Mom didn't! She went flying out of the chair!

"Oh my God" I thought, "What have I done?" In that same split second, I shamefully looked around to see if anyone had witnessed the incident. To think that I had just thrown my mother out of her wheelchair was unforgivable! Landing on the gravel with her hands and knees, Mom started laughing hysterically. I ran to her, bent down and immediately checked to see if and how she was hurt, or even worse. But thank God, all was okay. In fact, she wasn't even bruised. We sat there on the gravel laughing until we cried, at which point, my nerves calmed down and I got the strength to lift Mom back onto her chair. I was so grateful that I *was* lifting her onto her chair and not seeing her carried away by ambulance! All of a sudden, her heavy load didn't feel so heavy after all.

Husband Versus Mother In Law

The problem with spending so much time with Mom was that Bill felt more and more neglected. "Poor me," he would say, "I am the forgotten man." "No one loves me!" Lucky for me, Bill loves to shop. So we made it a point to take Mom shopping with us whenever we could. Better yet, it was a way of spending time with both Bill and Mom. I never knew what might happen, as with Bill's quirky sense of humor and Mom's lack of filter in her speech and actions, anything was possible. Bill had a particular ring tone on his cell phone for each person. The one for my mother was the 1961 hit song "Mother-in-law," sung by Ernie K-Doe. Now, if you haven't heard of it or don't know it, please do look it up on the Internet. Even better, you should listen to the song.

One day, while waiting to checkout at Costco, Bill decided to entertain himself by playing "Mother-in-law" while he, Mom and I waited in a long line. As soon as the music started playing, some guys behind us began laughing while giving thumbs up to Bill. He became an instant hero to many men standing close by. It was an unforgettable moment. My mother never did understand the words that were being sung except for the "mother-in-law" part, and when she did hear them, she gleamed with pride! Oh, if she had only known! Humor always helped Bill to ease any tension.

Would I Have Been As Able?

I often thought about what made Mom the way she was -- her spirit, her drive, her determination and her uber-controlling ways. Reflecting on stories told of Mom and Dad's immigration to the United States, I thought about how they left everything behind in Germany, arriving with only 25 cents in a pocket, a sack full of personal belongings, and two very small children in tow. Mom was in her late 20's, and Dad nearly 50 years old. Filled with hopes and dreams of a bright new future, they endured some exceedingly rough years. But they persevered and prevailed, overcoming numerous hardships while raising two young daughters. I thought of how I would have handled those circumstances. Could I have endured what they did? Compared to what they had gone through in their past, it made my caregiving duties look easy. I felt humbled by the experience of Mom's "need" for me. I had never felt that before.

Countless hours were spent taking Mom to and from doctors and the hospital. Diabetic foot wounds that wouldn't heal led to infection of the bone in her right leg. Amputation became necessary. At 83, Mom made an amazing recovery, and doctors were in awe over her attitude. When phantom pains occurred, Mom would say that she didn't miss her leg at all because it felt like it was still there. Tasks such as bathing, using the facilities and getting dressed became more difficult though. We tried hard going through extensive rehabilitation to use a prosthetic device, but it was of no use. It was simply too painful and difficult for Mom. She remained wheelchair bound.

Of Chicken Soup And Red Hair

Without much warning, gallbladder problems of my own landed me in the hospital for surgery. Bill had driven me there early in the morning, arriving before dawn. Waiting in the dark at the entrance were my mother and Otto. I was in disbelief. Just seeing Mom there brought tears to my eyes. After prepping and before wheeling me into surgery, Mom looked at the surgeon and emphatically said, "Doctor, this is *my* daughter, and I expect you to take very good care of her." He did. And when I opened my eyes in recovery, there was Mom, making sure that all was well. The frightened little girl inside of me was so happy to have her close by, and her presence was comforting. Once again, the caregiver was being cared for.

The day after my surgery, Mom was there again. I was vomiting from the effects of morphine and not doing very well. Seeing this, Mom told me that she was going back home to make me some chicken soup, and would return in a couple of hours. I watched the clock. 3:00 p.m. was the designated time. When Mom and Otto didn't show up right away, I wasn't too concerned, but after an hour and a half passed, I began to worry.

Minutes later, Otto slowly wheeled Mom into my room. I thought I was hallucinating, as Mom's blond hair looked as though it was streaked with red! I asked her to wheel herself to the side of my bed and lean in. She did. To my absolute horror, blood was oozing out of the top of her head, streaming down her hair and face. I yelled out, "What happened!"

Otto spoke up, telling of how the wheelchair had run away while Mom was going down the ramp in the garage. She had fallen out of the chair, skidded across the garage floor on her side and slammed into the spokes of their van wheel with the top of her head. I couldn't believe what I was hearing and seeing!

Mom was sitting in her wheelchair with a pot of chicken soup on her lap, a huge open gash on the top of her head, and blood streaming down her hair and face. I was shocked! I sat up in pain, and immediately summoned for Mom to be rushed to her doctor's office, which by chance, happened to be on the fourth floor of the same hospital. Many stitches and care later, as she was wheeled back to my room, Mom made it a point to say that it was her intention to bring me a pot of chicken soup, and nothing was going to stop her! It was the talk of the hospital for weeks, and a most unforgettable event. "Only Mom," I thought to myself.

Holding Steady And Holding On

With each passing month, Mom's diabetes took a greater toll on her kidneys. By then, we were making weekly and biweekly visits to the hospital for special shots that helped to maintain her kidney function. With so much time being spent there, I felt the need to make our time at the hospital as fun and special as possible. Dressing up on holidays seemed like a good idea, so I bought costumes. One Halloween, we arrived in (good) witches' costumes, dressed in long flowing cloaks and tall pointed hats with spiders, coils and sparkly baubles dangling all around them. Piled high on Mom's lap were decorated boxes filled with candy as well as tins of her heavenly signature cookies. Strolling through the halls, we passed out goodies to all. Nurses anxiously waited in the lab for their special treats. Lavished with hugs and appreciation while undergoing treatment, Mom fascinated everyone by sharing stories of her life in the old country before coming to the United States. All took delight in listening to her, and just seeing the enchantment on nurses and patients faces brought love and warmth to my heart.

Time passed, bringing with it yet more challenges. Otto started developing swallowing difficulties, amongst a host of other problems. By surprise, an ultrasound for his kidneys showed suspicion of lung cancer. He refused any testing, stating clearly that he would not allow himself to be poked, prodded, snipped, clipped, cut or burned in any way. Otto was an old soldier, and one tough and resilient guy. He agreed only to allow CT scans every 6 months to watch the progression. Eventually, a feeding tube needed to be inserted. We were grateful that he agreed to that as well.

Although Otto had to rely on nutritional liquid supplements, Mom still loved spending time cooking. Each and every day, she had something delicious and ready for me to eat. Even with her advancing health problems, she could still get around in that wheelchair and cook up a storm! Her spirit was simply amazing. Not only that, her mind remained as sharp as a tack.

Our afternoon coffee or tea times together brought talk of life, time lost, regrets, accomplishments, happiness, joys, wishes, and what the future may hold. On our outings, Mom more keenly took notice of the beauty of this earth and nature, saying things like, "Gaby, have you really noticed just how beautiful things are?" as she would point something out. It was stunning. She spoke in awe of all the talents she didn't know I had, what I was capable of, and the breadth of my knowledge. Feeling humiliated by the amount of work that was involved with her personal care, she constantly and tearfully expressed gratitude for all that I did.

The Inevitable

Mom's kidneys failed. She was given the choice of either going on dialysis, or letting nature take its course. At first she said she wanted to just die, but then changed her mind and opted for dialysis. I moved into the guestroom at Mom's, as I had to have her at the dialysis clinic three times a week by 5:30 in the morning. Nearly every weekend after dialysis started, we ended up in the emergency room, as her blood pressure dropped dangerously low. Less than two months into dialysis, my mother suffered from cardiac arrest, passing away just over 48 hours later. The hours leading up to her death were the most agonizing time of my life, as one thing after another went wrong. My grief was beyond anything I had ever known. Otto passed away 15 months later.

Renewal, Revelation and Transformation

Commitments made and promises kept changed the entire course of my life. The combination of a new marriage, an overload of work, misfortune, and giving up my career in order to care for elderly parents appeared to create a recipe for disaster. But quite the contrary occurred in a most unexpected way.

"Why do you have such big feet?" wasn't a question that I ever expected to be asked, but it was one that I *needed* to hear. My divinely inspired answer stating that God had given me big feet knowing that I would have heavy loads to bear, had nothing to do with the size of my feet. It had everything to do with the foundation of my faith and the strength of my spirit. God was calling me into action. His timing was perfect, and the message was clear, coming at a time just when I needed hope and encouragement the most.

With renewed spirit, I approached my role of caregiving with a different perspective, trying to better understand where others were coming from instead of allowing my ego to get in the way while drowning myself in a sea of self-pity. Physical work and care were the easy parts. Dealing with the peaks and valleys of daily emotional drama were my greatest challenges. Compassion, empathy and humor helped to ease tense situations, providing medicine for our souls. During the process, a difficult mother and daughter relationship took on new life, creating enjoyable experiences that brought laughter and joy. Old wounds began to heal, fears diminished, and my self-confidence grew as time went by.

My life in the caregiving zone ranged from downright hilarious moments to those of heart wrenching grief and sorrow, but I received vastly more in return than that which I ever gave. I was needed and loved, and my family relied on me for their wellbeing. I chose forgiveness in lieu of resentment, and love in lieu of anger. The loads I carried were none too great.

Life is unpredictable. You never know what circumstances, events or obstacles might come your way. Rest assured, knowing that whether any challenges you face are greater or lesser, you too have big feet! Look down, observe and love those miraculously designed pads upon which you stand.

They support you each and every day. Let them be a daily reminder of your true foundation, that of your faith, and of the strength and spirit that dwell within you. It is always there for you. All you have to do is put it into action.

Time and again, when I share stories of my life's experiences, people ask me, "How did you stand it?" My answer is easy. "I have big feet!"

About The Author

As an award winning Realtor, Gaby Rotter built a successful business in real estate specializing in exclusive properties, country estates, ranches and land. She abruptly gave up her career in 2002 to become a full time caregiver for her mother and stepfather. The eleven tumultuous years that followed became some of the most transformational years of her life and are the subject of her chapter in this book.

Gaby is intensely interested in integrative, alternative and nutritional medicine as well as other healing modalities, having been deeply influenced by an uncle in the medical field. She enjoys cooking, sewing, crafting, engaging in great conversational exchange and is passionate about writing, speaking and inspiring others with stories of her life experiences. She most especially loves spending quality time with her family and friends. The Florida Treasure Coast, where she grew up, is her favorite vacation spot.

Gaby lives in the beautiful countryside of eastern Kansas with her husband, Bill, and adores spending time in nature. She is a trilingual mother of two grown sons, a seasoned traveler, a philanthropist, and a lover of art and music.

Gaby is currently working on a blog, to be launched in the near future: http://gabyrotter.com

You may contact Gaby at: gaby.c.rotter@gmail.com

CHAPTER 4

A DEADLY COMPROMISE
Dr. Jill Morris

You are about to read about one of the most important things you can do for the health of your children or grandchildren. You will discover what may be wrong with you as an adult. You will be shocked that this health solution is so simple and cheap, especially if the problem is caught early. There is a part of you that is taking over a job that it was not meant for, robbing you of your health.

My breath struggled to swim through the sea of phlegm, finding only nooks and crannies to flow. Like a narrow straw collapsing from too much suction, I could not breathe and I panicked. Eight years old with no one else at home, was this my time to die? With steadfast patience, a voice inside my head told me my only way to survive was to relax.

Where it all began

My problem began at birth like most of the people who come to me for help. Our lives would be very different if only we'd done one simple thing as children. I think back on that scary day so long ago. Both of my parents had jobs and we lived on a small farm in Indiana. It was cold and snowing outside and I couldn't have called on the telephone for help even if I wanted because I'd lost my voice. I had a horrible infection and I couldn't breathe. At one point I panicked and started to have an asthma attack as I wheezed in air. I told myself to calm down and try my best to breathe past the phlegm.

During the winter months, whenever I would go outside to take care of the animals or play with the other farm kids, constant mucus flowed from my nose. It was pretty gross. My coat sleeves would be stiff from the frozen snot I wiped from my nose that constantly flowed.

It first occurred to me that something was different when I was standing at the bus stop with a group of kids. One of the kids had a cold and blew her nose. I thought, "Wow, how'd she do that?" I didn't know you could blow air through the nose. For years I didn't know you could take in any air through the nose because mine was permanently blocked. I thought that was normal.

Operations and Nightmares

When I was four years old, the doctors operated to remove my tonsils and adenoids. They held me down on the operating table putting a rubber mask over my mouth and nose with air that smelled sweet and thick. I was claustrophobic after that. Around this time I started having terrible nightmares almost every night. I remember staring in the bathroom mirror and pleading with myself not to have a nightmare tonight. I was afraid to go to sleep. I shared a room with my older sister who said I would scream so loudly they had a hard time waking me up.

Breakfast

Every morning before school I would make myself a bowl of boxed kid's cereal, but first I would coat the bottom of the bowl with a layer of sugar. We ate a lot of meals from boxes, drank sugary Kool-Aid and ate very few fresh vegetables. We had milk at every meal. My parents thought the milk would help us grow. For me, it just created more clogging mucous. Most of our vegetables and fruit came from a can since my mom and dad did not have time to cook.

If only my teachers had known

It was just after I started school that one of my teachers complained to my parents about how disruptive the sound of my breathing was in the classroom. When mom told me, I was so embarrassed I would try to hold my breath in class and feel miserable. It was impossible to do for very long.

I would suffocate when I brushed my teeth. When I ate a meal, I would gasp for air as I chewed with my mouth open. My sister always complained, saying I was gross.

In elementary school, after we received our class pictures, I started to dislike my teeth. They were crooked and gummy and my chin was back. I wondered why my teeth didn't look like my friend Becky's teeth. Hers were lined up nicely. My mom, dad, brother and sister all had straight teeth. None of them had ever had braces, either.

Playing sports was difficult for me and I was pretty puny. My shoulder blades and spine poked out. I would have frequent allergy attacks if I over-exerted myself and would have to stop frequently to catch my breath.

More surgeries

When I was nine years old, I was hospitalized again because I wasn't losing my baby teeth on time and they had to surgically expose the permanent teeth. Because my mouth was open all the time in order to breathe, the doctors said that my teeth were not stimulated enough to encourage normal loss of my baby teeth. I remember my Mom stopping the car on the way home so I could throw-up because the anesthesia made me sick.

My parents divorced when I was in middle school and I moved with my mom to Florida. At this time, my dentist was afraid my permanent teeth would never come in unless he did something about it. I would walk from school to the dentist's office and he would pull four of my baby teeth. Afterwards, I'd bite on cotton and walk to my Mom's office and wait for her to get off work. I did these trips four different times for a total of 16 extractions to the best of my knowledge. By the time I started high school I had a total of 4 front teeth on top and 4 front teeth on bottom. I would practice smiling in the mirror so the other kids wouldn't notice all my missing teeth.

Having all of the baby teeth removed at once meant that my permanent teeth would come in haphazardly and very crooked. Also, my jaws were narrow and there wasn't enough room for my permanent teeth. By the time I was 16, my teeth were so crooked I was ashamed to smile and felt like I didn't have a chin. Finally, the day before my senior pictures, I got braces to straighten my teeth. I was thrilled because the braces hid my ugly teeth.

As an adult in my twenties, I had a bad bite and temporomandibular joint (TMJ) pain. Dentists at top dental schools told me that they needed to surgically break my jaw to correct everything. Thank goodness I elected not to go down that path because I found non-surgical solutions for myself.

All of these childhood problems eventually led me to become a dentist. I became a well-known teacher in the field of cosmetic dentistry because I knew how much my ugly smile affected my self-esteem. I still didn't know why this had happened to me since everyone else in my family had naturally straight teeth without braces, so I continued my education in naturopathic medicine to discover what could have caused my problems. Over the last thirty years as an integrative dentist, I slowly discovered why I had so many problems.

I discovered the answer

There was one element in my life that was different from the experience of my brother and sister that could explain why they didn't develop my problems. It is just a theory. When I was a toddler, my mother was a teacher for special needs children that were mentally retarded. She would bring me to play with them frequently. They were all mouth-breathers. I may have mimicked their mannerisms until it became a habit for me. Mouth-breathing created larger tonsils and adenoids which defended against the unfiltered air entering my lungs. My childhood diet of processed high sugar meals made me prone to allergies. My allergies created the nose-clogging mucous. The reason for my nightmares was because of the lack of oxygen reaching my brain when I fell asleep as a mouth breather. I would also frequently wet the bed at night because of my abnormal sleep patterns.

I also learned that the reason I still couldn't breathe through my nose after my tonsillectomy was because no one taught me how to breathe through my nose. Mouth breathing had become a habit. The doctors didn't know that if I continued to breathe through the mouth after surgery, my adenoids and tonsils would grow back. Bacteria and fungus-filled air passed through my mouth unfiltered, causing an immune response of the tonsils and adenoids that caused them to enlarge and grow back again. They were stimulated by all of the germs. If I had learned to breathe through my nose, the nasal passages would have filtered contaminants in the air. Breathing through the nose is vital to the growing child's health, school experiences and self-esteem. These have lifelong consequences for the well-being of the adult as well.

I learned that genetically, I was supposed to have straight teeth, but this would never happen as a mouth-breather. My gummy smile and recessive chin developed because my top jaw was narrow and my face grew long. My tongue was never resting in the roof of my mouth to guide that growth. This created my narrow arches. There was not enough room for my teeth. Holding my mouth open caused my face and cranium to grow long, backwards, and narrow.

Kids are in big trouble
In America, our children and grandchildren are heading down the same path. Today's kids are in big trouble. Experts

estimate that 75% to 80% have crooked teeth or bad bites. These children have mouths perpetually forming an "oh" and red circles under their eyes. They have slumped, rounded shoulders falling from a neck thrust forward hoping for more air. They may wake up with wet bed sheets and frustrated parents. They have trouble concentrating in school. He may be the last one picked by friends in the neighborhood ballgame. She may be left out in the game of good looks and popularity. Teachers assume a slowness of wit and intellect because the mouth is hung open. As he grows to adulthood, his job promotion is lost to the one with the chiseled chin and powerful posture. The same thing happens to her. Their posture lacks confidence. Self-esteem crumbling with each rejection. The inner spirit is crying to break free.

Why God gave us a nose

There are several reasons for the cause of open mouth breathing. In the 1950s, women were told that baby formula was better for their babies so many women used bottles instead of breastfeeding. The cow protein in the bottle formula creates an overload of mucus and allergens. Holding the correct tongue position in the roof of the mouth is impossible for the growing infant and child who drink from a bottle, sippy cup, thumb sucks or uses a pacifier. The tongue is a strong muscle that applies 500 lbs. of pressure to the top dental jaw, helping it to grow wide and opening the airway. The tongue resting in the roof of the mouth with nasal breathing leads to good jaw and facial development. When the airway is properly developed, the posture of the child is good as well. When I was around seven, our pediatrician told me that my posture was terrible. He had me stand against the wall to teach me good posture. My doctor didn't know that if a child is a mouth breather, the lower jaw grows backward, closing the airway off, restricting the size of the windpipe. The child must hold the head forward in order to open the airway to breathe better. This leads to slumped shoulders and a recessive chin along with spinal and neck changes. As an adult, no matter how hard I tried, years of poor posture made it too painful to stand correctly.

National Geographic Smiles

In tribal cultures, each time the baby was full after nursing, the mother would gently close the child's lips with her fingers. She would repeat this each time she saw her baby's mouth open until the child formed the habit of breathing through its nose with its lips together. Correct tongue position with the tongue resting against the roof of the mouth is therefore learned. A correct swallowing pattern is developed which results in broad dental arches with plenty of room for the teeth and an open airway. Look at the smiles of tribal cultures and you will see this. No buck or crooked teeth!

Crooked teeth are a modern phenomenon. Tribal people had strong chins, good posture, wide dental arches and straight teeth, correct nose size and high cheekbones. Mouth breathers develop long faces and weak chins, sometimes straining to close their lips.

Breastfeeding

My practice also includes the growing infant and child. I want to spread the word about this widespread problem. Up to 75% of American children have crooked teeth or bite problems.

Breastfeeding for two months is not long enough. Breastfeeding needs to be encouraged today. When my three children were infants, I continued to work full time as a dentist being the only dentist in my practice. I found the time to nurse by a process called "night time nursing." All of my children slept with me and I would nurse during the night and pump during the day. I did this for seven and a half years. My oldest child nursed for four years and my youngest for three and a half years. My children did not develop any food allergies and received my antibodies against colds and infection. Since they were drinking my breast milk through a bottle during the day, they were not learning proper tongue position and swallow, so they did develop malocclusion. At the time, I did not know how to train my children to breathe through the nose like I know today. Establishment of nasal breathing as early as possible is imperative for good health. Good breathing is achieved when we cannot hear or see it.

Don't worry if your infant wasn't breastfed. There are a lot of situations that make it impossible. Nasal breathing with the mouth closed can still be taught to the child for proper growth.

The processed American diet leads to childhood allergies and mucous in the nose causing mouth breathing. The food is sticky and processed, saturated with chemicals and foreign globs formulated by scientists, that our cells struggle to recognize. The food seems vaguely familiar. Pieces of this undigested food slip through the weakened intestinal wall which guards our insides from the outside, setting off a chain of allergic reactions. We are starving to death for something nutritional. The natural intelligence of our system yearns for whole foods teaming with live enzymes and nutrients. Instead, these undigested foreign invaders set off an allergic reaction creating the mucous that wreaks havoc on our system.

Many parents have told me that they were told to wait until their child is 12 years old before they start braces. Wrong, wrong, wrong!! They have missed years of growth opportunities of the jaws as well as training of the tongue position. By the age of 12, the majority of the cranium is developed. Sixty percent of the facial growth takes place during the first four years of life and ninety percent by age 12. The important cranium houses the brain, eyes, ears, pituitary and nose. We like to start the child with training to correct habits as soon as the parent sees they are sleeping with their mouth open or mouth breathing during the day. An infant should have its lips together when it sleeps. Many times the jaws will grow with proper training so that braces are not necessary. I cannot stress it enough to start early training with your child. Jaw development affects posture. Crooked teeth cause a crooked body.

Many of my colleagues have reported a decrease in ADD and ADHD symptoms when the child's airway and nasal breathing is improved. This could be due to a better level of quality sleep and concentration. Bed-wetting has also decreased in many of these children.

The diet is also vital. Removing processed and mucous forming foods with dyes and preservatives is another key component to the establishment of nasal breathing.

When deciding upon orthodontics, more than just the mechanics of pushing the teeth around should be considered. The skeletal and jaw development should be corrected first whenever possible and then the teeth moved into ideal position in the dental arches. Orthodontic extractions alone, to create room for the crooked teeth, can narrow the arches further and create a smaller airway. Headaches, ringing of the ears as well as head, neck and back pain, can become a lifelong result.

The Trouble with the Tongue

Most people don't know that 90% of orthodontics relapses if proper nasal breathing is not established. It's not that the teeth are too large for the jaws, but the jaws are too small for the teeth. A tooth can be moved with 1.7 grams of force. The strong tongue applies up to 500 grams of force expanding the top dental jaw when the child swallows properly 2000 times a day. Dr. John Flutter, the Australian orthodontist, says "every child's face has the growth potential to match its own set of teeth." Mouth breathing causes crooked teeth because the tongue is not stimulating the growth of the top jaw! Healthy children breathe through their nose with their lips together. Their tongue rests on the roof of the mouth.

Chronic over-breathing is a result of mouth breathing and occurs when we breathe in more air than our body needs. The brain resets to this concentration, making us feel as if we need to breathe in this much air all the time. The problem with this is it causes a decrease of carbon dioxide in the blood, tissues and cells. Carbon dioxide is needed in the tissues in order for the red blood cells to release oxygen. Thus our cells, brain, and organs become oxygen deficient. Breathing more often and deeper does not increase the oxygen in the tissues, it does the opposite. Heavy breathers have less oxygenation of the brain leading to poor sleep and daytime sleepiness.

How we treat Children

Any child with crooked teeth is a sick child. My dream is for families to return to a simpler diet of whole foods, breastfeeding when possible, and seeking help early if their child is a mouth breather. Treatment is not complicated but does take commitment from the child. In my office, to teach nasal breathing and correct tongue position, our children wear removable appliances overnight and one hour during the day. They have exercises on computer apps where they earn points and we can track their progress. The average treatment time to create the proper tongue position, swallowing, and breathing habits is anywhere from six months to two years according to the child's age and compliance. Improper breathing should be corrected as early as possible. Even if the child is in high school, they can be corrected. Just straightening their teeth is not correcting the root of the problem. They may look better, but they have a lifetime of health and dental issues that could have been avoided.

Mouth Breathing is Expensive

The lifetime progression of problems costs a lot of money. Children stay in braces for years, sometimes repeating treatment in their twenties due to relapse. They are more prone to decay because of dry mouth. They are being drugged for their ADD or ADHD symptoms. Through the years, they grind and clench their teeth so that they go through expensive dental procedures. As they age, they put fillers in their cheeks and folds to support the sagging skin because the jaws did not develop properly. They are treated for sleep apnea and high blood pressure. They miss work because of headaches. They may be too tired to enjoy activities with their grandchildren.

I meet adults with these problems at least once a week. They make an appointment for various reasons, but the cause and solution is usually the same. They are going to die prematurely. They don't know they have a problem so dangerous. They exhibit the tell tale signs of bags under their eyes, exhaustion, poor sleep, recessive chin and weak facial profile, and crooked teeth. Some have face pain and headaches. If only they had known that doing one simple thing as a child could have profoundly changed their lives forever. They may have a productive life now, but who knows what their full potential could have been?

This Mom stopped smiling

Vicki is 45 and doesn't like her gummy smile and has never liked her teeth or chin profile since she was little. Now she has TMJ pain and her teeth are crooked even though she's had braces twice. Most people don't know that ninety percent of the time after braces, the teeth will get crooked again if proper nasal breathing is not established. She came to see me for cosmetic dentistry. She made sure that her kids had good dental care and now that they are grown it's her turn.

His wife was afraid he'd die alone in a hotel room

Another patient, Sam, came in because he has sleep apnea and he's tired of breathing on a CPAP machine at night. In fact, he's just tired. His wife hates the sound of the machine all night long, but is glad it keeps him alive. She's heard the statistics that sleep apnea causes premature death through stroke or heart attack. He travels nationwide for work and carries that darn machine everywhere he goes. He wants off of it.

Cindy's teeth and face were collapsing

Another lady, Cindy, is 52 and wants a wider smile. Her orthodontist pulled her teeth in high school to fix her crooked teeth. Now her teeth are worn down and she has a collapsing bite and face. She has already spent a lot of money on her dentistry and facial fillers.

Mary doesn't know what's wrong

And then there is Mary who breathes like she has just run out of a burning building. Her speech stalls between breaths. She is unaware that she chronically over breathes. All she knows is she is here for help. Her bite feels off. Her teeth are discolored. She wants her toxic corroded mercury fillings replaced after reading about their dangers on the Internet. It's hard to believe, but all of these symptoms are preventable and caused by one simple thing.

Believe it or not, these problems stem from the same cause. I will discuss later what the cause is and how I helped these people.

There is a skyrocketing trend in adult sleep apnea and TMJ pain. Many of my adult patients had crooked teeth due to their mouth breathing habits, which lead to the extraction of four permanent teeth in their teen years. Removing these teeth allowed for the needed room to align the teeth in underdeveloped, small jaws. Unfortunately, the dental arches remained narrow, the lower jaw receded, and the elevated palate impinged on the nose airway. The teeth were straightened, but the poor tongue habit worked against the correct alignment so the teeth relapsed and became crooked again. The lower teeth are trapped inside the cage of the top teeth. The lower jaw and chin are forced back against the skull. The sore muscles work tirelessly positioning the lower jaw back to fit inside the narrow top arch. The teeth slowly collapse inward over time, becoming jagged and crooked. Years later, TMJ pain, crooked teeth, worn teeth, high blood pressure, and sleep apnea developed in a large percentage of my patients.

During sleep, the tongue is sucked backwards, like a stopper in a bottle, plugging off the airway and causing sleep apnea and suffocation. The suction pulls the stomach acid into the esophagus causing GERD. The brain sounds a warning siren when the oxygen gets dangerously low. The blood thickens and syrupy clots form, causing heart attack and stroke. If the person is lucky enough for the hundredth time that night, the teeth gnash forward, rescuing the tongue by sucking it out of the throat and breaking the seal so oxygen can flow again. The poor soul's teeth continue to crumble, flex, and deflect while the sore, fatigued muscles labor to save the life. These events, repeating hundreds of times every night, are triggered by our innate drive to live.

Most people aren't aware that at any age, the body can be stimulated to grow. Although, with older people, we don't have the same influence on the growth as we do with a young child, we can still grow and widen the top arch making room for the teeth and a better bite. This opens the airway naturally. We teach people to breathe through the nose while keeping the mouth closed. We wake-up their stem cells, which know exactly what to do. The result is a wider smile and cheekbones that support the face. As the lower jaw moves forward, the posture gets better. Many people with sleep apnea can get off their machines. They have more energy and sleep better. Because they sleep better, they release hormones that allow for weight loss and they heal better.

We work with adults to correct habits also. They wear removable appliances that apply light pressure to the dental arches that create positive skeletal and airway improvements. They see a decrease in the levels of sleep apnea and achieve a wider, better-looking smile. Usually the expansion takes approximately a year's time with regular wear. I wore these appliances at age 53 for health reasons. My posture is the best it has ever been. I no longer have the facial or back pain I used to have. It is easier to breath with my lips together. My oldest patient to receive this treatment is a grandfather in his sixties.

"Don't let what happened to me happen to you or your kids"

I wrote this chapter to help grandparents, parents, and children. I want adults to know why they have their problems. I want parents and grandparents to know what to look for in their children and grandchildren. I want them to spread the word to a friend who may have a child like this. I want the school nurses to know what to look for. If problems can be caught early, what happened to me won't happen to them. Here are the things to look for if you have a child or grandchild. See if they are breathing through the nose with the mouth closed. The mouth should be closed during sleep as well. Snoring, attention deficit, bed-wetting, allergies, asthma, or crooked teeth point to mouth breathing. See if they slump and have poor posture. Learning to breathe through the nose is simple and inexpensive and will change the rest of their lives.

When growing up, you may not have had exactly the same experiences as me, but if you are experiencing TMJ and headaches, I encourage you to also get a sleep test as there is a link to sleep apnea. If you are grinding your teeth, or tired during the day and find that your teeth are getting more crooked as you age and your face seems to be collapsing, there is help to reverse this as well. There is light at the end of the tunnel. I have whole families, both parents and children, in treatment. I have grandparents in treatment with removable retainers that expand the arches and open the airway.

Lost Futures

Sometimes I wonder if a child could have developed into a great athlete if treated. Or perhaps they would have grown to their genetic potential and would have been a more attractive adult. Psychology has proven that attractive people have an advantage in the work force over unattractive people. The good guys in movies are usually attractive and the bad buys are ugly. Or perhaps if that child would have gotten more oxygen to the brain during those formative years, could they have been rested and attentive and done better at school? I believe mouth breathing is an epidemic in America and it's keeping our children from reaching their full potential. I certainly see all of the patterns in my adults. They have face and jaw pain, headaches, sleep apnea, caffeine addiction, worn down teeth and bites collapsing. Sleep apnea alone can shorten lives by 15 years, let alone the cost of dental work to repair the cracked and worn teeth. This gets expensive along with the lost time at work due to headaches.

As a dentist, I feel like I can make big improvements in my patients' lives at any age. There is hope for all. It's never too late. Actor Jimmy Durante' used to say "The nose knows." We just need to learn how to use it. God gave us a nose for a good reason! The title of this chapter is "The Deadly Compromise". You've probably figured it out by now. Every time we breathe through our mouth either out of habit or necessity, there are health consequences. It's time to let the mouth eat, talk, drink and kiss. Let's return the business of breathing back to the nose.

About The Author

Jill Morris, DMD, ND, CCHT, is the founder of World Class Dentistry™ in Sarasota, Fl. She is an integrative dentist and national educator known for her pioneering techniques in whole patient dentistry. She has the unique combination of degrees in dentistry, naturopathic medicine, and clinical hypnotherapy. She is an accredited member of the American Academy of Cosmetic Dentistry and fellow of the American Academy of Dental Facial Esthetics. She is a member of the International Academy of Biological Dentistry and Medicine and the International Academy of Oral Medicine and Toxicology.

She has taught dentists from around the world live patient treatment in cosmetics, facial esthetics, and holistic dentistry. Throughout her more than thirty years in clinical practice, she has pioneered the partnership between cosmetic and holistic dentistry to improve the well-being and spirit of her patients.

Her focus for children in her practice is to create proper habits for straight teeth and facial growth resulting in a lifetime of excellent health. She practices with her husband, a dental implantologist, and three children who are entering the dental field as dentists and dental technicians. Together they live in Sarasota with their two dogs, three cats, and Sebastian the snake.

Visit her website at www.SarasotaDentist.com

CHAPTER 5

YOUR STRUGGLES CAN BECOME YOUR GREATEST STRENGTHS

Tracy Laura Webster

My screams echoed down the corridor and my legs collapsed onto the sterile sheets. I gripped my sister's hand in anguish as my internal tremors turned into uncontrollable shaking. I was stone cold and the smell of the hospital room made me feel sick. They could not detect a heartbeat and when the doctor ruptured my water it was black. My baby had died in utero. The night before I went into labour I'd sobbed as I lay in my childhood bedroom. It was because she had died and at a deeper level I knew.

Just as her heart had stopped beating I felt that mine would too. How could I give birth to her knowing that I wouldn't hear her first cry, touch her soft warm skin and hold her close to me. I felt that I couldn't do it. The doctor said that it would be better for my recovery to give birth naturally rather than a caesarean. My recovery? I felt that I'd never recover from this! I didn't know if I should hold her once I'd given birth. I didn't know if I could bear it. I didn't know what to expect. I felt in that moment that I too just wanted to die.

As I looked at my sister I could see the reflection of my pain in her eyes. It was her love and strength that helped me through the traumatic labour and give birth to my beautiful little girl. My instinct to immediately hold her consumed me. They placed her limp little body in my arms after cutting the cord. It was wrapped tightly around her neck. I kissed her little face and looked at her perfect features and touched her tiny hand and then they took her away. I had never felt such immense pain in my heart before.

I named my daughter Laura and as we lay her to rest I knew that she would forever be in my heart but I couldn't imagine how I would find the strength or desire to go on. As my milk slowly dried up I found some comfort from the love and kindness that surrounded me. Two months later it was bitter sweet when I held my newborn niece in my arms and my heart felt raw and exposed. The memory of her first flutters and joy that I'd felt carrying her swept over me.

My dream of becoming a wife and a mother had come to a dramatic and devastating end. I still yearned for motherhood but I had to move forward with my life. I needed to suppress those feelings, pick myself up, put on my happy face and start over again.

I could not accept that the cord had caused Laura's death and I began searching for other possible causes. I was unaware of my self-blaming pattern bubbling under the surface. Standing in my childhood bedroom brought memories of my life flooding back. As I stared at my reflection in the mirror, I saw a young woman with her whole life ahead of her. Yet what I felt in my heart were the same unhappy feelings that stirred within me as a young girl when I had stood in that very room and wondered what my life was all about and how if felt like a struggle.

The Voice That Matters Most

The voices of my parents and siblings rang in my head. 'Why are you never happy or content?' I heard this question so often that at thirteen I went searching for the answers. Something stirred within me when I read my first self-help book *I'm OK You're OK* by Dr. Thomas A. Harris I felt there was a part of me that was not OK. I felt this inner unhappiness and how my life felt like a struggle. Yet on the outside it didn't appear that way. I was seeking the meaning of life and why I felt that something was missing from mine.

I grew up with a strong foundation of love and valued kindness and seeing the best in others. Friends, cousins, aunties and uncles surrounded my life. I played lots of sport, had the freedom to cycle to the beach with friends, swim in the warm Indian Ocean and return home to our sparkling blue pool that dad built us. I had many fun adventures. One of my favourites was catching a train with my cousin to her granny's farm. We'd wake up to the rooster's call and morning star, help milk the cows and play until sunset. Yet still I yearned for something and couldn't understand what.

Even though there were signs of financial struggles, with no matching Ken Barbies like my cousins had and no family holidays, it didn't seem to matter. Our home was filled with lots of love and laughter and the hustle and bustle of family and friends. From the outside looking in I appeared to be a happy girl and was fun to be around. But my life had become fragmented into my external 'happy' world and internal 'unhappy' world. My unhappiness revealed itself when I was at home without the busyness and distractions. My mom bore the brunt of my moods, defiance and discontentment. Up until the age of two I had been a happy, content toddler. Then mom was hospitalised and in traction for two months from a slipped disc in her back from picking me up!

My parents expected things to return to normal. But something in me had changed. My negative behaviour escalated and my parents were at a loss as to what to do. Nothing seemed to work and everything became a struggle. I continued to find ways to push my mom to the brink of despair. My negative behaviour and mom's negative reaction, followed by my remorse and her forgiveness became a vicious circle. I wanted to be more like my well-behaved sister but the harder I tried the more I seemed to fail and the worse I'd feel about myself and so the sabotage of my own internal voice of self-loathing began.

I was too young to understand why I was not Ok and the simplicity in what I was seeking. My self-destructive, self-loathing patterns continued to weave into the fabric of my life and at sixteen I developed Bulimia. The very thing I was searching for and what I valued most in giving others was unconditional love and kindness. What was missing was my belief that I deserved it myself. It took many more years of struggle and further searching to reach that realisation.

As we all got a little older and wiser, I was reminded in jest about the turmoil I had put my family through. The words 'your time will come when you're a mother one day' felt hurtful somehow but I smiled anyway. It was unbeknown how that would manifest in my life and how the self-blaming and feelings of unworthiness had already deeply rooted themselves into my personality.

New Beginnings

Many people suffer from the fear of finding oneself alone, and so they don't find themselves at all. Rollo May

My books have been my companion and teacher of valuable insights throughout my life. The ones that I've learnt to practice and experience are the ones that have become part of who I am and have helped me throughout my life. This insight has helped me choose being alone over staying in disempowering, even sometimes comfortable situations. It's given me the courage to immigrate to new countries, to find new beginnings but most importantly being alone has finally been the key to my true self.

I felt happy and revitalized after my skiing trip in Austria. It had been two years since the loss of Laura. My best friend and I sat with a glass of wine in the beautiful courtyard adorned with palm trees, background music and people's laughter. We looked up to see two guys approaching us. My friend had gone to her high school dance with the one. The other became my second husband and we married in the same courtyard two years later.

As tension grew in South Africa we felt concerned about our future. I wanted to immigrate to America as I valued being near family and knew that my sister was moving to California. My husband's first choice was Australia because of the similar culture. We literally flipped a coin and I won. On the other side of the coin was the pain and hardship of knowing that our close-knit family was being torn apart, along with leaving our beautiful country of birth and all that was familiar.

In our new land although we found wonderful new friends, I could not have imagined how much I would miss and yearn for our family back home. There was a huge void in my life. It felt like I had been unearthed and was walking around in another dimension. I wanted to belong. I wanted to feel settled and put down roots in my new home but up until immigrating I hadn't realized how much being apart from my family was my biggest struggle.

Christmas time was especially tough and so my sister and I spent a lot of our time visiting each other between the East and West Coast of America. Ironically fate had us on opposite sides of the continent and although my personal journey of self-discovery continued, my time alone was consumed with wishing that we could live closer together. That's when my yearning to become a mother returned with full force and to find contentment in creating a family of our own.

Empty Baby Shoes

I was swallowed up with unbearable grief and I wanted my life to disappear and never face the world again. Memories of Laura came flooding back. Not even my husband's love and reassurance could soothe my pain.

I woke up drenched in sweat. Was it all a horrific nightmare? The drone of the morning news and smell of freshly brewed coffee made my stomach turn. As I lay my hand on my empty belly, tears streamed down my face.

My husband's hand softly touched my cheek. I looked up at him through puffy eyes as he gently said, "Trace, Princess Diana died from the accident, they couldn't save her." My heart ached for the loss of such an incredible woman and mother taken in the prime of her life. My throat was tight and strangled with sadness as I thought of her sons.

To escape my pain, I wished that I could fall back to sleep. I heard the call of a Mourning Dove and noticed that he was sitting on our windowsill as though he could sense my pain and the fragility of life. Was his presence and song a message of hope that I would one day become a mother?

My baby books were piled high on my bedside table. Why had I lost another baby? I had been taking good care of us. Did I cause this from my years of bulimia? The little denim baby shoes, that I had surprised my husband with when I found out I was pregnant, sat on our bedroom shelf. Empty.

At eight weeks there was a strong, fast heartbeat. At my three-month ultrasound appointment I lay on the table staring at the screen, excited to see an image of our little one. Then came the nurse's voice. "I'm sorry but there is no heartbeat." I lay there alone with the same paralysing words echoing of when I lost Laura. I was booked in for a D&C to scrape and clean my uterine lining. As they wheeled me in for the procedure, it was the first time that I had seen my husband cry. Choked up he said, "I love you Trace. I'm so sorry."

As December drew nearer and my pain was easing we prepared for our second winter wonderland in Baltimore. My dream as a young girl of having a white Christmas had come true. Wearing my warm down jacket and gloves, I felt the soft whispers of the snowflakes on my face. I looked at the winter trees standing bare. I knew spring would bring them new life and I felt a twinge of hope.

As the months passed, my specialist suggested further testing as I had two more early stage miscarriages. I was diagnosed with Grave's Disease, an autoimmune disease. I had mixed feelings of concern and relief but at least I had some answers and a cause for my miscarriages. I received two rounds of Radioactive Iodine Treatment. Left with a dysfunctional thyroid and deemed radioactive, I had to stay away from people for seven days and not conceive for six months! I think it was a much-needed break for my poor husband! As I yearned, I noticed pregnant women and chubby little baby feet in strollers, everywhere.

After our six months we conceived but again I miscarried. The treatment had killed off too much of my thyroid. As the doctors tried to stabilise my levels with medication we underwent various tests with a top fertility specialist. I needed to inject myself with Estradiol to stimulate egg production. With fragile faith, I went through the motions but I feared another miscarriage. I also feared another stillbirth. I felt my dream of becoming a mother slipping away and I knew that this was our last hope.

Miracle Christmas Sock Baby

I was excited that I had several viable eggs but I was afraid of getting my hopes up. We had thirty minutes to get to the doctor's rooms with the little plastic container wrapped in a Christmas sock. A part of me had begun to let go of the outcome. Maybe it was from the past disappointments but it's as if I'd started to accept that if I wasn't going to be a mother I had done all that I could do. I'd even started to think of how we could travel around the world! Then I missed my period. Usually when I was one day late I would do a pregnancy test. I never did one and at my doctor's appointment she suggested we did.

I was pregnant for the sixth time! I passed the three-month mark, then the six-month mark with a new glimmer of hope. Finally our little miracle Christmas sock baby arrived. Our long wait was over and we had a healthy 8.8-pound son. We thought our hearts were going to burst with love and relief. He literally paved the way for his siblings. He was such a delight and an easy baby I felt I could manage a second. The sooner we tried the more chance we had of conceiving naturally. Now at sixteen our eldest son likes the fact that his parents didn't have to have sex to bring him into the world!

When he was only four months old, I stopped nursing him. Although I was sad, my continuous mastitis had taken a lot of the joy out of breastfeeding. Our second son was born fourteen months apart from his brother. He never breathed straight away and what seemed like a lifetime was seconds in slow motion. After the mucus was suctioned, he began whaling. It was music to our ears. He weighed 8.2 pounds and was a lot more vocal than his older brother (and still is). We could tell then that he was feisty and his name means

Spirit of Battle, as we would find out later in his life. We had wondered how we could possibly love another little being as much as our first, but our hearts just kept on expanding.

My parents visited us for the birth of each of their grandsons. They were such a great help and support to us. I longed for my children to experience what I had growing up around extended family but our lives were made up of hellos and goodbyes. Until six years later my husband had a job offer in California. I was pregnant with my third child when we moved from Maryland to California to be near my sister and her family. My dream had come true. My husband on the other hand felt it was closer to Australia where he ultimately wanted us to live.

Ever since losing Laura, I yearned for a daughter. So this time around I tried all the methods of how to increase our chances of conceiving a girl. I decided to find out the sex of my baby and although I knew that I'd love the baby whether it was a boy or girl, it was my last chance for a daughter.

My sister-in-law was expecting a girl and I felt a pang of jealousy as I apprehensively awaited my results. I was horrified at my reaction. I was filled with guilt, shame, and disappointment. I could not forgive myself for feeling that way. My dream of becoming a mother had come true and my third son was healthy. Why could I not be content and happy? What was wrong with me? I was disgusted with myself. When I calmed down, I spoke to my baby and told him how much I loved him but I felt like a fraud.

The pregnancy continued smoothly and I eased up on myself as his little flutters reminded me of how fortunate I was. As we said our goodbyes to our friends in Baltimore, we looked forward to our new adventure in California.

Our blonde Californian boy arrived right on time but with a very scary entry. My husband agreed that it would be wonderful for my sister to experience his birth. My labour was progressing fairly slowly and they went out to grab a quick bite to eat. When they returned I was on oxygen with eyes like saucers! His heart rate had dropped and he had gone into fetal distress and had passed black meconium. He gave us quite a scare! His mucus was suctioned and then he was safe in my arms. In that moment as I held our newborn son, I knew I was truly blessed and my life felt complete.

Hellos and Goodbyes

My sister and my young sons and I flew to South Africa. My dad had stage four cancer. We knew it would be our last time together. We treasured every moment and found some peace in the thought that he would be reunited with his brothers and Laura. As a family, we had so much love for each other. Nothing needed resolving, we had no regrets only an incredible sadness that he was leaving our world for another. I had always watched people at airports seeing the joy of their hellos and the sadness of their goodbyes. It was the hardest trip I've ever made.

When I returned home a big decision loomed over us. We sat absorbed in the aroma of Starbucks and deep in thought. Our green cards for the United States and our permanent residency to Australia had arrived two days apart. We had to choose one over the other. My heart was torn in two. I wanted to stay where my support and extended family was but I knew my husband was unhappy and longed for his familiar cultural roots that Australia tempted him with.

If I dug my heels in, my husband might end up resenting me so once again we said our goodbyes. I thought we could always return if it didn't work out! It was that false belief that helped me get on the plane. Brisbane was unbearably hot and humid. I felt miserable. I felt like I had made the worst mistake of my life and I resented my husband for bringing me to this new land that felt so different from 'home'.

I learnt that one needs a strong marriage to survive immigration. Even with a family of my own, I missed my extended family. I missed what had become familiar to me in America. Again I found myself living from one visit to the next. Although I made wonderful new friends my yearning for family descended upon me in waves. It hit me the worst when my sister was diagnosed with breast cancer and then again when my mom moved to America. I exhausted myself with scenarios of going back so we could all be together again, that I could be there to support my sister and be with my mom in her golden years. The realisation that the core of who I am is about family and yet I moved away from that and that there was no return. I had never felt more on my own than ever before!

Eventually I knew that I had to close that door for the sake of my family and my sanity. I'd reached a point of acceptance and was able to let go. I finally allowed myself to fully embrace the beauty and find the joy and gratitude of my new home in Australia. It's a good thing that I did because I needed all the internal strength that I could muster for what lay ahead.

Discovery

I felt like pulling my hair out. I could hear my mom's words in my head. As my four-year old screamed to go home with me from school, my two-year old screamed to stay and play in the sand pit. As these episodes grew in intensity and frequency, I knew in my gut that something bigger was at play.

We saw allergists, doctors, and behavioral psychologists but nothing substantial was found. Even my closest friends did not know the full extent of what our family was going through. From the outside our sons seemed well mannered and respectful but there were signs of social anxiety and we never overstayed our welcome in fear of outbursts.

As they grew a little older my youngest son seemed miserable from the time he woke up until he went to bed. The arguments, sibling rivalry, hypersensitivity and screaming were relentless. The impact that it had on our family was huge and we became exhausted. It seemed the only time we still caught glimpses of his beautiful smile and any light-heartedness was when he was with his friends over the weekend. So we welcomed sleepovers and friends into our home. It gave us a break from the turmoil. I wondered where my happy boy had gone and I wanted him back!

I blamed myself. Had he bore the brunt of my misery moving to Australia? I thought about when he was in my womb in the early stages and wondered if from a cellular or energetic level whether he had memories of feeling unwanted, feeling unloved. Was the unhappiness and the behaviour in his outer world a reflection of feelings and beliefs he held in his inner world? My friends and family thought I was crazy but my research led me to Dr. Alex and his amazing work on cellular memory.

As his mother I felt at a loss, but I kept on searching. My husband suggested medication so that we could catch our breath and figure out what to do next. I was concerned about the side effects. I researched, attended talks, read books on parenting, nutrition, ensured a good diet along with nutritional supplements and different parenting approaches. I would get excited with small improvements only for it to suddenly get worse again.

Up until the teenage years we lived in survival mode until the relentless screaming and anger outbursts reached the point of neighbourhood disturbance. It felt like our family was falling apart. I noticed white specs on their fingernails. My youngest were the worst and his nails were covered in them. The more I researched the more evidence pointed to the link between zinc deficiency and anger. My endless pursuit trying to find the right help for my sons finally led me to a practitioner specialising in imbalances and deficiencies based on individual biochemistry.

We tested positive to a genetic chemical imbalance involving an abnormality in our hemoglobin synthesis. We produce a toxin in the body that binds itself to important essential nutrients that we need but instead are excreted in our urine. The more stress we have the more toxin we produce and the more deficient in zinc, B6 we become. We are unable to efficiently create serotonin (a neurotransmitter that reduces anxiety).

It was a big missing piece of the puzzle and also one of the reasons for my mom's, sister's and my platinum blonde hair that people admire and which I don't mind keeping!

For the first time in a decade of struggle, I felt hopeful as a mom. What first appeared as history repeating itself has become a journey of discovery and the potential to change our family's future.

To Love & Believe

Figure out how your life is speaking to you. There's a flow trying to guide you in the direction to your higher self. Know that you become not what you want or desire but what you believe. Oprah Winfrey

My life had been speaking to me through my struggles. Two years ago I fell down a driveway and fractured my ankle. I was forced to stop! The messages from my outside world became loud and clear and I had been given the gift of time to reflect on my life and it's direction.

Overlooking our beautiful park abundant with trees and birdlife I could practice stillness and meditation and feel the simplicity of each moment, each breath, each day.

As I sat quietly on my veranda one cloudy afternoon it came to me. Just like the sun was always shining behind the clouds, what I'd been searching for since I was a thirteen-year-old girl had always been there. It was a foundation of unconditional love for others but my self-sabotaging beliefs had been blocking out my sunshine and ability to love myself.

As I continue my journey through life, this is what I know, believe and hold true - that your struggles can become your greatest strengths. They carry messages that can connect you with your heart to heal your wounds and make you stronger. It's in the stillness where we find clarity and see the lessons they bring, as they are our greatest teacher and they can be your greatest teacher as well. It's in the awareness of our sabotaging beliefs that we can free ourselves from them.

Love is still the greatest gift in the world and it begins with loving the true essence of who you are! The simplicity and freedom that comes from loving and accepting oneself, as the unique being that you are and choosing words, thoughts, feelings and beliefs wisely as they will come to pass.

My hope is that you find comfort in the flow of your life and know that whenever you feel pain know that there is also love. Wherever there is blame there is also forgiveness. Wherever there are problems, there are also solutions and how you choose to look at your experiences and your life's struggles will bring you anguish or comfort.

Now twenty-six years later I believe, Laura was my guardian angel. From her conception and first flutters I could no longer ignore the disrespect from my husband. She gave me the strength to leave an unhappy marriage, as I wanted the very best for her life... and mine. She stayed with me until it was her time to go and I have found peace in the thought that she set us free and I know in my heart that one-day we will be together again.

The flow of my life has been guiding me to this point. Even though the clouds will continue to come and go, my compass is set and my heart can shine with renewed strength, understanding and belief in myself. In reading my story I would hope that you might find your compass to discover the incredible strength and love that lies within you to allow your heart to shine. This I feel is my greatest learning and one that I wish to pass on to my sons and to you and together we can create a better world.

About The Author

As a certified Life Coach for parents and youths Tracy's motto is *Connecting Hearts For A Better World.* She believes that the true essence of who we are is found within our spiritual hearts. Her journey of discovering inner peace and freeing her own heart of emotional pain and deeply rooted sabotaging patterns, have helped her self-worth, inner strength and confidence soar. When we can view life in a reflective way our struggles become our checkpoints, our strength builders and our guides to a life of unfolding fulfilment.

Tracy is married with three teenage sons and lives in Brisbane, Australia. Having years of invaluable parenting experience, her mission is to help families with similar issues. Her heart centered approach is based on finding the truth and the root cause of any overwhelm and to help others build stronger connections. It's in the contrast of her life, with the trials and tribulations that have made her stronger and wiser and has brought incredible purpose to her life.

For Tracy, being a part of *Stories That Heal* is a dream come true. Her passions for writing and healing mind, spirit and body and her continual quest in obtaining knowledge have been at the core of who she is since she was thirteen.

Her vision is to make a difference in people's lives and believes living happy and inspired lives is our birthright.

Contact Information:
www.traceignite.com.au
traceignite@gmail.com
+61 434 533 480

CHAPTER 6

THE LEAP TO FREEDOM
Anne Barton

When you come to the edge of all the light you know and are about to step off into the darkness of the unknown, faith is knowing one of two things will happen: There will be something solid to stand on or you will be given wings to fly. Barbara Winter

I'm feeling stuck, lost, unfulfilled. Running through my head are the familiar, nagging, fear-inducing questions "How am I going to pay my bills? How am I going to support myself?" From the depths of my soul I know I have more to offer, I have a specific purpose in this life, but I have no idea how to express it. I want to live a joyous and enthusiastic life, not one of fear and dread. But here I am again, feeling this tightness of anxiety in my chest, clutching fear in my gut.

I know I can always get a temp job. It's an easy way for me to get work, always has been. But I know where that leads because it's been my pattern and 'safe bet' for most of my adult life. I'm well educated and organized, easy to get along with and hard working. Usually a temp job turns into an offer for a permanent job within days. And within a year I'm miserable again, frustrated because I'm doing work I don't love. I only ever make enough money to get by, nothing extra. I can't get ahead and create new options.

There is a deep wound in my heart that comes from a pattern of suffering in silence and never asking for help. I don't let people know how I truly feel. Instead, I just put my head down and work. I know I'm selling myself short but I'm afraid I don't have what it takes to build a business. Can I really market myself, step up when necessary and do what it takes to be successful, no matter what? The fear and doubt keep me cemented in the known and comfortable.

After repeating this pattern for decades, I find myself, yet again, standing on the edge of that deep chasm of dark, bottomless fear. On the other side is freedom. On the other side I have my own business. I'm working from home, serving people, using my gifts and skills to make a good living. I'm my own boss. I just need to take a leap of faith. I know this but I've never been able to summon that level of trust. I've always stepped back instead. I've done what I told myself I have to, to pay my bills and be responsible.

This time, I jumped.

Asking for Help

Back up a few months. I could feel myself approaching that place where I would be facing the decision again - leap or step back. I didn't have enough work, I was running out of money and I really wanted to try starting a business again. A year or so before, I'd participated in a three-day workshop on starting a small business and I heard there, for the first time, the words 'Virtual Assistant.' Something clicked inside me. It sounded like the perfect business for me. Before the workshop started, I'd already decided on a business idea to pursue and I worked through the workshop exercises with that business in mind. However, I continued to dream about what I saw as a perfect match for my skills and my desire to work at home–supporting clients virtually. I didn't know how that would work exactly, but the seed had been planted.

Then an opportunity for some work presented itself. A man I'd met at a real estate workshop (yes, I was trying a lot of different things!) asked me if I would help him put together some spreadsheets for a few new deals he was pursuing. He lived in Southern California and I lived in Northern California. It was an ideal opportunity to try out working virtually and I started right away. He was thrilled with my work and continued to come up with more projects. I was learning how to manage projects with phone calls and email. It seemed perfect. Then he started having back pain and pretty quickly the work came to a halt.

The days of no work stretched into weeks. He seemed to be getting worse, not better. I had a thought that perhaps the reason we were put together was for me to find a way to help him heal his chronic back condition once and for all. Within 48 hours of that thought, I received an email from a woman I'd been following for several years, inviting her followers to a special call that week to share her healing story and introduce Dr. Alex Loyd. I signed up.

On that call I heard about The Healing Codes for the first time. My client had said he was open to anything and everything so I immediately called him to share this program I thought could help him. He told me to order it but have it sent to me, because he "didn't want to read some manual." I was happy to oblige.

A few days later I'd received and read the manual, so I called my client, excited to teach him how to use this simple tool. It turned out he wasn't really open to anything and everything. He was off the phone within minutes, not able or willing to try. I was disappointed and frustrated, but I decided "OK, I'm going to give this tool a try." I started that night and decided to work through the codes, one a day. After a couple of days, I noticed I was feeling a little differently about my situation. I had the thought "Why don't I just create a flyer, send it to everyone I know and announce 'I'm a Virtual Assistant!' What's so hard about that?" Creating a flyer might seem like a fairly easy and perfectly logical step, but it was like standing in front of an auditorium filled with strangers to give a speech, without any preparation or notice of the topic beforehand! It was an invitation to be judged and exposed as not good enough. The perfectionist in me never felt ready for such steps. However, I could feel something had shifted within me because now, instead of feeling too risky, this idea felt exciting, like an invitation to a new life. I sent out the flyer the next day.

Two months later, I'd received lots of positive feedback from my flyer, lots of encouraging replies like 'Oh, that's perfect for you!' Plus I'd received one check, from my best friend who wanted to be my first paying client. I didn't have any clients beyond that, however. I'd been doing the Healing Codes daily, and I continued to feel shifts 'from within.' I got completely honest with myself and knew I wasn't fully committed to the Virtual Assistant idea. There was still some fear and doubt. Deep down what I really wanted to do was become a health coach. But it took money to go to coaching school, so I couldn't seriously consider it. In that small business workshop a year before, we were encouraged to pick something as our business we knew we could get paid for tomorrow. The reasoning for this was that you needed to choose something you knew how to do really well because there would be so many new business building skills to learn and master at the same time. Doing administrative work was what I knew how to do with my eyes closed. It was the logical choice.

Facing the Fear

Then a new opportunity presented itself. I was on a free teleseminar with a business coach I admired and had been following for quite a few years. She taught a variety of energy tools and I always resonated with her work. At the end of the call, she offered a free 30-minute business coaching session to the first three people who contacted her. I called her the minute she ended that teleseminar. I was so quick to dial that she was fully taken aback when she answered the phone. I hadn't given her time to breathe after finishing her teleseminar. This was such unusual behavior for me–to be the first to respond, to dial without even thinking. Shifts were continuing to happen deep within me.

That business coaching call was scheduled for two weeks later. I had bills due now and I had no way to pay them. I was at the precipice faced with the 'leap or step back' choice.

When I jumped, this is what it looked like–I decided to ignore my bills, trust they'd get paid and commit to being as prepared as possible for that 30-minute coaching call. I did The Healing Codes. I walked, meditated and journaled. Each time the anxiety and fear pressed on my chest I closed my eyes and did visualizations until the anxiety subsided. I chose to trust the Universe would provide.

This was the visualization I created that worked best: I'd heard from another coach that the Space Shuttle is off course something like 80% or more of the time and the pilot's job is to keep that 'stick' aligned with their course. He is working against a constant pull away from the course, to get back on course. The visual I had when I first heard that was from the movie *Apollo 13*, when Houston is trying to solve the problem and the three astronauts are floating in space, waiting to hear what they are supposed to do next. They are finally told they need to find a fixed point to direct their capsule towards, so they are aligned with a specific course when they re-enter the atmosphere. They look out their little triangle window and see Earth. Then all three astronauts work together to keep Earth centered in that window. That's what I did. I visualized Earth in that window–that was my place of peace, trust, and calm. My anxiety threw the capsule off course and I meditated and visualized until Earth was centered in the window. I practiced until I could feel a click in the center of my chest when I was on course, and the anxiety fell away.

Choosing a New Path...
And the day came when the risk to remain tight in a bud was more painful than the risk it took to blossom. Anais Nin

By the end of two weeks, I was pretty good at releasing any stress I was feeling. My bills were officially overdue now, a hugely anxiety-producing state for me. But I was in a place of trust. Time to talk to a business coach and figure out my next step. I don't know exactly what I was expecting out of that call. Probably way too much! I hadn't looked beyond it so I had my whole life sort of depending on those 30 minutes. Not a particularly realistic expectation. I learned this woman had a similar history to mine. She'd been an administrative assistant, office manager, executive assistant and then decided she wanted to be a coach. She found a part-time job working for a philanthropist in her home office and earned enough to support herself and go to coaching school. She thought I should pursue something similar. She believed I needed to go to school to be a virtual assistant or a coach, and I'd have to get a job to help make either happen.

Well, that's not exactly what I wanted to hear. I didn't want a job; I wanted a business. I wanted multiple clients, not just one. However, I took some practical actions as a result of that call. The next day, I called my credit card company and made some arrangements to reduce my monthly payment. In the past, I'd never imagined making such a call. That would mean admitting I couldn't handle my finances; that I needed help. At this time, it felt natural and necessary. And the fact that the economy was falling apart worked in my favor. Everyone was struggling and the credit card company was sympathetic and helpful. Next, I went to Craig's List and the newspaper and applied for a couple of jobs. My heart was not in that, and surprise, surprise I never heard back about any of those jobs!

Later that day I sat down with a blank piece of paper and I wrote what my ideal work situation and clients would be. I included things like "Work from home," "Work with people who can afford to pay me," "Work with people who don't require a resume," "Work with like-minded people who are supportive, appreciative and positive." I remember very specifically thinking, "I just want to be paid to work."

The Universe Responds

Before I went to sleep that night, I read my list aloud. The next morning, I received a phone call from a man I didn't know who opened with, "I woke up in the middle of the night last night and thought 'I need an assistant.'" He proceeded to share that he'd contacted a friend first thing in the morning, someone I'd met a year earlier in my real estate dabbling, and she had sent him my flyer. She told him 'she's a member of the GSD club–Gets Stuff Done.' We talked for an hour and then he asked me to work on a project for him. He sent me a check for five hours of work.

This man lived five minutes away from me. He was a newly licensed business coach and he had just purchased membership in an online administrative system for coaches. He offered to pay for half if I was willing to take their 8-week virtual assistant training course. I happened to have exactly half of the cost because he'd just paid me, so I agreed. As a brand new coach, he also told me he couldn't afford to pay me for regular work right away, however he suggested we might consider trading services. I honestly believed the only way I'd be successful at building this business was if I had a business coach, but I'd not even considered yet how that might come about. We created an agreement and have been working together ever since.

After completing the virtual assistant training program, I was invited to be part of their certified virtual assistant team and was given three new clients almost immediately. Seven years later, I still work with two of those three coaches. I could go on to tell story after story of the miraculous opportunities and successes along the path of building this business. The responsibility and focus required to tackle the endless stream of day-to-day decisions and challenges push me to build on my successful results and continue to take leaps regularly. This process has been transformational.

That is not to say I never face challenges or fear. I often say being an entrepreneur is a profound exercise in personal growth. I've been on a personal growth/spiritual journey for more than three decades and I've had other healing successes. But these deep-seated issues in my life - lack of self-confidence, dependence, and settling for less—came into full focus in the past seven years of growing my business.

The most interesting realization of all is that by choosing to do what I knew—organizing and building administrative systems—instead of focusing on my inability to do what I wanted—become a coach—I ended up with something totally unexpected and even more valuable—learning how to build a coaching business.

Reflecting on the Journey

Wisdom doesn't come from the experiences in our lives. It comes from reflecting on our experiences. Jane Fonda

In looking back at this time in my life, I can identify that my key behavior change each step of the way was asking for help. I didn't fully realize this at the time. When it was happening, I was on this amazing ride, watching miracles unfold each step of the way and not fully analyzing what I was doing. After that initial leap, everything felt so new and life affirming.

I asked for help from energy tools. I asked for help from the Universe. I asked for help from experts. I asked for what I wanted.

Even seven years later, I'm still struck by how that leap totally changed the culture of my life. I feel such gratitude for where I am in my life. I talk to and work with amazing clients daily. These are men and women who are committed to supporting transformation in the world. They express their appreciation to me regularly. I have a team of amazing women who support and inspire me. I feel part of a powerful circle of respect, support, love and gratitude. It's such a gift.

If you've ever felt stuck or unfulfilled, like you have something valuable to offer but finding and expressing that true purpose feels daunting and unattainable, I would encourage you to take a leap of faith and pursue your dream. I believe it's why we are here; to share our gifts in our own unique way. There are people in the world waiting especially for what you have to offer.

I've learned that true freedom goes hand in hand with discipline. Perhaps these steps I've learned to take will work for you too!

❖ **Ask**–This means I set my intention and decide what I want, focusing on how I want to feel, not how it's going to happen.

❖   **Acknowledge/clear any debilitating fear** before acting. (Energy tools, prayer, meditation, walking in nature all help with this. I believe *very* strongly that energy tools are a vital part of any daily routine.) The key here is 'debilitating' fear, which comes from that part of us that wants to stay in the known and safe, rather than a natural fear that comes with doing something new and potentially life-changing. I equate it to the stage fright many performers feel. Despite that familiar anxiety, they find the strength to step onto the stage, because they know as soon as they do the fear will fall away.

❖   From this state of calm, I have **trust and faith** that what falls in my path is worth my consideration as the next step on my journey, even if I can't see how it will help.

❖   **Choose and act** from a place of enthusiasm and joy. Ask this question, if you aren't sure about the step: "Is this taking me towards my dreams or away from them?"

❖   Find something to **express appreciation** for, every step of the way.

I feel like this set of tools allows me to meet any challenge I face. And in the past seven years, I have built *my own* history of evidence, which I believe is the most compelling kind. I love reading other people's stories and I can track so many of my behavior changes and successes to the healing story of someone else, motivating me to take a new step. But having my own success stories is what keeps me leaping forward! I feel excited about the opportunities ahead, knowing I can create whatever I ask for. In fact, I'm often a little careful when I ask, because I know I'll get it!

If one advances confidently in the direction of their goals and endeavors to live the life they have imagined, they'll meet with success unexpected in common hours. Henry David Thoreau

About The Author

I believe the 'start a business' seed was planted by my father, who was part owner in a business when I was very young. He ended up returning to a corporate job, something I think he may have regretted later in life. Somehow I feel like I can fulfill what he started with this small business I am building.

It is my intention and vision to partner with coaches and other soul-aligned service professionals to support their business growth. As a team member who can manage the day-to-day administration of their business, I provide them with the freedom to do what they do best - help others live their best lives.

Working at home allows me to live green and healthy. Working virtually makes use of my many years of administrative experience in a new realm. Working with like-minded professionals allows me to share my interest and growth in the personal/spiritual development realm.

I've trusted that all of the pieces to this puzzle of my life would eventually come together in a really exciting way–and now they have!

I am a native Californian, born and raised in Southern California and now living outside of San Francisco, where I've been an active part of the village that raised my two nieces–champion water polo players. We are a musical theater-loving family that also enjoys cooking vegetarian meals and baking together.

Contact Information:
Email: annebartoncva@gmail.com
Web: https://annebarton.coachesconsole.com or http://buildingwellth.com

CHAPTER 7

UNIMAGINABLE: THAT CAN'T HAPPEN TO ME

Bayne Doughty

By the time February of 1952 arrived, so did I–ostensibly against all odds. Although I had no notion of it at the time, my parents had been trying to have a child for nine years. They were living in St. Louis, Missouri, my father's hometown. Eight years earlier in the hours before dawn on June 6, 1944, my father was poised in the doorway of a droning C47 in the darkness over Normandy (France) in the last seconds before parachuting into an abyss of flying bullets and bomb bursts. The sky was illuminated with the flash and concussion of antiaircraft barrages from the German-occupied French countryside below. As he led his men out of the fuselage of the plane into the burning night sky, the tail section had been hit and was engulfed with flames. Many men did not make it to the ground alive that morning.

Others who had jumped with the 80 pounds of gear they needed to carry could not jettison the heavy leg bag which was supposed to release and fall to the ground before the paratrooper made his landing. These men broke their legs upon landing and were sitting ducks for enemy bayonets. The four other officers with whom my father had shared living quarters and friendship before the war did not survive D-Day. Somehow he survived. He discovered that his rifle had a bad firing pin and he discarded it, using his pistol to get through the first days of the Normandy invasion. On the ground he could locate only eleven of the two-hundred men in his Company. When they took position under the bridge which was their assigned objective, it was bombed because the Allied Command knew that the ranks of 101st Airborne had been decimated. Somehow he survived.

I continue to be amazed that my father survived D-Day and then the remainder of the war. He was wounded in Holland in what he related as "the most horrible artillery barrage he could ever have imagined." He had set up a command post in a small schoolhouse which came into the trajectory of a German artillery shell. The schoolhouse came down all around him and he was hit with shrapnel which lodged in his forehead. Somehow he survived. Then there was Bastogne, the epic "Battle of the Bulge" which claimed the lives of thousands of American soldiers surrounded by the Nazi troops and tanks in the Belgian Ardennes. Somehow he survived.

Between the utter perils my father confronted head-on throughout WWII and the apparent issues which prolonged my parents' ability to conceive a child, I feel very lucky to be here at all. Dr. William Masters and Virginia Johnson, famous for their clinical studies on human sexuality, also had a sterility clinic at Washington University Medical School in St. Louis prior to their landmark work with sexuality. I'm told I was a product of that sterility clinic. Somehow I made it into this world!

That God has put me on this earth for a reason is something I don't question. I can safely say I have been tested in ways that I never imagined. I've experienced life events which as a younger man I would have said, "THAT's not going to happen to ME!." And yet multiple "THAT's" have run their course through my life and provide me the basis to want to help others whose lives are visited in unexpected, challenging, even devastating ways by life events. My mission in authoring this chapter of *Stories That Heal* is to deliver a message of encouragement, hope and gratitude; and an exhortation that's it possible, if not imperative, no matter what illness or life calamity has found its way to you, to understand the power and necessity to heal our spiritual hearts. We can live a life free of fear and darkness. We can rise up and boldly walk through unimaginable life circumstances with love and truth as our constant companions. When you think your life is about to be over, it has only just begun.

We had been married 15 happy years when my beautiful wife began to have severe headaches. They got worse. And then she began to have violent nausea and vomiting along with the pain in her head which mostly did not subside. We pursued a string of medical appointments and referrals in an effort to get her relief and find out why she was having such horrible head pain. The answer turned out to be three metastatic brain tumors from an egregiously aggressive cancer in her uterus–stage 4b cancer. It ultimately took her from me and our two daughters who lost their precious mother at the tender ages of 13 and 9. She was only 39 and in the prime of her beautiful life. I had no idea how I would ever survive this loss, how I would be able to raise my daughters without her, how I would ever be able to have any happiness in my life again. The grief and sadness I felt for my young daughters having to live their lives without their mother was overpowering. And yet I knew it was imperative to move forward and through whatever our changed life presented, and find our way through it with courage and strength and hope–just as she would have.

She was amazing in every way, a stalwart, beautiful spirit. She never gave up, she soldiered through every minute of what she had to do to try to heal and survive. I only wish she could have had the toolset of The Healing Codes to help her on this journey.

Eleven years later I had remarried. We had envisioned being our own version of the Brady Bunch. "Faith, hope, love, joy, happiness and FUN" was the motto we wanted for our eclectic family. My second wife of then six years had two young sons to whom I very much wanted to be a real father. My daughters were now young women and largely on their own pursuing their dreams in life. It had not been an easy time, and yet it did become exceedingly more difficult. Cancer reappeared in its inexorable way and once again the woman to whom I was married received an ominous diagnosis. After double mastectomy surgery and chemotherapy, she emerged determined to heal and keep cancer at bay. I could not believe that once again this horrible demon had invaded our lives. I was upset and mad with God.

My stepson loved his mother with all his heart–an exceptionally tight bond, particularly so with a father who had been less than present in his life since a small child. Now at age 13, the stark terror of a cancer diagnosis for his mother led him into experimentation with drugs. His schoolwork suffered. All of the relationships in the family suffered. What had been "not easy" became horribly difficult. It became readily evident that he was using drugs in our home and elsewhere. By the time he was 14, both he and his mother were seeing a chemical dependency counselor in an effort to turn his life around. Our marriage relationship suffered. Our family relationship suffered. I felt desperately unhappy. I was filled with fear for both what could happen and what was happening.

The phone call came at 2:30 a.m. "Mr. Doughty, this is Officer Kreiling with the Hopkins Police. I'm standing in your kitchen and I need to tell you that your house has been broken into and you have had a great deal of property damage and likely many things stolen. You need to come home and secure your house and property as soon as possible." I was stunned. I had gotten this call in northern Minnesota at our lake property. My father and I had left for the weekend to open the Minnesota fishing season on our favorite chain of lakes. I was speechless except to rouse my father and tell him we needed to head home.

The police said that there had been as many as 50 people in our house the night of the break-in. And from interviews they conducted, they established that there had been known drug dealers present at certain times during the night. My wife and stepsons had also gone north for the weekend but to Duluth. We both needed time apart to think and reflect. Our marriage was at its lowest ebb–or so we thought until the 2:30 a.m. phone call from the Hopkins Police.

We arrived home at approximately the same time that morning. It looked like a war zone. There were cigarette butts and burns everywhere–in the sinks, on the countertops and hardwood floors, all of which were used as ashtrays. There was broken glass everywhere. What had not been stolen had been smashed. The basement door had been pried off its hinges and lay in large splinters. Every drawer in the house had been turned upside down, ransacked and emptied. There was vomit on the walls and on the floors. Every bed in the house had been used for sex. Liquor bottles and evidence of drug use was everywhere. It was unimaginable. I did not know how we would get through this horror or how we would ever be able to put our home back together again as a family.

The police wanted to see my stepson at the police station to question him. Three hours later, my wife pulled up in the driveway with both boys in the car and said she was going to go live with her parents for a while. Three days later I received an email from her requesting a divorce.

The divorce was final 60 days later. We did not fight each other. I would retain the house, but in so doing I had to sell the cabin property to accommodate my ex-wife's financial interest in what had been a marriage just short of eight years. All of the events at hand devastated me. The end of a marriage dream, the horror of a teenager deeply ensnared in drug use, the utter destruction and desecration of our home and belongings, having to sell the cabin property that I dearly loved, and for which I had greatly sacrificed to be able to have. It all seemed impossibly, irreparably dark. I did not know how I would be able to go on; just that I must. It was another occasion in my life where I admitted to myself that I did not recognize this as MY life, this was not supposed to happen to ME. But it *was* my life and it *was* happening.

"I can pay cash for a property like yours" had read the small printed card that was attached to the gate to my cabin property. "I would never sell this property" I remember saying to myself at the time. It was pristine, beautiful northern Minnesota property–33 acres and 1500 feet of lakeshore on a beautiful lake which was part of a chain of lakes formed by the damming of the Mississippi River. And yet here I was, preparing to meet a realtor who had been highly recommended to me because what I never dreamed possible now *needed* to happen. I was getting a divorce, and I had to sell the cabin. Both scenarios were unimaginable to me under any circumstances and yet here I was doing two things which only a short time ago were the unthinkable. And I was still in the process of dealing with the insurance claim and cleaning up the aftermath of the break-in and devastation of the home in Hopkins. The losses had totaled over $30,000, and after writing the check, the insurance company promptly and tersely informed me that they would no longer insure me. I was numb and filled with disbelief.

The real estate agent was friendly, pleasant, professional and provided much encouragement that the cabin property was "premium" real estate and there would be no problem in dividing the lakeshore into lots and selling it at top dollar. He came out and met me at the lakeshore to see the land and discuss possible options. We walked almost the entire parcel and then sat in front of the cabin looking at the lake. We talked shop and much more. He had many ideas for possible division. We went on to talk about hunting and fishing and discovered that we had much in common with love of the outdoors. We ended up talking about a lot more than real estate that day. We talked about our families and about events which had happened in our lives. He seemed like a really nice person with whom I had a lot in common. I was very happy I had met him and I thought "God puts people in your life for a reason; maybe he is one of them."

Over the course of the next few months the property was divided, listing agreements were signed and prospective buyers lined up to see the beautiful lake property which was no longer to be mine. Within mere weeks of listing, offers came in at the listed prices. Overnight envelopes began landing on my doorstep which contained checks for proceeds from the sale of the lake lots from closings that I did not even have to attend. Everything seemed to be falling into place and exactly as advertised.

About a month after the first closing, my new realtor friend, who I now had known for six months, started talking about investing in real estate. I explained that I needed to retire some debt associated with my divorce, but that I wanted to be a good steward with the remaining proceeds from the lot sales. It was important that I invest wisely and hopefully have a chance to own a place on the water again some time in my life. I did not know it at the time, but from that moment on, what would happen over the course of the next three years would drastically alter the course and trajectory of my life.

It was the night of the Customer Appreciation Dinner for the realty company with whom I had done a great deal of business in the past three years. I had driven to the northern Minnesota home of my realtor friend and his wife who was also a real estate agent. We had become close friends to say the least over the course of the three years. We had vacationed together and recreated together and spent a great deal of time in one another's company both personally and professionally. When I had real estate business to attend to up north, I stayed at their home in a guest room which they came to refer to as being "your room." A bond of friendship and trust had formed and cemented over the course of three years and a series of over fifteen real estate transactions, which at the time of the Customer Appreciation Dinner, found me owning two sizeable lakeshore development properties. This night when they greeted me, the look on their faces let me understand that something was terribly amiss. They were breathless and visibly agitated. They did not seem themselves as I had come to know them. Something seemed terribly wrong.

Something *was* terribly wrong. The FBI had raided the realty company that day with 10 federal agents who executed a search warrant and seizure order. The FBI agents confiscated over 150 files of closed real estate transactions and conducted interviews with numerous personnel who worked for the realty company, including my realtor friends. Upon obtaining a copy of the FBI search warrant, I later came to find out that two of those files were transactions where I was the buyer of the real estate which involved a high value lakeshore development that I had purchased and been working on for the last nine months. A third file was that of a recently completed transaction as a buyer of a golf course investment property with deeded lake access to a major Minnesota landmark lake.

Some days later, articles appeared in both newspapers in the Twin Cities and the northern Minnesota town describing the FBI raid and the criminal activities that had been taking place. I recognized names of people I had come in contact with in the course of buying real estate over the last three years with what had been my highly trusted friends. About a week later I received a copy of the FBI Search Warrant Affidavit.

By the time I read the newspaper articles[1] and the FBI affidavit, reality was setting in. I felt as if I had been hit in the solar plexus with a battering ram. I felt certain that any semblance of my life as I had come to know it was OVER. It suddenly washed over me like a gigantic ocean wave which sucked all oxygen out of my lungs. I had lived through cancer with two wives, had seen the mother of my precious children slip away in a brain-tumored morphine stupor after having endured unspeakable pain and trauma in the course of her illness; had helped my second wife endure the horrible ravages of breast cancer while witnessing a teenage stepson self-destruct with drug abuse; I had received the email that informed me I would be getting a divorce after the destruction and desecration of our home; I had been forced to sell the cabin property that I loved so dearly and had worked so hard to be able to own; and now, having

---

[1] Bemidji Pioneer, 2008; Mpls Star Tribune, 2008

worked and studied and strived for three years in an attempt to rebuild dreams and reassemble a life and pass on a legacy of love to my children and the family I had wanted to build, I realized that I stood to be financially ruined.

The FBI Affidavit told the grim tale of Mortgage Fraud, otherwise known as "Fraud for Profit, that involves industry professionals and usually includes numerous gross misrepresentations... The property value is often inflated through appraisal to increase the sales value... and to generate cash proceeds... Common professional fraud schemes include... Property Flips: property is purchased, falsely appraised at a higher value and then quickly sold... The schemes typically involve fraudulent appraisals, doctored loan documents and inflation of the buyer's income... the artificial and fraudulent sale of a property between a group of conspirators for the purpose of fraudulently raising the price of the property.

Such a conspiracy will often involve the connivance of an appraiser, a realtor, a mortgage or loan officer and an investor. In the common practice of such a conspiracy, a property will be 'sold' between a group of conspirators, including sham or 'straw' buyers, several times within a short period of time... The conspirators may use false or 'straw' sales to collect real estate commissions, loan origination commissions or appraisal fees, especially in the case where one of the conspirators may actually obtain a mortgage from a financial institution at the inflated price; in effect, receiving a loan in excess of the actual, known value of the property. Such 'flipping' transactions will ultimately require a legitimate, end buyer of the property in order that the conspirators be relieved of any financial liability regarding the property transaction, including taxes and mortgages, and to provide the conspirators with their expected profit for their role in the conspiracy..."

In this moment of realization, I understood that I was the "legitimate end buyer" and had been used and manipulated and orchestrated into purchasing the properties that I now owned at prices in great excess to what they were actually worth. I felt sheer, unadulterated terror invade every cell of my body. I physically and spiritually realized betrayal and hopelessness and destruction in one crashing, engulfing, all-encompassing moment. Destruction, hopelessness and betrayal of everything I had worked for and achieved in 56 years–evaporated, poof, gone.

It was Christmas morning four years later when my smiling eldest daughter handed me a wrapped gift with light dancing in her eyes and said, "Here, Dad, this one's for you." In the intervening four years, I had found my way through the unimaginable events associated with the real estate fraud. It was by no means "over," but as had come to be my bent in life I was "still standing" and working diligently through the issues. I underwent two cardiac ablation procedures the year before, but I still could not shake the occurrences of what is known as atrial fibrillation every couple of months. My heart would beat wildly in a very inefficient rhythm that was extremely uncomfortable. The stress in my life was immense. Inside the wrapping was a hardcover book titled *The Healing Code* by Alexander Loyd, PhD, ND and Ben Johnson, MD, DO, NMD. With the book was a card from my daughter and her husband which I taped to the inside cover which read:

Dad, Merry Christmas! I read this for research this semester [as she studied for her Master's Degree in Holistic Studies at St. Catherine's University in St. Paul, MN] *and it was kind of a doorway to health and healing I hadn't considered before. I believe there are some very valuable concepts to ponder in it, and wanted to share it with you---someone who is also constantly seeking a better path. I ask that you approach this with a completely open heart and mind, and to read it cover to cover. Thank you for all you do. We love you!*

Read the book I did! Today this book is ragged and dog-eared; the jacket cover is taped together and many (approaching all) pages are flagged and tabbed and underlined and highlighted. Actually I read the book soon after receiving it and I was thoroughly intrigued with everything it said; so intrigued that I also purchased it as an audio book and listened to it on long road trips. Then I read it again some months later. Somewhere between the third or fourth reading I realized that I was in fact "stalled." I read the book, I understood the book, it made sense, it was filled with cutting edge science, it was filled with God-centered wisdom, it provided a medically unprecedented path to heal physically and emotionally as experienced by hundreds if not thousands of people, but I was stalled because "as powerful as *The Healing Code* principles are, they won't work by themselves. You must diligently practice the Healing Code techniques and use the tools such as the Heart Issues Finder"[i]. And although I had read and understood *The Healing Code* concepts, I took no action.

Yet another trip to the doctor with my racing heart found me on a Sunday at the ER. When my afib issue presented itself during the week, I would be treated by the cardiac clinic doctors and staff. On the weekend I had no choice but to go to the ER. I learned that day that protocols varied between the clinic and the ER. Everything proceeded in the fashion to which I had become unfortunately accommodated until the point I realized that I had just felt, in real-time, what it was like to be awake for the hit delivered by the paddles pushing 200 joules of electrical energy through my chest.

Therein lay the difference in protocols followed by the ER versus the clinic. The ER used a different drug to put me asleep and they used a sparing dosage which did not have me completely "asleep" compared to what took place in the clinic.

This experience gave me pause. It had become time for me to step back and take a look at my life–"a fearless personal inventory." I didn't feel healthy, I didn't feel GOOD in the manner that I had for most of my life. About two years after the death of my first wife, I began to experience severe instances of atrial fibrillation where my heart would reach rates of 130, 160 or even 200 beats per minute. And it would continue for days unless I got to a hospital!

With a procedure called "electro cardioversion" a person suffering atrial fibrillation is placed on a series of cardiac monitors, is anesthetized for a brief "nap" and then administered an electric shock ("the paddles"–150 to 200 joules) which stops and (usually) starts one's heart beating in a normal sinus rhythm. Since 1997, I have undergone this procedure over 30 times in my life. I have also had four cardiac catheter ablation surgeries–two in 2001 and two in 2010 which had me on the operating table under a general anesthesia for a total of 36 hours between the four procedures. The procedure calls for the insertion of a catheter in the groin, neck or arm through blood vessels which lead into the heart where radio frequency (RF) energy is used to destroy small areas of heart tissue where abnormal heartbeats may cause an arrhythmia to start. *The Healing Code* discusses energy of all types and discusses the role of energy in healing our spiritual hearts.

After my first two catheter ablations in 2001, I lived a life free of any symptoms of afib for many years. It was the day in June that I met with the realtor to discuss the division and sale of the cabin property in 2004 when we walked the property. While driving back to Minneapolis that afternoon, I felt the switch flip inside my chest and my heart began beating frantically. I pulled off the road and called my doctor at the Minneapolis Heart Institute. Afib was back in my life.

As I thought about the events of my life, I realized that there were many things which had occurred which still carried a hurtful emotional charge in me–energy which was destructive. There were things in my life about which I was angry, bitter and resentful.

And I concluded that it was obviously having a deleterious effect on my health. I thought it was interesting that my heart was apparently bearing the brunt of this load, and I was getting tired of being recognized on sight and known by my first name at the Minneapolis Heart Institute–"What? Back so soon?" It was as if I had become the character of Norm Peterson in the television comedy "Cheers," except substitute a major cardiac care clinic instead of a drinking establishment. I remembered that *The Healing Code* discussed stress in great detail as it related to illness. I opened the book again. The words leapt out at me because I had already highlighted and underlined them:

According to Stanford University Medical School in research released in 1998 by Dr. Bruce Lipton, a highly renowned and respected cell biologist, stress is the cause of at least 95% of illness and disease.

Stress affects you emotionally, as well, marring the joy you gain from life and loved ones.

In other words, whatever problem you have, somehow or another, it probably came from stress.

Then it hit me. I had been living my life filled with stress and fear and a sense of impending doom–not consciously, because my self-talk for my whole life has always been about doing the right thing with strength and courage, and doing what must be done even though the task might be onerous.

I had always tried to emulate the example of courage and strength provided by my father in WWII. But I knew that I had been living my life for the last 23 years in a state of constant stress brought about by the events of my life–death of a spouse, cancer with two wives, drug abuse by a stepson about whom I cared greatly, divorce, having to sell the beloved lake property, fraud and deception by people I thought were trusted friends leading to enormous and catastrophic financial loss.

I had made it through it all "still standing," but what was my heart having to say about all of this? Every couple of months it would just haul off and beat incessantly out of control and would not stop until it had been hit with a freight train of an electric shock! Something had to change. I realized that my self-talk these days was often very angry and full of profanity. What I had been doing for the last 17 years was not working. Getting more catheter ablations and cardioversions did not seem to me to be a sustainable model for my health.

I opened the book again. I reread "The Three One Things" and especially One Thing #3: "There's one thing on planet Earth that can turn One Thing #1 (the immune and healing systems of the body) back on. What is it? Healing the issues of the heart!"

"The Healing Codes can turn the immune and healing systems back on because it heals 'issues of the spiritual heart'. The Healing Codes® encapsulates the discovery of a system that's been in the body since the dawn of time. How do we know that The Healing Codes can turn them on again? Because when we use a gold standard medical test that does not respond even 1 percent to the placebo effect, the results are unprecedented in the history of medicine."

I reread the inspiring story of Dr. Ben Johnson and his amazing journey through and deliverance from incurable ALS. Like Dr. Ben, it was time for me to "take the plunge." I signed up for Dr. Alex's LT3 course and spent 5 weeks immersed in study and practice of The Healing Codes and had five one on one sessions with Dr. Alex. I also came away with lifetime healing codes developed by Dr. Alex just for me. What an amazing gift it has been!

My results are amazing to me. I no longer have atrial fibrillation beyond a couple of stray beats every now and then. I feel it occur and then just about as quickly as it starts, my heart rhythm corrects back to its normal 58 beats per minute. I firmly believe and confidently assert that the work done with The Healing Codes has changed the energy patterns and frequencies in my physical heart because of healing which has taken place in my spiritual heart. I hasten to add that I am no longer upset and angry with God.

I now thank Him continually for the many amazing blessings He has placed in my life. None of the doctors or medical professionals I started seeing in 1997 ever mentioned a word about healing one's spiritual heart–nor perhaps would we expect them to. Instead, there were myriad cardiac pharmaceuticals, "drugs du jour" and my "Norm Peterson-esque" trips to the ER or the Minneapolis Heart Institute to get hit with the paddles once again. But maybe the day will come when many others like me will be able to reverse symptoms of stress manifested with irregular heart rhythms by healing the issues of the spiritual heart. Maybe then the doctors of the future will help us heal our problems at the source by helping us heal our stress.

Atrial Fibrillation (also "Afib" and "AF") has been described as "the epidemic of the new millennium," with projections for up to 15 million Americans expected to be affected by 2050.[2] To all those who may be already, or who become so

---

[2] KPCNews.com, Dr. Terry Gaff, April 18, 2015

affected via whatever life circumstances creating the stress which takes unruly control of their life, I offer my story and my heartfelt exhortation to "take the plunge." When you think your life is about to be over, it has only just begun.

About The Author

J. Bayne Doughty continues to enjoy what has become a 40-year career in information technology (IT), having begun his career with IBM in 1977. Today he works for an IBM Business Partner firm headquartered in Hamel, Minnesota, Evolving Solutions, Inc., helping large corporate clients solve business problems utilizing IBM and other leading edge IT providers to create enterprise IT infrastructure solutions.

He is a proud father of two daughters and a "still speechless" grandfather to four grandsons who he refers to as his "Band of Merry Men" He is an avid outdoorsman and adventurer and can be found on the water or in the woods when time permits.

His interest in health, wellness and nutrition has become a lifelong quest for knowledge. He aspires to become a certified Healing Codes Practitioner with hopes to give back to those in need and serve those who seek help.

jbdoughty@comcast.net

CHAPTER 8

THE SHADOW OF ILLEGITIMACY
Ruth Duffield

Blighted by shame and the negative consequences of believing the lies you tell yourself.

Setting the scene

The teenager was sitting on the big shiny dark red mahogany dining table, carelessly swinging her skinny legs, wondering what her Dad wanted to talk to her about.

It all started out innocently enough as he talked about her birth certificate that she had never actually seen. She had no idea what he was talking about until he bluntly told her that the reason she had not seen it was because it stated that she was adopted.

Lifeshock! She vaguely heard the grandfather clock in the corner chime but for her, at that instant, time stood still! No air to breathe. She was suffocating!

Such cold words, no hug, no kiss, no comforting endearments of love to soften the blow, and her mother was nowhere to be seen.

He went on to say that her brother and sisters did not know and we would not tell them in case they said something unkind to her. Apart from revealing that her birth mother was a nurse and her birth father was a doctor, that was the end of his monologue. She was rendered speechless as he walked out of the room, leaving her on her own to digest what he had told her.

She went out into the garden, feeling dazed and numb. Gradually the numbness turned into bewilderment and insecurity. She could not cry. There was nobody to talk to about this bombshell. At least it made sense of why she always felt the odd one out. She *was* the odd one out after all.

The death of innocence

It had been a secret kept from her for sixteen years and now she was told it would remain a secret from her siblings. It was *never* spoken of again *ever*! For that teenager it was the birth of shame and the death of her innocence! Just at a time when she was leaving school and needed every ounce of confidence to go out into the world.

Yes, you have guessed it–that teenager was me. It was like having a hand of silence placed over my mouth. Can you believe that my brother and three sisters did not discover the truth until after my adoptive mother died? At this point I was twenty-five and married.

The day she died, three months to the day after my wedding day, I distinctly heard a voice in my head, obviously hers, telling me she could go now that I had someone else to look after me.

What I made it mean

I am telling my story because of the lasting negative effect this secrecy had on me. My self-esteem plummeted as I made up a story that I am unlovable if my birth mother gave me away and there must be something fundamentally wrong with me. That was the start of my Core Shadow Belief. And if there is something wrong with me then I am not deserving of all the good things in life. This life-shock moment and the meaning I put on it has played out in every area of my life.

Turning the clock back

The shame I felt growing up started long before that pivotal moment when I discovered I was adopted. In fact that same dining table, where I innocently sat swinging my legs in curious anticipation of what Dad had to tell me, was the same table I frequently hid under to avoid his belt when I had displeased him.

Dad was a lay preacher in the local church and well-loved in the community for his generous acts of kindness, but behind closed doors a different side of his personality emerged. He was also a harsh disciplinarian who ruled us children with his belt.

Stepping back in time, I thought my parents would be proud of me as I rushed home to boast that I had passed the eleven plus exam to go to grammar school. But my joy was crushed when instead they told me not to get too big for my boots. Only in later years did I wonder if it was because my older brother could not read or write. At that time–dyslexia was not known.

It was left to a kind neighbour to take me to visit my new school in their car. She gave me a hockey stick and even bought me a little blue case for my schoolbooks. I have not forgotten the giddy joy of being the centre of attention for a change.

Know your place

It was drummed into us that there was a wide distinction between them and us - meaning the rich folk and the poor folk. Now as an adult I understood that it is a culture thing because mother worked as a housemaid and dad was a gardener for the same household. They assumed these roles were always our station in life.

Consequently, I developed a poverty consciousness very early in life, and always felt ashamed of being brought up in extreme poverty. Whether it was being seen to have free school dinners or being mocked for wearing homemade school uniforms. There was no way I would invite friends home because our toilet did not flush and it meant pouring buckets of water down it. Also we used newspaper for toilet paper. I was also self-conscious on parents' evening when Dad in his heavy hobnailed working boots would be heard clumping noisily down the school corridor. Thinking about that I also remember that Dad repaired all our shoes. I would admire that now, but at the time, I felt it brought unwelcome attention to me. One of my jobs as a teenager was to cycle to a relative's house on a three-wheeler bike transporting dustbins of pigswill. I lived in dread that classmates would see me.

There were occasional carefree days too. My fondest memory was haymaking in the summer. Dad would hand up pitch-forkfuls of hay onto the cart as I was atop the hay, spreading it evenly. When the cart was full, he would dig two pitchforks into the hay, and I would slide down them to the ground. My sisters tell me they hated having to drag the heavy cart, but I never minded that.

Hardship

All our clothes came from jumble sales, even my first bra. I can see it now–one of those circular stitched pointed bras that Madonna wore on stage. At least as the eldest girl I did not suffer further hand me downs like my younger sisters did. I can still recall the sheer bliss I felt when I bought my first coat in installments from a shop after I earned my own money.

My childhood seemed to be one humiliation after another.

Our mother had no housekeeping money and had to put the groceries on the bill that Dad settled on payday. I recall telling my children if they did not finish their meal they would have it later–so concerned was I about wasting food, having grown up in the days of rationing and little money to put food on the table. I still don't like to see people pile food onto their plates then throw half of it away. I have just had a light bulb moment–maybe that is why I always cook big portions. As children, our weekly treat was an orange or a Mars bar cut into five pieces shared amongst us all.

Humiliation

It was during my first job as an office junior that I was summoned into the welfare office because someone had complained I had body odour. I felt utterly humiliated as I lied about which deodorant I used when in truth we had no running hot water or toothbrushes.

I was equally embarrassed when the local paper reported that my brother, who had got in with the wrong crowd, had been sent to prison for petty theft. At the time I could never understand why my mother visited him when he had brought shame on the family. I had no idea then how strong the love of a mother is for her child regardless. All I could fearfully think of was that if people read the article they would judge me as being tarred with the same brush. In my ignorance and feeling victimised, the strategy I used to tolerate the situation was to silently judge my family.

Making my escape

Not long after that I eagerly left home to work at a holiday camp followed by a spell abroad in the Navy, Army and Air Force Institute. Just before being posted to Germany we lodged in a hostel where I had my first experience of a shower instead of a strip wash at the kitchen sink–bliss!

The NAAFI did not work out so my friend and I broke the two-year contract. To my surprise, my Dad found the money from somewhere to pay my airfare back to England. Knowing there was no likelihood of my 21st birthday being celebrated at home I soon took off to find work in London.

Falling in love

My next adventure was working as a waitress in Jersey, where I met my future husband Eric. Along with some girlfriends I had already paid ten pounds for my passage to Australia for two years. He said if you are not back by then I am coming to get you. No need because by this time I had fallen in love and cheerfully waved my pals goodbye. I never regretted that decision.

One of the questions he asked me was if I had left home because I was adopted. I truthfully told him that was not the reason. I left home because I was fed up being bitten by the fleas in my bed. This truth would be hilariously funny if it weren't so embarrassing.

On a visit to my parents' home with Eric, I noticed there was a bucket on the table to catch the raindrops from the leaking roof, as we ate our meal in the verandah. As if that wasn't embarrassing enough, I saw my brother outside and my brand new fiancé remarked there was a tramp coming down the garden. I wanted the floor to swallow me up, as I had to admit it was my brother. Just recently that embarrassing memory was triggered when I was offered a lift to my sister's funeral, which would save me three train changes. I found myself making excuses because I was worried about being judged when she met my brother who is still scruffy. The old shame was re-ignited until I plucked up the courage to tell my friend the truth.

My body speaks for me

After I married and had our daughter I developed ankylosing spondylitis, an exceedingly painful inflammation of the entire spine. She cried a lot and as a new mother with no family to turn to I struggled and felt resentful that she stopped crying the minute her Dad walked through the door and picked her up.

My emotional pain was primal but I was unable to say I felt hurt when he gave the baby more attention than he gave me. My body spoke my mind with the ankylosing spondylitis, because he had to help me in and out of bed and chair. Looking back, what a dysfunctional way of getting someone's attention. Perhaps my body was indicating I needed a backbone not a wishbone. It was seven years before that arthritis burnt itself out after which I was left with a number of fused vertebrae. At that time I worked as a waitress while a child minder looked after our daughter. I refused to give in to the pain. That is how unworthy of self-care I believed I was. I am still stoical by nature and I know that is not a good thing when taken to extremes.

Abandonment Issues

I remember an odd occurrence when we took our baby daughter Kim out for the very first time and I was suddenly physically incapable of pushing the pram. To this day I don't know what came over me. Many years later when describing this to my therapist, she wondered if it could have been a symbolic way of not wanting to push the baby away from me as had happened to me.

Years later I could not bear to be left out when Kim decided to research universities by herself. This was perfectly understandable given her independent nature. But the rejected inner child within me felt compelled to take a day off work to follow her. Bumping into her in the street in another town stopped me in my tracks. I did not know what to say so walked away without saying a word. I was appalled at my behaviour but felt helpless to deal with it at the time. Naturally she told her Dad and he gave me a hard time when I got home. I was unable yet again to explain my inner anguish and so continued to believe in my tortured mind that he would always put her wishes first.

By chance it was Kim, not me, who got to spend her Dad's last night on earth with him, and I felt jealous. It seems to me that complex generational unseen cosmic forces took over my female line and that not only my birth mother and my adoptive mother, but also Kim and I have a sacred contract to be played out for my soul's growth.

Long-term effects of believing I am unworthy
I have no doubt that Kim is my earth-bound guardian angel and on one memorable occasion a few years ago, God used her to rescue me when I was almost at death's door with pulmonary embolisms in both lungs. Despite living five hundred miles away, she put the wheels in motion to alert my son, who was only an hour's drive away, to come to my aid. It was typical self-sabotage as I did not take proper care of myself.

I still find it easier to give than to receive. It recently took me weeks before I could comfortably accept financial help from Kim and her equally loving husband for some work done in my house. Such is the power of still believing the lie that I am unworthy and that life is a struggle.

My healing
Most of my healing started over twenty years ago when I began training as a transpersonal psychotherapist, and we

were obliged to have weekly personal therapy. I got in touch with the inner wounds caused by my dysfunctional upbringing. However, it is one thing to understand intellectually that your parents do the best they can, given their own upbringing, but that is to overlook the lasting emotional impact.

I am forever grateful that I had a very good therapist who held my feet to the fire and made me face my demons. She also metaphorically walked beside me as I, tentatively at first, searched for my birth mother after both my adopted parents had died. It would have felt disloyal to do it whilst they were still alive.

That was a very emotional journey for me. What if my birth mother did not want to meet me? Could I cope with a second rejection? It turned out that she had already died. Even though they had not known of my existence, her family nevertheless made me very welcome. It was fascinating to be shown where she had lived, where she had gone to school and the hospital where she died. Even more fascinating to be told that I had so many of her mannerisms. I was on cloud nine for ages after meeting them. It filled that empty void in my heart, particularly when they hoped I would stay in touch.

Getting it all into perspective

What is abundantly clear to me now is that the shadow of illegitimacy negatively affected my birth mother as well as me. The stigma in those days of having a child out of wedlock meant that she would have suffered in secret the heartbreak of having to part with me. Chances are that she would not only have been unable to support a child financially on her own but it could also have reduced her chances of marrying–who knows? I learned from her family that she had had a hard life. I am so grateful to her for giving me life whilst sacrificing her own.

Understanding the Shadow

The Shadow is a term coined by Carl Jung that refers to the traits we try to hide or deny because we deem them unacceptable. They arise when our early caregivers, though well meaning, sometimes give us a message that we need to be a certain way to be loved. Since we depend on them for our very survival we bend ourselves out of shape to be acceptable.

Unconscious shadow beliefs drive our thoughts and behaviours. Even now, despite working in a profession, I still think of myself as working class.

My personal dysfunctional behaviour used to be to people-please, hoping to be loved. That is very tiring and does not work anyway. Thankfully I have outgrown that particular habit. Also I have had a lifelong habit of buying top of the range stuff in order to mask my feelings of inferiority. I remember diligently saving up for a coveted Burberry raincoat that I felt would make me somebody. Eventually I realised it was still only a raincoat. Similarly I hankered to live in Surrey because it is considered to be a posh area. I smile looking back of course because it is actually no different to anywhere else.

Recognising the Gifts

In hindsight, the gift of growing up in my particular family and not wanting their lifestyle has encouraged me to work hard. More importantly, I have compassion when I see others labouring under the illusion that they are not enough! I firmly believe that everything in life happens for a reason. My individual experiences definitely taught me compassion for others–even some for myself, though that is still a work in progress I have to admit. Shadow work is undoubtedly the work of the heart warrior.

I saw my father badly treating my mother and, because he held the purse strings she never had any money. I 'vowed' that I would never have a life like hers and determined to 'have what I want when I want it.' Because this 'vow' became buried in my subconscious I had no idea my teenage self was running the show with my finances.

I am inclined to believe my soul's task is to transform the negative lies I have told myself about being unworthy and unlovable. I cannot change the facts of my birth but I do have the power to change what I make it mean.

Do you have a childhood imprint that is holding you back?

Healing the Inner Child

I am telling my story because of the far-reaching negative effect my self-invented Core Shadow Belief had on my self-esteem. My self-esteem plummeted as soon as I made up a story that if my birth mother gave me away then there must be something wrong with me, and to assure you that there is a way we can heal ourselves.

In fact, all the so-called negative events in my life are only painful because deep down I have laboured under the illusion that I am not enough. But what if there was never anything wrong with me in the first place? What if we all chose to see ourselves as God sees us–perfect in every way?

We tend to live unconsciously - simply taking on board whatever cultural beliefs we were exposed to as children, when we were like sponges, soaking up everything we were told.

It turns out that all events are essentially neutral until we assign them a meaning. The good news is that we can choose to assign a more positive meaning any time we like.

Insights

Now I realise that having been given away at birth for reasons that made good sense to my birth mother at the time, I have unwittingly abandoned myself for most of my life. I believe it was all in God's plan for my soul's evolution because now that I am older and wiser I get to transform my illusions into the truth of who I really am.

That is why I have come to the conclusion that our childhood traumas are an integral part of our soul's journey. What is the lesson my particular trauma was sent to teach me? I think it has a lot to do with realising I can choose to esteem myself, not look for external validation. I confess I am still working on that one.

Some Remedies

As an incurable workshop junkie I have been blessed to benefit from many great teachers, and discovering along the way that there are a number of ways to heal our false Shadow Beliefs. For example, Dr. Alex Loyd's 'Greatest Principle' teaches us that it is not our fault that our negative

Shadow Beliefs get programmed into our subconscious mind. His particular method of healing involves 'deprogramming' the lies we tell ourselves and reprogramming ourselves with the truth of who we are. It involves utilising his Energy Medicine Tool, his Heart Screen Meditation and a Reprogramming Tool, all of which are very effective.

There is also Colon Tipping's Radical Forgiveness Healing Tool, which helps us to understand that there are no mistakes and everything is exactly as it should be, so there is actually nothing to forgive. Marisa Peer, a well-known English transformational hypnotherapist instructs us to write 'I am enough' in lipstick on the bathroom mirror, where we see it every day. This action is so simple but so effective.

As a certified Shadow Coach, trained by the late great Debbie Ford, it is now my privilege to guide others to become more self-accepting and to see the gift in their various Shadow Beliefs.

The Enormous Power of Interpretation

Of course, there is an enormous shift in attitude now compared to when I was born in an unmarried mothers' home in England nearly eighty years ago. I feel thankful that there is no longer a stigma attached to a woman bringing up a child on her own.

As I look back over my life I realise that most of my emotional pain has been caused less by the events than by the meaning I put on them.

Your situation might be completely different from mine, but what I hope you get from my story is that whatever negative meaning you have assigned to a difficult situation in your life, it is never too late to choose a more positive interpretation. It could prove to be your salvation.

About The Author

Ruth lives in Egham, Surrey, England, just half a mile from where the Magna Carta was signed. She works face to face or worldwide over skype as a Transpersonal Psychotherapist and Integrative Coach (Shadow Coach, Best Year of Your Life Coach, Courage Coach, and Relationship Coach). Her coaching training with the late Debbie Ford gives her a strong platform for partnering effectively with clients to move beyond their limitations, accessing their own inner wisdom, in the discovery of their heart's desires both personally and professionally. If you are interested in working with her, please see contact details below.

She was awarded an MA in Transpersonal Psychotherapy for her Research Paper on 'Retirement–Is it a time for Self-Discovery?', which she presented to the BACP Conference in 2000. Ruth also trained with Caroline Myss as an Archetypal Consultant and is a qualified Hypnotherapist. Her favourite hobbies are cooking and dining with friends and family and facilitating book study groups.

Contact Information
Telephone: 44 – (0) 1784 472069
E-mail: ruthduffield@icloud.com, Skype: rutheric
Website: www.ruthduffield-livingconsciously.com
www.thefordinstitute.com/coaches

CHAPTER 9

LIFE BEYOND MY WILDEST DREAMS
Patricia Iorillo

The downtown train came screeching to a torturous halt, piercing my ears with unendurable pain. Wincing, I covered my ears with freezing hands as my mother kissed my father goodbye. One more icy winter day in the suburbs of New York, hands chapped from the dry wind, I managed to sit on them for the drive home, missing my dad. His sacrifice gave us more than heart could wish. Our New England waterfront home had twenty-five rooms and five bathrooms. While sitting in the office of Mother Superior, my stomach turned when asked why I wanted to come to her school.

"I don't!" My candor surprised her. I continued, "It was my mother's idea!" The youngest of five, all of us went to private school except me. I was fourteen, tired of the rigors of religion, and hated those mean nuns.

A providential seed was growing inside me that I just could not bear. It was simply getting too big. Crying out to God on the inside, I wanted to know, "What is true?" Why didn't I see evidence of this loving God in the people around me? Especially those teaching me? Educated in a sea of humanism, I was all but lost in its undertow.

Soon spring broke forth with its promise! The fresh, clean balmy air was hypnotizing. Somewhere between skipping and dancing my mile walk home from school, every tree and flower beckoned me to embrace new life. A spiritual high lifted me into a dream as I thought, "I'm going to meet with God!"

Entering the house without interruption, and keeping my promise to pass the refrigerator, I fell to my knees alone on my bedroom floor. With intentional effort, I shifted my mind and heart. It had been a long time. I hadn't bothered the Almighty in quite a while. "God?" I meekly cried, "What is the Truth?" I paused to collect my questions, then continued.

"I mean, everybody believes *something* ... and of course they all *think they're right*!" I gave the Almighty some examples, just to be clear, then continued, "I don't want to be like that. Teach me *the* truth." Finally, I added, "Like ... about *everything!*"

The very next day, sitting alone in the school cafeteria, I felt a huge burden had lifted from my shoulders. I sat back with my newly acquired Kurt Vonnegut novel when two girls approached me. "Have you ever read the Bible?" one asked.

Ecstasy overflowed my heart with joy for all the amazing things we talked about that day. Think of it! Truth! All laid down for everybody to read and live by. How can it get any better? I was high on her love all afternoon. Pure love and true kinship made those next few years glorious! My new friends were the best friends I'd ever had, so unlike the spoiled rich kids in my neighborhood.

Love's GPS System

Soon enough, life's harsh realities began to set in as my innocence gave way to seduction. Pain replaced pleasure as heart-felt relationships were gravely challenged and life was somehow not so simple anymore. Good friends went off to college one by one. My parents and siblings grew more distant than ever. All this stuff about "living in love" was just too much for them. My heart broke time and time again as their disdain for my viewpoints became more and more apparent. I felt so alone.

Efforts to connect with my mother seemed nearly impossible as our differences increased. I entered college hungrier than ever to find answers. The deadline to declare a major hovered me as I lay in bed trying to sort out my day one morning. I prayed, desperate and helpless to determine my own path.

That day, my advisor's office was dark, shades drawn and dusty, hindering my vision as I pushed my file back across her desk asking her, "What do I look like?" Over the rim of her glasses, her glance told me she understood. "Well, you've got enough credits in the direction of psychology."

Silently I thought, "I'm glad that's what *you* teach." I liked her. I thought she'd be great to have as a teacher. I was longing for someone to teach me, to reach out to me and show they really understood and cared.

"At SUNY, psychology is considered a Natural Science." She continued. "What does that *mean*?" I inquired. "Well, we don't teach from a Social Science standpoint. Our emphasis is not on Freud, though we will cover it. We emphasize the hard science, the studies and experiments." "Wow! That sounds great! Let's do it!"

"Well, we require a Field-Exam your junior year, and a Senior Project where we require you to do a year-long Final Thesis as well as an oral dissertation."

"Really? At the Bachelor level?"

Without the help of my boyfriend I could never have done it. After we were married, I continued on to get my Master's, and desired to get my PhD I was intrigued by science of the brain and heart.

My boyfriend's loud, Italian household was quite different, very intimidating. Shocked, I discovered their lack of education only more deeply cemented their family bonds. Yet, somehow I seemed to sense he was hiding a secret. And he did have a secret.

His mom had devastating pancreatic and liver cancer and was given six months to live, and that was eight months ago.

At that time, the drugs were experimental, and very harsh. She would vomit for hours while he would hold her over the toilet. She lost all her hair and her teeth would bleed. It was a horrible thing! Her doctor appeared on the *Today Show* describing the experimental drugs in use. This was supposed to be promising. "But what is this kind of *love*?!" I thought to myself. I had never seen such devotion and sacrifice given with such joy from a young man.

One afternoon, tears overflowed my reasoning. Through the taste of salt, and fighting a runny nose, I pleaded, "Take me to her! I can lay hands on her and she can be healed!" Oh, the zealousness of youth! Have you ever spoken so fast you'd wondered what took over your tongue? He hesitated, "I'll have to ask her."

Climbing the narrow rickety stairway of an old townhouse, we entered from the second floor, in a part of town I never knew existed. Crowded by furniture, I had barely enough room to pass through. Yet, the entire family was there, waiting to greet me. Surroundings clean and neat, but a little claustrophobic, I gathered myself with respect to my promised duties that evening. With much premeditated thought, I'd prepared my moment, but butterflies filled my stomach as events took on life of their own.

On cue, and in synchrony, the whole family marched in unity into the narrow den as soon as I arrived. It was as if they'd had it rehearsed. Everyone sat down and held hands. Not what I pictured at all, but I was willing to go with it! I started off in prayer. Suddenly my eyes burst open as around the room, each in order, one by one prayed, heartfelt prayers, pleading with God, Mary, Saints, *anyone* who would potentially hear, with abandon baring their souls. At one point, I saw a picture in my minds' eye of a green mist flowing out the window. I never said a word about it. I was sure somehow this was a sign.

That night my boyfriend's mom was miraculously healed and she went on to live ten more years. She'd always said she wanted to live to see her sons marry. She *really* wanted *me* to marry her son.

Today, we have been married for almost 35 years. Years later we were driving home when my husband said to me, "Hon? Do you remember that day you prayed for Mom?"

"Yeah?" I said. He continued, "I saw a green mist leave her body that night." In shock, I shouted, "I saw that too!" Amazed, locking eyes, in unison we shouted at each other, "YOU *SAW* THAT?"

"I didn't want to freak you out!" I exclaimed. "I didn't want to freak *you* out!" he shouted right back at me. *I couldn't believe it!* "What are the *chances*?" I thought, "Wow! There must be so much *more* to this universe than we realize."

From Depression to Destiny

…unless a grain of wheat falls into the ground and dies, it abides alone; but if it dies, it bears much fruit. John 12:24

Many more encounters with the supernatural turned prayer into a passion. I was convinced that God was there to answer. I'd left my boyfriend to attend Bible College in Kansas. Faithfully, he waited for me, but inside I was craving more of something he just could not provide. Sorting out relationships was difficult for me. Realizing I needed to make a decision about the future of our relationship, I did the only thing I could–I cried out to God. Suddenly, feeling a nudge in my spirit, I jumped in my car and drove to his office. He was alone, working through lunch. Once again, my prepared speech concerning our future took a twist. "You don't want to marry *me*!" He said.

"Meet me at the church in two weeks!" I blurted out. Yikes! I did it again! But now I had to hold to it. In a moment, all at once I realized love meant commitment, for better or for *worse*. In a flash the thought arrived deep down on the inside of me. "Oh my gosh! So *this* is what it's all about!"

You know that "deep in your gut" feeling that comes up leaving you breathless? Have you ever felt like you suddenly have to face the truth? Butterflies in my stomach increased trying to anticipate what would happen next.

"Really!" Almost insulted, he tested my resolve. "In two weeks?" He pulled his pencil from in back of his ear, sliding his forearm across his desk blotter revealing a fully-scribbled calendar. Circling the given day, "Okay! The seventeenth!" His anger cut me to the quick.

He called me later with an open heart, giving me a chance to back out. No hard feelings.

We were married despite much opposition and subsequent miracles! Loading a trailer with whatever we had, our arduous journey to California was filled with adventures. Amidst culture and climate shock, I found a few colored pencils and a piece of heavy paper. Promptly a hand-made sign went up on our new mini refrigerator declaring, "Never Underestimate the Power of Prayer."

A package came in the mail the next day. Opening it, I discovered the latest *National Geographic*. As I fanned the pages, a beautiful color insert fell to the floor. My heart skipped as I recovered it, opening the page carefully so as not to tear the treasure, I beheld The Silicon Valley laid out in blue hue, lights appearing as colorful falling stars. The time-elapsed photograph was taken at night. My mom had sent it.

Barely aware of where God had landed us, our future was set to burgeon while Hewlett Packard was in its infancy. Ten years later, my husband was traveling–wheeling and dealing for all the hi-tech companies, like a high-powered marriage broker. I was lonely, a fitness instructor, all my dreams of attaining a doctorate had vanished. In bed at night, feeling the sting of going nowhere, once again, I prayed.

"God, I want to go to Israel! I want to see the Holy Land! And, I want *You* to pay for it!" With that, I nodded off to sleep. Awakened suddenly, knocking over the phone, I managed to eke out a sleepy, "Hello?"

"Allo? Allo? Ees Reek dere?"

"Uh, no he isn't" I replied, recognizing it was another foreign caller.

"Oh...you must be Pah-ti!" His strong accent was hard to decipher, "Theese is Dohv, I am calling from Isra-el..."
"Israel?! **I** want to go to **Israel!** I want to see the Holy Land!"

"You want to see duh Holy Land? I want to see *your* Holy Land! You know dere is two Holy Lands?"

"Uh, no."

"Yes, dere is, of course, here in Israel dere ieez da Holy Land, and den dere eez duh Silicon Valley!"

"Oh... uh huh..." I said, wondering about the rest of this conversation.

"I want to speak wid your husband, we want a start-up in the Silicon Valley, and we hear we should call him. I tell you what, I will pay for you and your husband to come and visit the Holy Land to talk about dis! You come as my guest!"

And there it was. Another moment transformed from depression to Divine intervention. My dreams started to bloom as I became the first to publish a small tech journal called, "Focus on Flash," featuring the innovative upcoming flash technology now used in mobile devices every day.

No Wiggle Room

Twenty years later, a sudden urge nagged me to resurrect the classical guitar I'd received as a teenager. Miraculously surviving the journey across the continent, it landed at the local guitar shop. The word "lessons" flashed in neon in the window. Cringing at the thought, I asked, "What about lessons?"

What? Did that just come out of my *mouth*? Have you ever felt that you're just not in *control*? "Oh, there's a 6-month waiting list." The shop manager said. I sighed with relief as he continued, "Do you want me to put you on it?" "Sure." I thought to myself, "This will give me time to figure out how to get out of this."

Promptly, I was contacted by the instructor, unexplainably my name was at the very top of the list. As if swept away in a dream, I was on a new journey, playing in their church band several months later. The Pastor really didn't like me, he knew I was somehow different. Seven years later, packing up my guitar after a set, I heard the announcement, "Patti is going to be teaching Bible Study on Wednesday nights."

Certain I'd misunderstood, Patsy, the church elder, approached me asking if this was true–or was Pastor referring to *her*?

No, it was *me*! Another one of those, "out-of-the-blue-I-didn't-expect-this" kind of moments. Have you ever felt like events were taking on a life of their own? Suddenly an average morning turned into another life changing adventure! This time I *knew* I was definitely not in "control" here. I'd survived the ridicule of winding up in a "biker" church, with a group of recovering addicts. Most of their stories were miles away from mine. They didn't understand me, and I didn't expect them to. But this was *really* tough. Now I had to stand in front of them and teach. How would they ever accept me? My heart sank to new depths knowing I wanted to teach the Bible from a *Hebraic* perspective. Have you ever felt like no one is ever going to "get" who you really are?

"That's what I was hoping you'd say!" Pastor responded. Shocked at his sudden interest in me, and no room to wiggle out of it, I thought, "How could this be *happening*?"

Teaching was going well, but to really illustrate my points, I needed more. "I need a white-board!" I thought to myself. I opened the large, old church door. Looking down the center aisle, there it was, a great big white board on wheels, with a bulletin board in back and a tray to hold pens and papers. Donated that afternoon, the Pastor's wife was wondering what to do with it. I was sure I knew.

Each lesson was carefully typed out in note form so everyone could follow. An overhead projector took care of the Bible verses, and now I could illustrate! Loving it, I grasped for more and more gems of Ancient Hebrew word pictures to bring the Scriptures alive! Google sent me right to someone named Larry Napier, and consequently to Dr. Loyd and The Healing Codes. "Wow," I thought. I'd remembered seeing Dr. Loyd on Jordan Rubin's television show. He was talking about something called *energy healing*. I was fascinated! Saying a quick, "I'm-sure-I'll-never-remember-this-but-I-know-God-will" kind of prayer, I pleaded, "God I want to *learn* that!" And promptly forgot it.

But, this Napier guy looks interesting? After all, I was looking for Ancient Hebrew.

Another year and a half passed and my passion for teaching only grew, as did my guitar and vocals. I was loving it, but inside I was longing to dive into Ancient Hebrew and The Healing Codes. The band leader was really struggling with my popularity. I mean, *really* struggling. The next thing I knew he called me to tell me he wanted to "share" something with me. I'd been asked to "step-down" from the band. I was devastated, sure inside that there was much more to the story. One incident after another confirmed my thoughts of betrayal by those I'd poured eight years of my life into. Suddenly, the storm of my life landed in unprecedented hurricane force.

Once again, the phone roused me into reality at the break of day. A student called to let me know to not bother coming to work. As of midnight, the company had been sold and the whole staff let go without notice. I'd been there 18 years. Trying to catch my breath, reality hit me–I had *nowhere to go.* No church, no job, no friends, nowhere to go, nothing to do. No purpose, no appreciation. My sense of value and meaning, accomplishment and connection–all *gone!*

My husband, having recently lost his job also, was not home. I'd been unable to bear children, and my family remained quite distant both physically and spiritually. My closest friends had completely betrayed and abandoned me, and two others I loved were fighting last-stage cancer. I lost them both. Still living in shock, one day I arrived home to find another close neighbor had just been robbed. Just four doors down, a gunman entered from the second-story window and surprised them. When his dad arrived home unexpectedly, both were robbed. In addition, a loose gunman had been awakening neighbors by doorbell and intruding. I awoke in a panic at midnight to the grinding sound of someone prying at our front door. Rousing my husband to his feet, he jumped out of bed from a deep sleep. Sliding uncontrollably, down he went and snap! His wrist fractured in several places. Throbbing and barely coherent, pain and swelling on the way, he tried to compose himself, sitting down on the side of the bathtub. Collecting his thoughts, he convinced me to let him drive himself to the hospital.

When is this nightmare going to end? Every two weeks another life-altering trauma, with no end in sight! Hours later still alone, once again, I cried out to God.

An emptiness pervaded my prayer. God seemed different somehow, *distant*. Unable to understand what we had done to cause this uproar, I pleaded, begged, for things to change. I wanted Him to take us *out* of this shock and drama. Instead, it seemed He would only take us *through*.

Where's The Silver Lining?

Dark clouds of reproach haunted us for the next two years. Looking for work, I introduced myself to a local chiropractic group. They were all consumed with something called "Energy Medicine." Leery, but interested professionally, I accepted their invitation to join their staff meetings. After several visits and lively conversations, one of them enthusiastically gave me a copy of The Healing Codes manual. Though I knew I'd been interested previously, I was now despondent. Despair made the new opportunity in front of me all but invisible. Though I was constantly prodded to try them, I procrastinated. Feeling alone and miserable, each day was a chore. I was simply devastated. It had been two full years since calamity first struck and here I was, emotionally stuck–no improvement. Even great opportunity would quickly and suddenly end in trauma. Prodded once again, I broke open *The Codes*. My husband volunteered to do them with me, and to tell me what he thought. I simply didn't trust anyone except him, not Dr.

Loyd, not even myself. My husband approved, remarking that he could "feel" energy leave his fingertips. Surprised at his approval, it was a happy thought for me. Maybe there *was* hope, and maybe I would even receive his support in this healing journey.

A month later, I received an email from Dr. Loyd inviting me to take a class where each student would receive special healing-energy training. This included one half-hour session personally on the phone with Dr. Loyd each week. I thought the phone calls would allow me to really "check him out" because so many had betrayed me. My husband didn't seem to care about the cost, and I was so encouraged by that! Knowing him, this *had* to be a sign! Something gave him confidence that this was from God, and would provide even more than just a path for healing.

Miserable, afraid and unsure, again and again I soaked my pillow in tears. Have you ever felt so alone, devastated, even traumatized? Like everyone you once trusted is suddenly against you, even talking about you? Maybe you've selflessly been there for others, but not one of those people had a bit of compassion for you? I was desperate, longing for help, not wanting to wear my husband out. My self-worth had hit an all-time low.

"But, Babe, I keep telling you, you had *to go through this*! If you hadn't gone through all this, you wouldn't have left your work, met the chiropractors, and found The Healing Codes!" My husband was confident.

"How can pain and suffering be *good*? "I wondered to myself, "How can I *embrace* this time of my life?" Certain there was a key point here that I was missing, I thought, "What does he know that *I just don't get*?" None of our own doors would open up. I kept longing to move to a distant place in the mountains, and write. "Look at the big picture." He said, trying to convince me.

I honestly just didn't get it. "What picture?" I thought to myself. He continued, "If this hadn't happened, you would never have found the chiropractic group, and then you would never have found Energy Medicine, or The Healing Codes, and you would not be starting on this new adventure with them." How did *he* know?

With help from Dr. Loyd's assistant, Cindy, I slid into the LT3 class just under the deadline. Another miracle! Hope was immediately rising. She even encouraged my husband to join in on the class sessions. This was a great boost –I really felt I needed him there. Diligent to do all my assignments, Dr. Loyd objectively measured our healing every week.

"Well, you're 9% healed." He said. "No wonder I feel so bad!" I thought to myself. It was my first session, a baseline measurement.

Every week my score grew by almost exactly 10%. After 6 weeks it was at 60%, just as promised. My husband really noticed a difference in me. "You smile more!" He said, knowing this is just the beginning. "Let's take a trip and look at homes in the mountains!"

The next three years we traveled every weekend, growing closer to each other with every trip. Great job offers came in, new friendships formed with great people, and life started to bloom. I continued to connect with The Healing Codes family, knowing that I needed their support. The truth is I really loved the help, so I continued to sign up for Johanna's classes. Her love and support was so *real*. There were times when she would spend time with me one on one, without asking for anything, just to help. She has been priceless to me and many others also. The pain had been so great I just couldn't wade through it on my own. With The Healing Codes, I didn't have to. I didn't have to dredge up all that mess. It's just pure, simple almost instantaneous healing. It was amazing! These people are the "real deal" and I was now connected with them! It took a while, but eventually it seemed I could *feel* love again.

The Only Way Out Is Up!

Love is the greatest answer in life. Cleansing all feelings opposed to love is not an easy task. But, energy medicine swept away the dross I longed to forget as simply as throwing a light switch. But to keep my healing, I needed a new perspective–I needed to *re-define* the way I looked at "love."

Scientists talk about "dark energy" and "dark matter." I remembered the words of Jesus, something about "if the light in you is darkness..."

"When is the light in you *darkness*? How can light be *dark*?" I wondered at this whole concept. "When can you be dead right, but dead *wrong*?" When you have no **love**. The answer was clear.

"How then, can you love without people and close relationships?" I pondered, not wanting to have anything to do with people.

Relationships had cost me. I had experienced that *pain*. Have you ever felt the pain of relationships gone bad? "More of *that*?" I thought, "What would I do to finally be free from *people*?" The answer remains. Learn how to **love**.

My focus had been on what I had lost. Now, light was knocking at my heart's door, the question was, would I let it in? Would I choose to re-focus, re-group, re-prioritize my life in **love**? And what would that *cost?* That was the question.

Life was not going to be about "Having what I *want*–which for me meant, having what I had *lost*." But instead, I would have to be able to live each moment, "wanting what I *have*."

This would mean letting go of the past to embrace a new perspective, a new heart, a new joy! Love takes risk. It does not hold back fearfully in that old, comfortable place. Love reaches *out*, to the one loved.

Have you ever had an "Aha!" Moment? Suddenly it dawned on me! It was like a light went on while hearing my husband's words in my head, "Embrace it!–Don't fight it!"

The connection appeared–embrace the possibility that these trials were meant to bring me *through* to a new *place spiritually!* The fight had been my *resistance* to the pain. I wanted pleasure, happy times again! That was over. I had to embrace the idea that this was going to be a difficult, yet great and memorable time of transition in my life.

Transition to even greater love, joy, peace and happiness than I'd ever known! I decided to embrace a life of living every moment in the present, no more focus on the past, or fear of the future. Living each day, one moment at a time, truthfully in love, would make all the difference. I didn't need to embrace the whole world at once, but I could start by just loving right where I am, in my small corner of the world. Who else would touch the everyday people in my life? The clerk at the grocery counter, neighbors, clients, coworkers, each a part of our lives, are placed there in front of us daily to be touched in love.

"You are always living *in* what you're giving *out!*" I thought to myself. Living in love basks you in a peaceful glow of true light, casting out any former clouds of darkness. Suddenly things were clear.

Elegant Simplicity
The light of the body is the eye: therefore when thine eye is single, thy whole body also is full of light. Luke 11:34

Nervous chills swept through me as, once again, I was put on-the-spot. My friend's voice rang out over me as she prayed boldly for me in front of her congregation.

"And I pray, Heavenly Father, that You will show her that this is not the end, *it is but only the beginning for her and her husband.*"

My gut was tied in a knot. Inside myself I was rolling my eyes cynically asking, "How long, O Lord?"

Have you ever felt like all eyes were upon you, and you just wanted to die? Her words would turn out to be both vitally important, and *true*.

An unhealthy yoke to those familiar things that I'd hoped would bring me comfort *were* indeed the source of my stagnation. Looking back at that moment, I knew I'd made the right choice to break away from all that had become so familiar, even my business and clients, and in one giant leap of faith, embrace something new. My perspective had to change, and I knew it.

With every passing moment I would ask myself, "What do I *really* want?" "Is what I'm doing right now in truth and love?" "Am I living in the 'now?'" Or, am I yearning to *make things go my way*?

With each passing day, courage to live truthfully from the heart was rising up inside. Somehow the sudden struggle to find myself had ceased. The fight had vanished. I was free again, even if it meant putting one foot in front of the other.

After much pondering, I realized I had been leaning on old familiar relationships simply because I felt I had no place else to go. I wasn't doing it for the right reasons. Wrestling with guilt, I made a decision to break free.

Free to recognize who I am in the midst of others. No struggle, just a genuine longing to help anyone who would ask. Once again, I wanted to tell the whole word there is hope. This simple Healing Codes process had opened up a new world to me, free from the prisons of my own heart.

Work turned to pleasure, as the next adventure unfolded. I felt more and more acceptance and respect from others than ever. Wonderful things just seemed to flow to me! New jobs, opportunities and relationships all turned into divine appointments. Life became like "greased-clockwork." Soon my business was built back to a greater extent than ever before. Time with my husband was no longer consumed with hopeless tears, but joy! We were young and free and in love for the first time–again! We have grown closer to each other in the last few years than in the thirty years previous – full of spontaneity, untied, *present* to what it feels like to love, *truly*.

The words, "EinGedi" kept whispering inside my ears. "What could be the connection?" I thought.

"Ein Gedi"- a place of beautiful springs in the midst of Israeli desert, is made up of two words- Ein, or *Ayin*, is the ancient pictograph of an eye. Metaphorically it's a *spring*, as the "fountain" or "eye" of the land. *Gedi* is a kid, a young goat. We often think of a "kid" as a child. The message was simple. "See through the eye of a child!"

Children are humble, naturally dependent. They know they don't have control. In simple trust they put their hand in their father's hand to lead them, to keep them safe. Ein Gedi is an oasis in the desert, a fountain of life, of refreshing springs! Oh, to be a child again! Living simply in the moment, fully trusting, free from adult entanglements! Life springs through our being as it flows out to everyone around us. Children change our world!

Paradigm Shift

And now abide faith, hope, love, these three; but the greatest of these is love. I Corinthians 13:13

Flying down the freeway, feeling the buzz of traffic around me, I felt "back in the zone" as I answered my cell phone.

"Babe, I found our house! And it's got a two-million-dollar view!" My husband had been searching tirelessly. "Wow!" I answered, thinking, "Could this finally be *it?*" Two and a half years of patient endurance had finally paid off.

Tired but excited, I had a peaceful calm about this evening, even though the Friday night drive would be arduous. Two of us and two ninety-pound Airedales piled into our pickup for five hours.

"Hey, you wanna sneak up and see the place? It'll be fun!" I asked, almost giddy with anticipation. "Yeah! Let's do it!" My husband was thinking the same thing.

We drove up almost a mile above sea-level. Breathless and mesmerized by the spectacular skyline panorama, in every direction, 360 degrees, we were spellbound by nature's beauty. I knew this was my house! I had to have it!

Nine months later we relocated. A year after settling in, I felt an urge to seek work at a particular facility that seemed to be calling out to me since we'd arrived.

"Would you excuse me a minute?" My future employer jumped up from my interview in haste. Interrupting a class, she quietly stepped in to speak to the teacher. "Just take a look at this resume!" She nudged her to take a look.

"Oh, my gosh! This woman's been living my life someplace else!" She exclaimed. A brand-new career relationship was on the way for me! My new friend and colleague called me the very next business day.

Like a divine connection, it seems they were seeking me as much as I was seeking them! Life was getting better and better every day. Finally a chance to start all over again! No relationships or reputation to lean on, I had a sudden "Aha!" moment!

Maybe you've felt that way.

Have you ever had one of those moments when all the lights come on? It's a lot like living through a storm where the electricity goes out. After enduring for a while, when you have finally given in and settle down to accepting life by candlelight and fireplace, suddenly, unexpectedly the lights come on!

At that moment, everything becomes clear. Things seem brighter than before. You now value something as simple as light! I finally realized all was *never* lost.

All the "good stuff"–those things we take years to acquire in character, skills, judgment, on-the-job training–all of it is sown down deep on the *inside*. There really *are* "hidden treasures in secret places"–inside of us!

Slowly with patience and peace, the job of my dreams began to emerge in a brand new community with amazing people. At the heart of it is beautiful, true, unselfish relationship.

All the pain and hardship you've walked through simply prepare you for where you are going. You have been heaping up "treasures" on the inside of *you!* It is hard to see the value in them because those treasures are not meant for you; they are meant for those people in your future who really "get" you, who will really appreciate your special gifts, knowing the price you have paid to acquire them.

For me, this healing journey isn't over, it's truly just beginning. And it may just be the same way for you.

I have learned from the greatest Source that we are all still children inside. Our heart's issues are their voices crying out for healing, for recognition, for love. I have learned not to ignore the cries of my heart, but to treat them with attention, kindness and gentleness. You might want to listen to "who" is crying out from the inside of *you!*

I'm sure you would agree there is too much hatred in the world, but self-hatred is among the worst. It eats us from the inside out. And I want to leave you with this thought, don't believe the lie that all is *lost*. Ponder the truth that you are a virtual "hidden treasure" to someone extremely special who is seeking you at this very moment. You have a fortune hidden on the *inside!*

About The Author

Patricia Iorillo, MS.Ed., has been a prolific writer for over thirty-five years, having published in the areas of education, health, science, physiology and technology, her writing has spanned both national and international audiences. She has served as a nationally certified instructor, coach, speaker and Bible College Educator specializing in a Hebraic perspective of Biblical truths.

By unlocking mysteries hidden in the language and culture of Hebrew text, deeper spiritual realities, otherwise veiled in modern language and understanding, begin to surface. This unique linguistic approach uncovers how our spirituality, physiology and psychology inter-relate to make us who we are–even on a daily basis. This empowering message embraces the individual in three dimensions: spirit, mind and body, while challenging notions traditionally accepted as truth.

"Snatched from the teeth of the enemy" in 1972 during the Jesus movement, Patricia moves with a prophetic voice and passion to provide keys to revealing how a new perception of ancient realities can free us to become who we are destined to be.

patricia.iorillo2@aol.com

CHAPTER 10

A LOVE THAT ENDURES

Holly Malmsten

Overwhelmed with Life

Trusting God may have been the most foolish thing I had ever done in my life and my family's future was ruined. Maybe everything I had ever believed in was wrong. Feelings of failure and defeat overwhelmed me and my body felt weary and heavy. What once was truth, was coming back to haunt me as falsehood, and questions ran through my mind. God must be cruel. Had he just abandoned me? Left me alone to figure a way out of this mess? Couldn't he have stopped such a huge and costly mistake? After all, we had fully believed that God had led our family to California and that he was going to take care of us there. Instead, we were struggling to survive each day, and it seemed like an invisible force was against every effort we made to establish ourselves in our new city.

I was desperately trying to help my four young kids adjust to their new life, but it seemed next to impossible to manage my household. Overwhelmed with everything, I was unhappy, and frustrated a majority of the time. Every day I carried the stress and fear about our financial struggles, guilt and doubt about making the decision to move, and feeling like God had bailed on us altogether. Just living became so draining on me ... I had nothing left to give my children who required every ounce of my energy. How was I supposed to pull myself up out of despair, while having to face the demands of my family? Was it even possible? I felt like I was climbing Mount Everest with four young children on my back, with no idea how to get to the top. It was a hopeless climb. I felt defeated and I was facing the possibility that my whole life may end in utter failure.

A Crucial Moment

I was paralyzed, and my hands felt like they weighed a thousand pounds, as I tried to start the dinner dishes. Ending an exhausting day with an enormous pile of dishes was always a daunting task for me, but I typically just trudged through it while my last bit of energy was drained. But this time may have been the worst exhaustion I had ever felt, and I couldn't move. I just stood there at the sink, unable to tackle the dishes, to mother my kids, or to see a way forward. All I could do was stare out the window. What could I do now? Give up my faith, and throw out my personal beliefs? How would that help? My history was God coming through, and being reliable. I certainly wasn't feeling his love, and didn't know how I would ever get past this disappointment. Confusion filled my thoughts and disappointment destroyed the trust I once had, and I was most disillusioned with myself and with God. Did I ever really know him? I completely misunderstood who he really was and must have made a naive and senseless decision to move away from everything that was familiar and secure.

What happened in the next moment, as I stared out the window in a paralyzed state of dismay, redirected the course of my life forever. Sometimes, we aren't able to see clearly, that God's ways are higher and better than we could ever imagine. Could it be possible that God was reaching out to me in a way that was more loving, more brilliant, and so everlasting, than my human mind was able to understand right now?

I was completely surprised that it was God's goodness and love that began drawing me deeper into a hidden source that I had never known before.

A Difficult Choice

In the past I was able to hold it together, when facing a struggle, and figure a way through a problem. But this time was different than anything I had gone through before. The reality of our savings being gone, and our bank accounts totally depleted, along with not having any real sense of home, friendship, or family, had taken its toll. I had never felt such a lack of security, stability, or support.

We had left our life back in Colorado, where my husband and I met, married, and lived for fifteen years. My husband's family had been close by, and his business had thrived and God had blessed us there. Breckenridge, Colorado had been our home, where my husband and I had built our life together, and where our four kids had been born. That may sound like a lot of children, but the most shocking part of all is they are all girls. That's right, four daughters, who were active, creative, and adventurous. They were mountain kids. The extreme weather conditions and outdoor lifestyle made them tough and this is what they knew. We drove away from Colorado, with our four kids in my car, embarking on our adventure. My husband drove his car, along with our two big dogs, and a trailer full of our stuff. We looked a lot like the Beverly Hillbillies as we rolled in three days later, with our big family, our dogs, and our belongings. Even though we didn't know anyone, and my husband was starting a brand new business from scratch, we just believed that everything would somehow work out. After all, we had trusted God and felt confident that we had been divinely led to Santa Barbara, California.

Little by little the newness wore off and the reality of the insanely high cost of living in Santa Barbara began to emerge. Unable to purchase a home, like we had planned, we jumped from one short term rental to another. How was it possible that our beautiful, newly built log home wouldn't sell? The housing was so expensive and no one seemed to want to rent to a family with four kids. Mentioning to potential landlords that we also had two labs usually ended in a hang up, without even the opportunity to explain ourselves. The only house we could find, where the owner didn't seem to mind our large family or the dogs, was an old white house that had been empty for a while. The elderly owner had moved into assisted living and was graciously welcoming of youth, dogs, and family. Our family moved into this old and neglected, shabby house. What a change from our beautiful log home we had left, that remained empty and unsellable.

Living in California had become a lot tougher than we thought. Deciding to pick up and move had been a mistake. Our future was ruined, along with the future of our children. All of our security was gone, and I felt like a complete failure. Our plan had failed, and the stress of the move and starting a business from scratch had beaten us down, and now I was even a failure as a mother with no energy to take care of my family. I had never felt so helpless, so desperate, or so deserted.

Now I was facing the most annoying and draining chore, for a tired mother. Having to wash the dishes after caring for the kids all day seemed like the worst job I could possibly have, and a horrible end to my tiring day. During that desperate moment at the kitchen sink, staring out of the window, I was forced to make a choice that was one of the most significant choices I would ever face. There were only two choices before me, and they were simple, yet both were terrifying. One was to just give up what I believed about God and accept despair and failure; the other, to trust and wait. A voice inside was telling me that I could not give up, and I knew that I couldn't. Undoubtedly, waiting was the hardest action to take, when in the midst of desperation.

This type of action, or should I say inaction, goes against our natural survival instincts to protect and rescue ourselves. I could feel my flesh squirming and agitated with this strategy, but my spirit was ready and willing to endure this trial. Although this tremendous battle was raging inside, waiting and trusting was the only light I could see at the end of the tunnel. As dim as it was, I made a choice in my heart to take a small, uncertain step in that direction. I didn't feel like trusting. I didn't know for sure if this was more foolish than before, and I didn't know if this path would be solid under my feet, or crumble. I was either going to find solid ground, or take a miserable fall. It was the hardest, most uncertain, insecure leap of faith that I have ever made. And yet, it was made in the secret place of my heart. Not even my family was aware of what was taking place on that hopeless exhausting night.

An Unexpected Message

So there I was, in an old worn down house, instead of our beautiful home back in Colorado. I regretted leaving this home that we had designed and built for our family. Now, it wouldn't sell in the middle of the housing market crash. How would we ever be able to buy a house in Santa Barbara? I wondered how we would ever feel settled, or how our kids would ever feel at home. There I was, in a similar condition to our deteriorating rental house, weary and worn down. We were ruined. However, I will never forget that particular spot, nor that moment. That spot at the kitchen sink, that moment of desperate staring, that kitchen window that looked out to our front yard, dirt and neglected landscape from our elderly landlord, it became the most beautiful and inspiring spot I have known. It was there, through that window, at that moment, that I noticed something I had not noticed before. The kitchen window looked right out to a giant oak tree.

My attention was suddenly drawn away from my problems and I was awed by the size and strength of this tree, and I was amazed at its grandeur, in the midst of desolation. It towered over our house, with branches stretching out over the entire front yard. There was no grass, no flowers, no color, or any signs of life or beauty on that land. But somehow, that oak had managed to thrive and mature. This captured my attention. That magnificent oak tree seemed to have a message to communicate to me, and I found that I could not take my eyes off of it. I noticed how beautiful it was and how strong and enduring it must be to manifest such incredible signs of life, in our front yard, where there was nothing else living or growing. It must have amazing longevity and ability to prosper, despite its external surroundings.

As I marveled at this tree, and recognized the symbol of strength and endurance that tree was for me, my focus miraculously changed. Instead of noticing everything that was going wrong, I felt peace and calm in my heart because I realized that there was something to learn from this magnificent oak. Through the stress, strain, weariness, and fear, I heard a still small voice speaking to me. The voice was calm, quiet, and steady and was different from my own voice, that was relentlessly chattering in my head about failure, our future, loss, and lack. There was only one voice that could communicate like that. I realized it was the voice of God, and He was trying to get my attention.

Did He really want to interact with me while I was in a state of fear and despair? Could He be that kind to want to be present with me at the very same time that I was doubting His love and His goodness? Could it be that God was using my most despised chore, at the most exhausting time, when I was feeling at the lowest point, to reach me with His extravagant love? Right in the midst of it all, He seemed to be right there. "What kind of love is this?" I wondered. It is unlike any love that exists on the earth. It is a love that could only come from above, from God who desires to make a deep and lasting heart connection with His people that He created to love.

I was instantly aware of His nearness to me, and His kindness in reaching me in that low place of depression, despair, heaviness, exhaustion. To my surprise, thankfulness filled my heart for that oak tree, for His unexplainable kindness, and for all of His goodness to me. That's when my heart opened, my understanding was flooded with light, and something pleasantly and surprisingly drew me deeper into His love.

I heard His voice so clearly and felt His loving kindness behind the words. They melted away the negative thoughts, emotions, and questions that had paralyzed me just moments before. It may have been an epiphany, an encounter, or an ah-ha moment. I cannot say for sure. Trying to come up with a word to explain this experience seems to only diminish it, but I know it was real. It was clear, and God spoke to my heart. His words carried emotion and had such gentleness and kindness, mixed with strength and power. God's words were simple and frank yet seemed to hold some kind of secret formula for progressing forward.

His words didn't come from the outside, nor did I hear them with my physical ears. His words came from inside my spirit, or my spiritual heart. I heard Him so clearly with a sense of hearing that existed in that same deep place of my heart. I am calling them *words*, but they were somewhat like thoughts that were just drifting through my mind easily and effortlessly. My own thoughts were chaotic, confused, and cluttered, it was obvious that I was incapable of contriving these thoughts on my own. They were coming from someone other than me. God was communicating with me heart to heart.

These were His initial words that were direct and upfront, yet full of support and care. "Stop complaining, turn your thoughts to thankfulness, let praise come from your heart, and I will teach you about the oak tree." I stopped dead in my tracks down the road of depression, defeat, and self-pity after encountering God's heart words and thoughts to me. If God was speaking to me and wanted to teach me something, then I was going to listen. I was determined about one thing. I was not going to miss one single piece that could be learned or gained through this struggle.

As thankfulness began to overrun my negative thoughts, I started thinking of every little thing for which I could possibly be thankful. I started to thank him for dishes, for a roof, for the elderly owner of our house who had shared his home with our family, for a tree in my front yard, for my amazing husband, and our wonderful children. With every intentional prayer of thanks, I felt my entire being lifting out of negativity into contentment and peace, despite my current struggles.

Praise even filled my heart and I just wanted to give God praise for His goodness and His love. The stress, exhaustion, and overwhelming sense of failure, just vanished in this atmosphere of God's presence and love. That place at the kitchen window, with the dishes piled up before me, was the most wonderful place in the world. The dishes no longer seemed like a daunting task. I now saw an amazing adventure ahead and felt privileged to stand there in that glorious place. It was at that very spot at the sink, with a mountain of dishes before me, gazing out at the tree, that I began to learn life-changing lessons from an oak.

Strength of an Oak

From then on, I couldn't wait to get to the sink, look out the window and learn more. I looked forward to every moment I was able to wash the dishes. That place at the sink was where I started spending time listening for God's voice. He spoke many things to me there as I quieted my mind and remained open. Every time I showed up to wash the dishes, which I had previously detested, I received downloads of truth, encouragement, and support for pressing onward. Inspired to find all the information I could about oaks, I researched and learned a lot about them. I learned that the one in our yard was a Coast Oak, which can live longer than 250 years. I became amazed at the strength and endurance of oaks and fascinated by their incredible root systems which anchor them through storms and the toughest conditions. Down below the surface, they remain stable and fixed.

I discovered that my spiritual heart was in the maturing process. I could embrace this season, knowing that I could fully trust this process and that it was designed for my good and for my well-being. It is much easier to undergo a maturing process, with the right understanding, when the process has meaning. Although it was difficult to withstand, I was going to end up with a solid unshakable faith and trust in God and His love that would never fail. I realized how valuable going through a process can be, even when it feels unpleasant. This is needed to produce the necessary endurance for reaching one's capability and potential. I could feel my heart growing hopeful. I could not explain it.

How could I have so much hope, when my circumstances were the same? The pressure of my external circumstances, which were paralyzing at first, were in fact causing a strengthening and deepening of my root system and driving me to the dependable source and supply for everything I needed to stand firm and unwavering through the seasons of life.

The most incredible part of the oak tree's growth is the development of the taproot. Everyone could learn something, I thought, from the amazing root system that becomes the inner strength of the oak. This brilliant process must have been created by God, to reveal something to us.

This discovery pointed right to the core of what I was longing for and what everyone really needs. At an oak's beginning stages, the taproot grows down in search of a dependable water supply and doesn't stop until it reaches one and taps into it. After the taproot is established and has reached its water source, an extensive root system begins to grow out horizontally. The roots may spread out to seven times the width of the tree's crown. These mature oaks are so solid. They seemed to be unaffected by their surroundings and completely stable in all situations.

I started to understand the correlation between the oak and my own life. How could my roots be strong enough and deep enough to serve as an anchor through tough times? My own strength crumbled under the pressure and stress of my earthly circumstances. Had I tapped into a dependable source?

The wondrous oak typically braves floods and hurricanes easily. It has the strongest wood, is clothed with the toughest bark, and even tends to survive fire. Even if the tree is burned, the roots usually survive and afterwards sprout quite vigorously.

Would you believe that, during this same time the secrets of the oak tree were being revealed to me, I witnessed a trail of oak trees that had survived a major wildfire? While chaperoning my daughter's field trip to the botanical gardens, I was left speechless. I had no idea what we would see on our tour, our guide showed us the path of the fire that blazed through the property a year before. She pointed out that the oaks were unscathed by the fire. It was evident that everything had burned in its path, except for the oaks that looked as strong as ever.

I wondered if there was anything that could affect a mature oak tree. I concluded that the ones that lived through every type of circumstance and reached maturity are negatively affected by nothing. Droughts also pose no threat to an oak. The mature ones have lived through countless droughts. An even more intriguing fact is that a drought is actually a benefit to a maturing oak tree.

When there is a drought, the tap root is forced to thrust down even deeper to seek water. It does not stop until it finds moisture. Thus, the drought at the surface strengthens the tree's roots, so the next season of drought has no effect on the tree. It is tapped into a continual water supply way below the surface. The deeper taproots become a stronger anchor. Wow! The oak tree is fully supplied and anchored, and its strength is way beneath the surface.

I was fascinated by what I discovered about the marvelous oaks and their display of longevity and strength to endure for hundreds of years. What a remarkable symbol of unwavering stability my oak tree became. I couldn't help but marvel at how a tree could endure so much. I longed to be that strong and able to persevere. The secret of the tree's stability and longevity was clearly in its sophisticated root system. I was driven on a search for my dependable life source. That's where I wanted my roots, and it clearly wasn't found in anything or anyone on the earth.

My physical house could not have been a dependable source, nor could a specific city, or friends, or even having family close by. Worldly success or a certain job could not possibly be a dependable source in which to be rooted. All of these earthly things could come and go and were susceptible to the storms, fire, floods, and droughts of life. I wanted something solid and secure that would fully supply me through it all.

How shallow and underdeveloped my root system had been. I delayed my own maturing process in attempts to avoid discomfort or loss of control. That was me five years ago. I believed that as long as I felt in control of my life and my family and our future was secure and predictable, life was good. Or, was it?

What I learned from that magnificent oak outside of my kitchen window, with its mature root system, and its enduring strength through every circumstance, transformed my life forever. And the message that God spoke to my heart during that time revealed the true source. It is the extravagant, unending, and fully supplied love of God.

Connecting with this love, at the heart level, seemed to cause the struggles at the surface of my life dwindle into an easy load to bear. Filled with that love, I confidently faced the future with peace and knew I would be able to keep going and thrive where God had planted our family.

Through all the trials and uncertainties I faced during that season,–a storm of stress, a flood of disappointments, a financial and spiritual drought, and a fire that burned away all temporary securities–the roots of my heart were forced down to the depths of God's heart.

Another level existed down below the surface of my disappointments that I never realized I needed. To reach God's love had just been a concept I believed, but had not actually been experienced to such depths. I would never again doubt God's love.

What I found, despite my earthly circumstances, was that a love existed which is deeper, stronger, and more reliable than anything this life has to offer. His love is the most enduring and dependable love that exists anywhere in the heavens or on the earth. Any hopeless situation, in which you are stuck and have no idea what to do, may be an opportunity to simply wait and trust.

By waiting and trusting through strenuous circumstances, I found a fully dependable supply of what I needed to live and thrive. And, a root system developed that is anchored in love.

We stayed in that old, worn-down, white house, and my whole family grew to love it. My kids thrived and viewed our home as their favorite house in which we had ever lived. They were happy, joyful, thankful and appreciative of everything we had. Our family easily and effortlessly settled into our new life. The location of our house allowed for us to walk to the beach, which became a regular routine. We couldn't imagine being anywhere else. Our house became a cozy home with a loving and peaceful atmosphere. We lived simply and without the stress from spills, mishaps, and damages that are common in a house with a family of six.

As far as my kids were concerned, we had the best backyard in the world, like a forest with so much to explore. Some flowers were planted in the front and the landscape was upgraded a little. I drove up my driveway at the end of every day feeling we were the luckiest family. I didn't even notice the worn look of the house or the property anymore. We decided to just stay in that house as long as possible, as we lived free from high payments and the extra strain of upkeep on the house. We could focus on our kids, have them in the best school, and enjoy our lives.

My husband worked steadily at building his business, which became the number one boutique real estate company in Santa Barbara. It is interesting timing that I finish writing this chapter five years after my life changing experience. We received a call, during the last week of my work on this book project, and were told the news that the owner of our house had died, at the age of 98.

The house would go to his children, and in four to six months, they would be taking it over. I have such great hope and expectation, and can only smile at the thought of God releasing us from this home, right as I finish writing my story. I am ready for the change and know that we are headed for an upgrade. I trust the good plans God has in mind for our family.

I am compelled to share this life changing text that God highlighted for me during our lessons at the kitchen sink. It is an ancient scripture from the Bible that became words of life to my heart and soul. These words have become much more than words in a book, they have become a living reality for my life. *The Spirit of the Lord is upon me, to preach good news to the afflicted, to bind up the brokenhearted, and to proclaim liberty to the captives and the opening of the prison and of the eyes to those that are bound...*

To comfort all who mourn, and provide for those who grieve - to bestow on them a crown of beauty instead of ashes, the oil of joy instead of mourning, and a garment of praise instead of a spirit of despair. They will be called OAKS of righteousness, a planting of the Lord for the display of his splendor. Isaiah 61:1&3

A Risk Worth Taking

I had faced difficult and painful circumstances in the past and was usually able to hold it together during a struggle and figure out a way through a problem. But this was different than anything I had gone through before. I never felt so unsupported, unstable, or insecure. It was the most stressful and desperate time I had ever faced. I felt alone and deserted.

Maybe you've never known the feeling of being stripped of all earthly security. And, you may not know what it is like to be a mom of four daughters, in a new place, separated from my support system of friends and family. Some may understand what it feels like to be living in an old battered house that is far from the comfort of a cozy home, no money in the bank, overwhelmed by the stress of feeding kids and paying bills, while totally exhausted and worn out. But most likely, you know what it is like to find yourself in a desperate situation, where you don't know what to do, or how you are going to be okay. To find yourself in this place is one of the lowest, most helpless, and powerless places imaginable.

It is like being at the bottom of a deep pit, that would be impossible to get out alone, and wondering if there is anyone who could pull you out. Or, like being stuck in quicksand and slowly sinking, without anyone even aware that you are stuck. Was there anyone who could pull us up out of this pit? Did anyone even know or realize how stuck we were and that my whole family was slowly sinking?

Taking risks sometimes leads to the greatest advancements. Everyone will take a risk at some point in life without knowing exactly how it will turn out. My husband and I took one of the greatest risks of our lives moving to California simply on a belief that we were being led and that God had a plan for us there. Sometimes, what may seem like the most foolish thing could be Divine Love's leading and bringing us into perfect alignment with the most brilliant plan ever designed: the plan that exists in God's heart and in His mind, waiting to be discovered.

What I found, after I gave up trying to rescue myself and my family and made the decision in my heart to simply wait and trust, is something worth sharing. I can't say that the risk was easy, or that it came without a cost. I also must admit that my situation didn't suddenly disappear or get resolved overnight. But what I will say is that it was well worth the risk.

Real Love

I will never regret the decision to move to California, and I am forever grateful for the richness of what I learned through that challenge. Understanding that there was a purpose for such a strenuous challenge made it possible and even enjoyable to endure. My desperate search for something dependable, then discovering the extravagant love that became the only real reliable source was worth every price. God desires to drive our roots deep into the truth of His love and strengthen our endurance so that we are unwavering through any circumstance. He hopes for everyone to encounter the truth about who He really is.

God is not a concept or a "what." God is a "who," a person who deeply loves every person He created. God is love. A scripture from the Bible implies that God is the very definition and expression of love. 1 John 4:8, says, *Whoever does not love does not know God, because God is love.* Who wouldn't want to meet this love?

Many adults most likely remember that popular country song, "Looking for Love in all the Wrong Places." I believe that this song may be true for too many of us. Where are we looking for love? Real love, that satisfies and fills every longing and every need, doesn't come from this earthly realm. It is from up above. It is a divine love that transcends our earthly circumstances, our human minds, thoughts, and limited human understanding. This love is almost unexplainable in human vocabulary.

But, when you find it, you know it. It feels like the most familiar, safe, secure, kind, gentle, protective, and at times, even fierce love that anyone could ever find. It is enough for any wound, injustice, lack, void, or fear. And, the very encounter with this love is strong enough and sufficient enough to override it all and to fully supply what we have needed and wanted all along. It is that strong. Through my experience that I shared, this is the love I found. Once a theory in my mind and a shallow faith that I thought I understood is now a living reality in which I am rooted. It is the source for everything that I need in this life. Best of all, this love is in the heart of a person who I know and am forever connected with.

Significant forward steps in life involve taking risks and simply following our hearts, even when it doesn't make sense. The risk that my husband and I took in picking up and moving our family to California was definitely a risky move. The plan we had in mind didn't exactly turn out the way we thought.

But, in my experience, the bigger the risk, even if it seems foolish, the greater the potential may be for a life transformation. I can honestly say now that I understand the benefit and appreciate what I gained through that unstable and difficult time. I will never again lack what I need to face difficulty and uncertainty.

Living each day anchored securely in love and trust, without fear, is really living. It is real freedom knowing that it is possible to be content in any situation. No matter what happens on the surface, my roots are deeply established in the source of love. This source will never dry up or run out.

It is available through the fiercest storm or the longest drought.

As I ended this chapter, I did in fact go out in my front yard and looked in amazement at my oak tree. Even though I have never considered myself a tree hugger, I couldn't help myself and gave it a giant hug. I thanked that tree for the powerful message that was released through it, and I thanked and praised God for the way He used His creation to communicate His heart and His love.

So my hope and prayer for anyone who reads my story is actually a prayer that is written in the Bible, and I am praying it for you all, as I write: *I pray that you, being rooted and established in love, may have power together with all the Lord's people, to grasp how wide and long and high and deep is the love of Christ, and to know this love that surpasses knowledge-that you may be filled to the measure of all the fullness of God.* Ephesians 3:17-19

About The Author

Holly Malmsten grew up in a family of strong faith and received her bachelor's degree in sociology, with a minor in psychology from the University of Oklahoma. She moved to Breckenridge, Colorado, to be a part of a ministry working with teens. She met her husband, Ryan, and married in 1996.

Holly received a Master's degree in clinical counseling from Denver Seminary and began working as a counselor in 2001. Working for Colorado West Mental

Health Center as a drug and alcohol group therapist and then starting a private practice as a Certified Counselor developed her passion for helping others heal. Holly spent several years investing in and raising her four amazing daughters and viewed her role as a mother a high calling and responsibility.

Her family moved to Santa Barbara, California, in the summer of 2008. She serves as the Healing Ministry director at the Santa Barbara House of Prayer. Holly has truly enjoyed this position for the past two years and has helped countless individuals with emotional and spiritual heart issues. Holly enjoys surfing with her family and leading an active lifestyle. She is currently building her business as an alternative healing practitioner and working towards certification in bioenergetic therapy techniques.

CHAPTER 11

HEALING ME
AND THE "STUFF" OF MY LIFE

Karen Saari Secor

After a relaxing evening in front of a campfire this Memorial Day, my daughter's comments left me speechless. Standing at her back door, Jen turned around, put her hand up, palm facing me, and said, "Mother, you changed." She paused, then flipped her hand and said, "You made a complete turnaround–a 180."

What Jenn said next hit me like a ton of bricks. "Where would I be if you hadn't changed?"

Wow! *What if I hadn't changed?* Where would we be? I didn't want to think about where we might be.

As I drove home I thought about things that helped me grow and change: books, tapes, teachers, lessons learned, and experiences–the good, the bad, and the painful.

Years ago, I didn't know I needed to *"change."* I knew nothing about the mind or the effect my thoughts and emotions had on my well-being. We weren't taught anything about our inner world in school. The focus was on the external world: get good grades, go to college, get a good job, get married, and have kids.

I went to college and got a degree in math and computers. I found a job working in a business systems' department writing software for the computer systems we designed. I was a logical, left-brain, in-the-box thinker. I liked things with rules, like math and English. So, I loved my job and the problem solving that was part of it–finding "bugs" in the code that prevented programs from working correctly. Little did I know that what I learned as a programmer would help me find the "bugs" in my thinking, and in the programming that was right between my ears.

After Jen was born, my husband Leo and I moved back home to northern Wisconsin. I got a job as the head of the computer department at a local college. Life was good; my life plan was working well.

Then two things happened that put me on a different path. Jen was four or five when she crinkled pages in my new book. My reaction was instant anger. But looking at my child's sweet, innocent face, I bit my lip and said nothing. As a child, I kept my books and dolls and games in perfect condition.

Next Jen spilled a bottle of Wisk on the basement floor. As I wiped up the sticky, blue liquid, I saw red and yelled at her as if she had set the house on fire. Leo hollered at me from upstairs, *"WHY* are you yelling at her like that? There's enough change on the basement floor to buy another *damn bottle!!!"*

In an instant, the anger changed to regret. I felt awful, and ashamed! I called my friend Bevie and told her about the anger, not just with Jen, but over other things that pushed my buttons too. "There's something wrong with me," I said.

I didn't expect Bevie's response. She said, "You have control issues and abandonment issues." I had never heard of *"issues."* I could relate to the word "control," with the crinkled pages, but not to "abandonment."

"My father died. He didn't abandon my mother and me."

Bevie's response, "As an eight-year old, didn't you feel abandoned?" Maybe a part of me did, but I didn't know how that was connected to anger.

"Why did I act that way?" I wondered. Instantly, the words "we don't waste" popped into my head. My mother and her family grew up during the Depression. They didn't waste anything. So growing up, I learned not to waste, which was a good thing. But the way I reacted to the spilled detergent was horrible! The adult in me should have been in control.

I had to find out where the anger came from and why it was there. I didn't know where to look for clues to find answers, but the crinkled pages and not wasting pointed to my childhood. Answers would come over time. Some came years later, and in totally unexpected ways.

The Seven-Year Itch

Two months before my 40th birthday, I felt weird at work–jittery, as if I had too many cups of coffee. I watched in horror as big red welts popped out all over my arms and legs. The itching was horrible, but the anxiety I felt scared me. In a state of panic, I drove to our local emergency room. The diagnosis was *"Urticaria (hives)–source(s) unknown."* Little did I know that hives would torture me almost every day, often several times a day, for the next seven years.

Other problems appeared: asthma, extreme fatigue, "spaciness," and memory problems. Testing at an allergy clinic showed I was allergic to house dust, mold, yeast, and oak trees. Further testing showed sensitivities to chemicals: ethanol, phenol and formalin (formaldehyde). Products with these chemicals were used in the auto shop, print shop, and cosmetology in our building. Sometimes the air-handling system didn't work properly, so the chemicals circulated in our air.

Even though others experienced problems in the building, I was the canary and had strange, scary things happen to me. At times, I felt I was in a war zone fighting an invisible enemy. I never knew when the next attack would come or what damage it would cause–tiny hives on my elbows, welts on the bottom of my feet, or an all-out, full-blown hives attack. Hives were just the tip of the iceberg. My only ally was my acute sense of smell. It warned me of potential danger.

During one registration, I felt *"strange"* as strong carpet fumes drifted into the room, from the new carpeting in the room next door. Panicked, I thought, "I have to get out of here. *Right now!*" But, I couldn't get my body out of the chair or open my mouth to ask for help. My body was disconnected from my brain. Fortunately, someone opened the windows in the room. After the fresh air blew in, I was able to get out of the chair and leave on my own.

There were times my sense of smell didn't have time to warn me. One day as I stepped into the doorway of a friend's office, I felt a karate chop to the throat, then a constriction around my windpipe as if I were being choked. I spun around and headed for the outside door and fresh air. Later my friend told me there was a jacket with a slight odor of mothballs hanging on a coat rack next to the office door.

Another day a wall of horrible, noxious fumes hit me as I entered the Academic Building. That triggered an all-out asthma attack. When I couldn't catch my breath, a co-worker rushed me to the emergency room. The fumes came from the stucco sealer applied to the outside of the building. Someone from the construction company forgot to turn off the air intake valves.

Unfortunately, my sense of smell couldn't protect me from odorless chemicals. They were a different kind of enemy; their sneak attacks came without warning.

After our walk one day, my friend Nancy and I stopped at a friend's office. Within minutes, I was lying on the floor. I couldn't speak, but I could hear some of their words and sensed the panic in their voices. Julie's boss carried me outside. With the fresh air, I had my voice back by the time the ambulance came. The chemicals in the room got into my bloodstream quickly to do their damage, probably because of our fast walk to the top of the hill next to the college.

Several weeks later, odorless chemicals struck again, this time in our computer room. Within minutes of walking through the door, I lost my voice. When that happened every morning over the next few weeks, I was afraid to work there. I requested a letter from my doctor, a clinical ecologist, then got permission to move to an office in another building.

That move worked well at first; then I noticed a pattern. When I drove into the parking lot, my mind was sharp. I mentally clicked off the things I had to do. By the time I got to my office on the third floor, my mental checklist disappeared. Many mornings I remember thinking, "Oooh, where I should I start? I dunno." Whatever was in the air hijacked my mind.

One morning, I saw the cursor zigzagging all over my computer screen. "What is going on here?" I said out loud. Several minutes passed before I looked down and saw my little finger resting on the arrow keys. "No one is going to believe this crazy stuff is happening to my mind!" I thought. There was nothing going on in the hallway.

Then the phone rang. The man refinishing my mother's dining room set wanted to know what color stain to use. I couldn't answer that over the phone, so left the building. When I got back to the third floor, I saw carpet-cleaning equipment sitting outside a room down a hallway just off the elevator. It was the chemicals in the carpet cleaner that affected my ability to think.

From that point on, whenever hives appeared or I felt "strange," I played detective and searched the building to see what was going on. One day, I found open containers of ammoniated stripper in the basement. The fumes eventually ended up on the third floor. I realized that my problems feeling "spaced-out" began in the summer when the custodians started their summer cleaning.

When school started in the fall, I requested a room with a window and got permission to move to an office on the first floor. That move probably saved my life, in more ways than one. It was how I met Sage.

Sage and Ishpiming

Sage, a used-book buyer, came into the office to talk to my officemate. Sage was a big woman with jet-black hair, spiked on top, short on the sides, and longer in the back. She wore black-rimmed glasses and a loose-fitting, bright-colored outfit with a long skirt. I don't remember exactly what she said, only that it included the word "healing."

"Follow her," the little voice inside said. When I caught up with Sage, I told her about my health issues.

"I have a healing center," she said. "Come and visit. Bring a friend." That visit was the first of many to Sage's healing center, Ishpiming, the Ojibwe word for "universe."

Sage was a fascinating woman and one of contradictions. She was friendly and helpful one minute, then brusque and "Sarge-like" the next. She said what was on her mind and used strange phrases I had never heard: *healing modalities, cellular memory, ego patterns, the Illusion, the Duality.*

Some things she said resonated with me and became permanent sticky notes in my memory:

"Be grateful in every moment."
"Everything is perfect purpose."
"Your thoughts, words, and actions create your reality."
"Don't be stuck in a rut. Change your habits. Start with little baby steps."
"Ego wants to keep you stuck."
"Listen to your word patterns ... if only, could'a, should'a, would'a."
"Stop doing what doesn't serve you."
"Love everyone exactly where they are and bless them on their journeys."
"If you don't learn your lessons, life will offer up more opportunities for you to learn them."

Her favorite question was: *"What are you learning from this experience?"*

Healing Modalities and Body Electronics

Sage was a walking encyclopedia for healing. I left her center with vitamins, enzymes, and chelated-colloidal minerals that pulled toxins out of the cells and flushed them through the body. Taking the horrible tasting liquid was the only thing that reduced the intensity of the hives.

Sage was trained in Reiki, kinesiology, iridology, reflexology, and Body Electronics, a healing process that released trauma and emotions stored in the cells. Dark spots in the eyes showed where blockages were in the body. Holding specific acupressure points released the blockages (the crystal formations) and everything stored with them: feelings, emotions, images, and even smells (e.g. operating room smells, flowers in a recovery room). When points were held long enough, a kundalini healing took place that released energy and intense heat as the crystals dissolved.

Reluctantly, I did several sessions, first as a "point holder," then as a "point holdee." I couldn't believe I was doing these sessions! They were totally outside my comfort zone. But desperate, I was willing to try anything. When I held points at the base of the skull on one lady, I felt a burning sensation on the tips of my fingers, as if they just landed on a hot stove. The lady who held my points had the same experience.

During that session, I felt nothing. Sage's response, "You were in a state of *unconsciousness*." Above unconsciousness, in the list of *States of Consciousness*, were apathy, grief, fear, anger, and enthusiasm. I had multiple stages to work through to get to enthusiasm.

The Workshops - The Inner Child and the Judge

Sage had a schedule of workshops with out-of-town presenters. My friend Faye and I signed up for the *"Inner Child and the Judge"* with Rick and Rosalie, therapists from Illinois.

On Friday night, Rick handed out paper and boxes of crayons and said, "Draw a picture of something you did as a child that was fun."

At first, I couldn't think of anything, then remembered the field next to my mother's house. Flowers grew there in the spring alongside a little brook. I drew a little yellow circle the size of a nickel in the middle of the big piece of paper.

The little circle was almost invisible in the green grass that filled the rest of the page.

"What is this?" Rick asked, when he picked up my picture.

"A picture of me in the field next to our house."

His next question left me speechless: "When did you go into your head?"

"WOW!" I had never heard that phrase, but something inside me *knew* that's exactly what I did. I went into the logical, left-brain side. It was my safe place where I had "control," or so I thought.

The Judge and the Prickles

Rick started Saturday with a guided meditation. "*It's a beautiful sunny day. You're walking through the woods. Then storm clouds roll in. Now you're in the middle of a thunderstorm. Where are you? Whom are you thinking about?*"

Next, he said, "Draw a picture." I saw myself in the hollow of a tree and thought about my mother. The picture I drew showed her face with glasses and a stern, worried look. Rick picked up my picture and held it at eye level in front of me. "What's this?"

"A picture of my mother. She's worried about me."

He asked the same question three times. Each time my answer was the same, "A picture of my mother." The fourth time, he held the picture slightly above eye level, like a parent looking down at a child who had done something wrong. Instantly, prickles went up the back of my neck. How could a picture I drew cause that physical reaction? I never thought of my mother as my "Judge." It was *that look*" on her face that reminded me I failed. No matter what I did, I couldn't make the hurt she felt go away or get rid of the sadness in our house. I was my own Judge, wanting self-approval as the little caretaker.

After Bevie told me I had "issues." I watched John Bradshaw's video, *The Family*, and read his book, *Healing the Shame That Binds*. The family, as a unit, wants to be in balance, or homeostasis. If something happens (death, divorce, alcoholism, abuse), family members take on roles, trying to get the family back into balance. After my father died, I took the roles of little caretaker and hero.

On my way to school, two blocks away, I'd sometimes stop at the house of my mother's best friend. "Irene, please look in on my mother. She's having a bad day." Besides keeping my things in perfect condition, I tried to be the perfect student and "Miss Goody-Two-Shoes." If only I could be perfect, maybe our lives would be perfect too.

Releasing the Empowered Self

Rick and Rosalie did another workshop that summer. It focused on ways to shrink the Judge, find the Warrior within, and free the Inner Child. Rick said, "The Judge is a psychological illusion that tries to control and sometimes terrorize us. It develops from our childhood experiences."

What stood out at the workshop was another lady's experience. Her Judge picture showed the top half of a black-cat face with huge, scary eyes. "I was shaking as I drew this picture," she said. "It scares me! I have nightmares about those critical eyes looking down on me."

"What do you want to do with it?" Rick asked.

"I want to *smash* it!!!"

Rick and her husband held the picture. Standing with clenched fists, she hit the picture–hard–and ripped it in half. Energy exploded outward and filled the room. "I just felt a blast of energy," I said. (I was sitting about six feet away). Her husband commented, "How would you like to be living with that?"

Witnessing this first hand showed me the power of "Judge-work," with art therapy, to expose the Judge, then shrink it, or get rid of its influence completely. It's powerful work.

"The Judge prefers to operate from deep within the psyche outside a person's awareness because it … has no real energy or power of its own. It feeds off the energy of our own anger and fear … It is only by confronting this powerful psychological illusion that we learn to claim our personal power as strong capable adult human beings." Shrinking the Judge, Freeing the Inner Child, Rick Malter, Ph.D., Rosalie Malter, M.A.

Holotropic Breathwork – The Tears

"There's a workshop coming up. You should go," Sage said in a commanding voice. I resisted, until the last minute, then called Sage the night before. "There's one spot left," she said.

The next morning, Joyce told us what to expect. "Holotropic breathwork is like hyperventilating to wild African drum music. It's supposed to put you in another state of consciousness where *'issues'* can come up. At some point you'll feel relaxed. When the session is coming to a close you'll hear English-like words in the music." Next she said, "You'll need a partner."

"Yikes!" There was no one there I knew. When Joyce matched me up with a tall, serious-looking man, I wanted to run out the door. Just thinking about "hyperventilating" in front of him made me feel stressed. I had to start over, twice, to finally feel somewhat relaxed.

At some point, thinking I heard English-like words, I opened my eyes and saw Joyce standing in a corner of the room. She seemed to be really far away, and I felt *all alone*. Seeing that I moved, Joyce came over to me, smiled, then put her hand right above my heart next to my throat. I don't know what in that gesture brought up emotions in me, but I started to cry. She put her arms around me and let me cry until the tears stopped.

As a child, I stuffed my tears. I never went to my father Isaac's funeral and never cried in front of my mother Lempi. I didn't want to make her feel worse than she already felt.

After the session ended, Joyce gave us colored chalk and a piece of paper with a large circle drawn in the middle. "Draw a picture of your experience," she said.

I drew a dam across the middle of the circle with a small amount of water trickling over it–the tears I cried. There was a lot of water behind the dam–my unshed tears. Next to the dam was a stick kid with a broken heart–me. Outside the circle I drew a picture of this pretty blond lady who gave me permission to cry. Above her, I drew a rainbow. I felt there was a light at the end of the tunnel for the sadness I felt.

Ten years later, something told me to call Joyce to thank her again. "I remember that trip," Joyce said. "It was the only one I made that far from my home base. I remember what happened too. The man who was supposed to watch over you got up to use the bathroom. That must have triggered something." Yes, it triggered feelings–including those of abandonment. Wow! Bevie had been right.

As we are growing up and experience things too painful for us to deal with, we stuff them and the emotions we're feeling. Even as adults we stuff emotions. Later as things happen to us that remind us of those things we've stuffed, our emotions often erupt. From *The Trash Can Theory*, John Gray

My explosive reaction to the spilled detergent was a good example of emotions that *"erupt."* The crinkled pages and the Wisk incident reminded me of my childhood and stirred up the anger that I stuffed so many years before.

Spiritual Healing – The Vision

Faye and I took the *"Spiritual Healing"* workshop next. Neither of us knew what to expect. Nancy started the first day with an energy exercise. "Put your hands together as if you're holding a ball. Can you *feel* the energy?" Faye felt the energy; I felt nothing.

On the second day, Nancy did a guided meditation: *"You're in a canoe floating down a river on a beautiful sunny day. You land on a sandy beach. You look around and see steps. You walk up the steps. They lead to a castle. Inside the castle there are libraries with books for your well-being. Go into the library with the red books for your physical well-being. What do you see?"* Expecting to see nothing, I saw nothing.

"Go into the library with the yellow books for your emotional well-being. What do you see?" Again, I saw nothing.

"Now, go into the library with the blue books for your spiritual well-being. What do you see?"

A vision appeared–out of nowhere. I saw my husband, my daughter and myself standing together holding hands in the presence of a brilliant white light. I felt we were connected to God, to Spirit and the Universe. The vision blew me away! I expected to see nothing, yet I was given this incredible picture.

I asked Sage later, "Where did it come from? What does it mean?" Her response, "Be patient and answers will come."

Several years later, Jen drew a picture of my vision (her interpretation). She and her father had it framed and gave it to me for Christmas. It was a special gift!

I found comfort in the picture. It validated my feeling that there was help from above. As I struggled with the health issues, things appeared–a person, an event, a book, even a word–that led me to the next clue, the next step, the next lesson. Everything fit together as if it had been orchestrated outside my control.

I believed there were promises in the picture too, that I would find healing for my body, mind, and my spirit.

Looking back, I saw how all the events I thought were separate, were not. So many things had to be in place for me to connect with Sage and have the experiences I had. I realized there was so much more I'd need to learn about my inner world.

Finding Me

In the movie, *Finding Joe*, there's a video clip of the Golden Buddha story about a golden statue in a temple in Thailand. Villagers found out that soldiers were coming to their village. Afraid they would take the statue, the villagers covered it with mud and concrete. The soldiers stayed in the village a long time.

Eventually, people forgot the statue was golden. One day when a monk went to the statue to pray, a piece of concrete fell off. Excited, he went to tell the other monks what he saw. They went back to chip off the rest of the concrete and revealed the Golden Buddha inside.

Alan Cohen said the story has a metaphor. "*The metaphor is that each of us is golden by nature. We were born golden, born knowing, born connected to our bliss. We were born knowing* truth. *We were born knowing everything that each spiritual master has ever said. We were one with the Christ, the Buddha, everyone.*" But early on, the programming begins from parents, teachers and others. "*So we developed a casing of stone over the Buddha to a point where at a young age (maybe 4, 5, 6, or 7) we believed that we were the stone Buddha not the Golden one.*"

The stone casing is what's inside, the "stuffed stuff." Our cellular memories hold everything that happens to us. But it's the negative and destructive memories, thoughts, feelings, beliefs, images, and emotions that form the concrete. After my father died, the grief, anger, and fear I felt were too painful for me to share *with anyone.* They added another layer to the concrete already inside.

The concrete influences our beliefs and creates filters–how we see ourselves and our world. When filters distort the truth or create limitations, they hold us back from being who we were meant to be.

A few years back, I attended the funeral of an educated, professional man who had a colorful, sometimes controversial lifestyle. During the eulogy, his friend, another professional, said, "*From where he sat, this is how he saw the world.*" That one sentence painted a visual picture of the limited view a person has from a sitting position.

I could picture my "old self" sitting in a comfortable chair and thinking, "I don't need to change. I'm good just the way I am." Resistance to change kept me stuck in my comfort zone. I didn't know what I didn't know.

Know Thyself

My story is about change–changing me from the inside out and changing the way I look at things. To know more about myself, I stepped outside the box and became the observer. I played detective, searched for clues and followed leads - looking for nuggets. I asked questions to get answers and find insights. "What am I learning from this?" was one of the questions. I also asked "What if" questions.

What if the Wisk incident never happened? I might not have known what "issues" were or where the anger came from. The Wisk incident was a driving force for me to learn more. What if I never had hives? Without them there would have been no desperation in my search for healing. They were a blessing in disguise.

"What if" questions and Wayne Dyer's words helped me see life through new eyes: *"If you change the way you look at things, the things you look at change."*

What about you? Are you willing to see life through new eyes? How do you feel about change? Are you willing to chip away concrete to find your gold inside? Maybe you already found gold.

Or, maybe you think you're okay just the way you are. But are there things you'd like to change: relationships, emotional issues, health problems? What if changing the way you looked at them helped bring about the changes you'd like to see? Positive change has the potential for unlimited blessings.

One of my blessings is the wonderful, loving relationship I have with my daughter. Together, we're finding gold.

The better you know yourself, the better you are at facing whatever shows up in your life. So to understand your true power to thrive, you must first understand who you are. Gregg Braden

As you journey through this life, my wish is that you *"understand who you are."* May you discover the gold within and find many blessings along the way.

Namaste! *The spirit in me honors the spirit in you.*

About The Author

Karen Saari Secor spent over thirty years in the computer industry developing software for business, education, and manufacturing. It was a career she absolutely loved. She received a degree in math and computers from the University of Wisconsin - Superior and an MBA from Lake Superior State University, Sault Ste. Marie, Michigan.

Karen has been a member of the Wisconsin Council on Physical Disabilities for sixteen years. She joined the Wisconsin Public Health Preparedness Advisory Committee in 2007 and has been involved with emergency preparedness issues for people with physical disabilities. She has been a member of the Education Foundation for the local school district since it started 16 years ago and just ended her 21st year as a City Council member.

Besides her love of computers, Karen loves kayaking, rock collecting, Scrabble, and continual learning.

She can be contacted via email at: BlessMyUSA@gmail.com.

CHAPTER 12

SPIRITUAL PARENTING: EQUAL SOULS, DIFFERENT ROLES

Virginia Grace-Braun

Instinctual Love

A mother's instincts are amazing. Trust those instincts. They can tell you what to do long before your head can figure it out. Janelle Ashmore, Doula

In the beginning, we feel so excited to become a parent. We discover depths and doorways within ourselves we never knew existed. When I first laid eyes on my newborn daughter, alive, purple, shaking her fists with the shock of first breath, I felt as though a treasure door suddenly slid open inside of me, revealing a depth of love I never before knew existed. Passion for life rose like a skyscraper in my soul, and all my former uncertain, treacherous thoughts about living, the awful pain of growing up, washed away and shed downstream. In that moment of commitment to her, I awakened into purpose–maternal love–fiercer than any love I had ever known.

I had chosen home birth as the only way to avoid the callous conditions of hospital birth at that time. Unlike hospital birthing rooms of today, the hospital birth of that time would have dictated a plastic examination table with my feet in stirrups, surrounded by anonymous staff, beneath bright fluorescent lights in a white-walled room, like a butterfly pinned down in a specimen display case. Instead, my daughter was born naturally and at home with a midwife and a doctor in attendance, but most of all, with my husband, who had cared for me with utmost love, attention, and thought to every detail throughout. To give me a firm birthing surface, he constructed a plywood platform layered with thick, dense foam to top the waterbed. If somewhat high, it was a comfortable, sturdy surface for birthing.

Some hours following the birth, I went to shower, leaving my husband seated on the corner of the bed, cradling our daughter in his arms, then returned to the room to dress. Twelve feet away, I stood at the door of the closet putting on fresh clothing. At that precise moment, I glanced around from dressing, just as my fatigued husband's eyes closed, his arms went limp, and our tiny infant was cascading to the floor head first. Dashing at light speed, I caught our newborn infant midair. That awesome, attuned connection of mother to infant had averted the worst kind of disaster. The bond a mother feels is to her infant is vast and inexplicable, powerful beyond words. I could not have reacted more quickly if I'd been an Olympic sprinter, or pulling my own hand from a searing flame.

I vowed from the start to be the best parent I could be. I began to study even before my milk came in. We all want to be a really great parent to our child. We picture ourselves being loving and understanding, patient and kind, never doing the hurtful things to our children that we experienced as children from our parents. We vow to be better to our child than our own parents were to us. And we struggle to deliver the right balance between firmness and kindness, strictness and encouragement. The truth is that parenting is trans-generational.

My love for my daughter and interest in the psychology of positive parenting drove me into a career as a counselor. When I began working as a psychotherapist, I was a young woman, petite and soft-spoken. My position was at a high school in California that pulled students in from 40 miles back into the mountains. One day when I returned from my lunch, the school's administrative assistant, who was a size that could have eaten me alive, informed me that a set of parents was seated in my office waiting for me. My heart pounded because a few days previous, a student had shown me black and blue marks and welts on his torso from a belt, and I had reported the case to Child Protective Services. These were the parents now waiting for me in my office. I wanted to skip school, but it was my turn to be brave. I entered my office expecting to be thrashed—at least verbally—accused, and maybe threatened. However, the parents immediately began to shower me with words, their hands spread open, palms up, reaching out. "We just want you to know we are not bad parents," they said. "We want to raise our son right. We are trying to be good parents. We want to teach him right from wrong."

I stood frozen trying to take in what was going on and follow their train of thought. The father continued, "We don't want to be too easy on him, because we want him to know how to behave, and know right from wrong, and not be a weakling, be strong." There I am, thinking they have been brutal to their son. As the conversation continued, the father related his story, "When I was a boy, I was strapped to the bed and my father whipped the daylights out of me. He slapped me real hard, and he used the buckle end of that belt, too. I never did that–swore to myself as a boy I would never do that to my sons. I made sure of it. I used the leather end of the belt on them. I wanted to be easy on 'em. I only use the leather end of the belt. But my dad, he strapped me down and he whipped me and he learned me real good–and he used the buckle end. Now me, I went easy. I'm trying to teach him right from wrong. I wanted to do right by him. But not too easy."

Now the mother chimed in, "We don't want to be too easy on him, but not too hard on him neither. When I was a girl, my mom would tie me to a tree, and then she would switch me with a willow switch. Did you ever get a willow switch?" she asked me sincerely, with a questioning look on her face.

"A willow switch ... well , no, can't say that I have. But I can imagine it hurts very badly."

"Well it does, stings and cuts real bad , stings like crazy and you bleed in little streamlets. I will never use a willow switch on my kid. I will never be unkind the way my mother was to me!"

At that moment, a wave of compassion and forgiveness swept over me. Can you imagine the humility of this man and this woman to come to me, spill this to me, a little miss from college, in her Macy's outfit and makeup? And then, what's more and beyond that, to take my advice, parenting instruction and guidance? I will never forget them, their hands open and beseeching for understanding, pleading with me to know they are not bad parents, their stories, and their dilemma of not knowing any other way to discipline and teach right from wrong than to belt their son, so that using the leather end of the belt was in their eyes an act of kindness.

Clearly these parents had the wrong methods and limited knowledge, yet their feelings and intent were the same as all parents–wanting to do the best right thing for their child, to make him a strong child, a good child, who knows right from wrong, and grows into a fine adult, and to be kinder and more enlightened to their child than their own parents had been to them. Parenting is a trans-generational accomplishment, transmitted from one generation to the next, and our internal model is the deeply emotionally embedded memories of how we were raised and parented. No matter how wrong or misguided our parents may have been, they, too, were most likely trying to improve upon the parenting they received. The goal is to infuse greater gold into each link of the generational chain of parenting, more gold, and less lead into this generational and genetic chain that reaches into the future.

Dealing with Feelings

Unexpressed emotions never die. They are buried alive and will come forth later. Sigmund Freud

All our emotions are natural and normal–some may be pleasant and comfortable, while others may be unpleasant and uncomfortable, but they are all part of being a human being. Everyone feels all the emotions, even though some are difficult to acknowledge. It's just as natural at times to feel angry, down, or guilty, as it is to have fingers and toes! Our emotions are there as a lifeline, teaching us who we are, what we need, and how to treat ourselves and others.

As parents, it's typical that we want to keep our children happy, calm, and peaceful. We don't want them to get mad, feel upset, embarrassed, or ashamed. We even fear that feeling those feelings will lower their self-esteem. But children need to experience all the feelings in order to know what's going on inside of them, and how to handle those feelings. That way they are less likely to be overtaken or blindsided by them. If a child doesn't experience anger, how will they know how to manage anger? Anger is at times inevitable. If a child is not allowed to experience a moment of shame for some kind of wrong action, how will they learn to inhibit a behavior that is unacceptable or out of line? In our effort as parents to support our children and keep their self-esteem growing, we often make the mistake of not wanting them to feel their own feelings! When our kids are small, it's natural to fend off tough experiences for them, but when do we need to step back and allow them to step up and take up more ownership?

One mom recently told me that she was going through continued stressful arguments with her daughter over getting up, out of bed and into the car on time to get to school. Her daughter was always late. Finally, one morning, after having explained to her daughter in advance that she was going to leave for her own work on time, and if her daughter wasn't ready, she would have to walk, the mom actually did it! This mom finally stuck to her word. She gave her daughter plenty of warning, but when it was 8:00 a.m., she walked out the door, put the key in the ignition, and drove down the road leaving her daughter still getting ready in the house. The mom agonized over it. She was used to catering to her rebellious girl, but it was the last time her daughter was late! This mom used her own feelings as an internal barometer. Her stored-up negative feelings were acknowledged and acted upon in a way that taught her daughter logical consequences and set an appropriate parental boundary. She could have done this a lot sooner and it would have worked successfully.

Another parent of two young boys who rivaled with each other was struggling with the emotions of wanting to be fair to both her sons. She would find herself trying to sort out their quarrels, and sometimes in the pressure of the moment, she would overreact by giving too hard a consequence. Then she'd feel guilty afterwards. Often she'd reverse her own decision, and end up feeling weak and ineffective. This is what I call "The Marshmallow or The Meanie" syndrome—the parent stuffs too many negative feelings, then reacts by being too strict, then feels guilty and takes it back, and finally ends up feeling weak and ineffective. After discussing the problem, she went home with some new tools. Here's how she handled it.

At a quiet moment, she told the boys she was going to teach them a trick for helping them each be more in charge of their arguments and fight less. The mom taught them a technique I call "The Five-Finger Vacation." She showed her sons how to take a deep belly breath, hold it, and let it out. The count for the breath is seven on the inhale, hold three, and exhale eight. On the fingers of one hand, count five breaths–the first breath is counted with the thumb pressing to the index finger, the second is the same position with index finger pressing to the thumb, then middle finger to thumb, ring finger to thumb, and pinkie to thumb.

The next time her boys came to her angry and upset and wanting Mom to referee, she had them go to separate rooms, think about it, and practice the five-finger vacation. She said that she would get back to them soon. She no longer put herself on the spot and in the middle by trying to reach a decision instantaneously. She used the vacation trick herself in the meantime. After a few minutes, she talked to her boys. "You can't expect to have 100% of everything you want, and you can't expect to have things go your way all the time. You have to take responsibility for contributing to the argument. And if you want to play with your brother, and have other kids as friends, *you have to learn to give.*"

She let them have turns and some input into how to solve the problem. She told them she would always try her best to understand both of their wants. Over time, she taught them to talk to each other so they could solve their own quarrels using conflict resolution skills. Teaching your children to use deep breathing, and modeling it for them, is a powerful tool. Having the ability to calm oneself is an amazing power. It can prevent someone's life from shattering in a moment of over-reaction. This mom gave a tool and a presence to her children that will last a lifetime. She did not try to be their friend or their judge. She practiced spiritual parenting; she saw her children as equal to herself on the soul level, but at the same time, she wisely fulfilled her leadership role as a parent. She practiced the responsible use of power and guided her boys by giving clear and firm direction. As a result, the boys settled down and gained their own positive personal power to play forward in their own lives.

Children grow strong when they earn their self-esteem. They earn self-esteem through developing skills, learning how to handle their own emotions, and working hard for good outcomes. They don't blame others when things don't go their way.

They earn self-esteem by helping their family and others, and acting with kindness. Inside of the child, as with all of us, is a witness which knows without a doubt when we are acting as a "good person," for the greater good.

Unearned self-esteem, overly-praised, overly-celebrated children know inside themselves that the words are lifeless and even phony.

Much of our joy in life is based on our relationships, and that means developing communication skills, emotional understanding of self and others, the will to do the right thing, and the desire to be kind. Kids who are raised without being held accountable actually tend to have weaker self-esteem, poorer relationship skills, be less motivated, and lower achievers.

A child will learn from everything they see you do. The best way to teach is by example, so you want to show them in your action what you want them to grow up to be. A parent needs to be thinking twenty years down the road. Have a vision for what you want your children to become. This is the responsible use of your power as a parent and the wisdom you have gained through experience.

Healing Ourselves Through Our Parenting: Mindfulness In Action

Nothing is so strong as gentleness; nothing so gentle as real strength. R. W. Sockman

I stood motionless at the kitchen sink in the midst of the dinner dishes–frozen, defensive, and self-justifying. I had just engaged in a ridiculous verbal fight with my twelve-year-old daughter over cleaning her room "You aren't acting like a twelve-year-old! You're acting like a six-year-old! You're not being truthful! I never have taught you to act like this! What is wrong with you! You can't just shove it all beneath the bed," I shouted. Though I was "right" in some ways, how absurdly and arrogantly I had behaved in my self-righteousness! Hadn't my own mother taught me on occasion to "clean the kitchen" by stuffing all the mess into the oven? No one looks in your oven, so it's all good until later, right? A flood of shame swept over me. Where had all that anger and punitive words come from? How could I have behaved like such a jerk? I was inert as a statue, but at last I remembered to suck in a deep breath, then let it go.

"OK Grace, it doesn't matter if you know where it came from," I inwardly coached myself. "It only matters that you recognize it in this moment, you are noticing it, that's really good. So what if there's a gap between the action and the noticing ... it's a step." I encourage myself with the reminder that soon the awareness gap will shorten, until the behavior extinguishes itself. I close my eyes and breathe deeply through my crown chakra, through my nose, down deep into my belly, allowing in the breath, allowing in the gift of light, and proceeding with the practice I hoped and believed would transform me.

"Thank You, Higher Power," I spoke silently in myself, "Thank you for bringing me this awareness. I send these energies and emotions and all the traces of them within me known and unknown back to the Source to be recycled, without the need to manifest them in my life ever again. And I thank You for this! So be it!"

And then another deep breath filling myself with light, calming down, attempting to feel better. At least now I could think a bit more clearly. The next step was to ask myself, how else I could have handled that angry moment? What other options did I have besides overreacting and blaming ? After all, my daughter had not *made* me become angry, she had not *made* me act pompously, *she* was not responsible for *my* feelings of anger. That emotion was my own, and there are always choices. I paused to think of two or three different responses I could have made. Had I pulled in any one of them, I'd be feeling nurturing, strong, and humorous now, instead of guilty and embarrassed. Nothing was worth feeling this way ever again.

There must be a way to do some repair work, I thought to myself, and I walk down the hallway toward my daughter's bedroom. I tap on the door, pause, silence, then gently open it, and see her teary face,

"I didn't like what just happened," I say. "I'm sorry for what I said. Your behavior doesn't excuse my part. I think we can both do better. What do you think?" I pause, letting my effort at repair work sink in. Silence. I wait. My heart strains with love, frustration and disappointment, not to mention shame. After a long pause she says, "Go get the singing bowl, Mom."

"Good idea," I say, and walk toward the living room. On the mantle above the fireplace is a Tibetan crystal bowl, and beside it is a white leather-wrapped wand used to strike it, swirl, and make it zing. I walk back to my daughter's bedroom, sit on the edge of her bed, and position the bowl in my left hand, firmly yet lightly seating it upon my erect fingertips. With my right hand I tap the midsection of the bowl, then commence to swirl the leather wand round and round the lip of the bowl until it sings and zings and peals like a great reverberant Om, pulsating, filling the room with its rich sound. I halt when the vibration has become so powerful I think the bowl itself might shatter. The mighty vibration gradually dissolves, attenuating into finer and fainter tendrils of silence. My daughter and I have done this before. When we have both reached the still moment, we open our eyes. We are ready.

"I want to go first," she says. I listen as she explains. I want to understand her, and I know that from her vantage point she has a truly valid point of view. Until she has spoken and been fully heard, she will not be able to see any other perspective, not able to move forward, she will be anchored to the need to express her perspective.

Even though my responsibilities and experience are so much greater, even though time is short, lunches still need to be packed, and it's getting late, even though I want to wipe away all her need for trial and error, I don't do that. I listen. It really only takes a minute or two.

Her soul is equal to my own. I listen. So much conflict is resolved by one person truly listening to another. Deep listening is an act of respect, an act of compassion, a way of alleviating a great deal of suffering in the world. Kids are really smart–they are really aware–they see everything about their parent, and when they are in the critical age of early adolescence, they can judge you harshly. They can be quite condemning and rejecting.

As parents we feel disregarded and angry when we feel we haven't been respected, and we tend to want to wipe away our children's need for their own experience by forcing them to learn from ours. The best way to teach is by example; the best way to learn is by experience. Equal souls, different roles. My job now is to listen and raise her up.

"I see your point," I said. You've been feeling misunderstood, that I haven't been giving you credit enough for all the chores you've done, how much you've been regulating your own homework, all the time you've put into caring for the animals, and so you put your own room last? Because you think if it doesn't get done, it doesn't disturb anyone but you?" She nods, yes.

"I do understand better now, I said. "Thank you for explaining, and for trying to do the tasks that help others first." Equal souls different roles.

I can see she now feels heard and respected. So I ask, "May I tell you how I think about it, how I see it?" I wait for her answer. Will she give the okay? Otherwise any wisdom I try to offer her will not penetrate; it will only close the door harder. "OKAY," she says.

Okay! Then and only then do I give my teaching, my guidance, very simply, condensed to her developmental level. I explain, "If you had told me–asked me about finishing your room at another time, that would have been different. We could have agreed. Next time, will you please ask me if you can finish it another time, rather than trying to pretend you had done it? That way you will feel truthful and empowered, and I will feel better, too. I will feel respected."

My girl reaches for me, head bent down, and hugs me. We are back together, restored.

She snuggles into her pillows, and I go back to the kitchen, then decide that lunches can wait, or heck, we can buy lunch. I go to wash up for the night, weary but thankful that I fulfilled my role, maintaining the boundaries for parent and child, so that she can feel safe and secure, protected and deeply cared for. She will grow from our interaction, and have a stronger handle on her own emotions and communications. For myself, I have kept awareness of my own emotional states, monitored them mindfully, upheld my responsibility as the parent I want to be and was meant to be, healing my own woundedness through the privilege of parenting my beautiful daughter . I think to myself, that in the end, time has been saved, not lost.

As parents we take so much of our self-esteem from how we feel we are doing as parents. Parenting is passed down, generation to generation, like our genes. I recall that,

"Nothing is so strong as gentleness, nothing so gentle as real strength." I know that tonight, more gold has been melded into the link of our transgenerational chain of our parenting–alchemy and transformation are at work! Tonight I've been a good mom for my incredible daughter–she will play it forward. Equal souls, different roles. I go to sleep smiling, knowing I can count on myself.

About The Author

Virginia Grace Braun is a Licensed Counseling Psychologist and Nationally Certified Mental Health Clinician, as well as a teacher, counselor, and public school administrator. Her mission has been to merge psychology and spiritual development to help bring about an accelerated transformational path for the people she helps.

Her daily philosophy is to give love and compassion to all whom she encounters, because even the smallest and most inconspicuous acts of service work to instill love to humankind.

She has spent the last seven years providing counseling services to our Military Service Members and their families.

Grace lives in Sonoma County in Northern California and can be reached at vgbraun@sonic.net.

CHAPTER 13

PAINFUL MEMORIES HEALED!
Denis Franklin

What kind of past have you had?

Have you ever had any painful memories from your past? Of course you have! We all have them, don't we? But some are more troublesome than others. Since I'm 73-years-old, it's no wonder I've had lots of negative, painful memories from my childhood and earlier adult life. But I now have seventeen fewer negative memories, ones that have now been healed. And you can experience a healing of the negative memories in *your* life, too! Let me tell you how some of mine were healed. But first, some background.

When was the right time?

Back in 1991 I self-published a motivational/spiritual booklet titled *Yes You Can–With God's Help!* It had just a small circulation of two thousand copies around Sydney and parts of the state of New South Wales, Australia, where I was born and raised. But I didn't get much feedback on it then.

In 2010 I felt the Lord was asking me to publish a Second Edition, expanded and updated into a book, with current photos. I soon completed the additional text, but then, as time dragged on, I wondered why He had never made it possible financially for me to accept a certain publishing offer in the U.S.

Then in 2015 I discovered why I had had to wait so long. I had to wait until Dr. Alex Loyd published his book *Beyond Willpower*! How I came to receive an email advertising this marvelous book, I don't know. (But I have a pretty good idea!) I just happened to receive it at the same time as an email about affordable self-publishing.

What if it didn't really work?

In *Beyond Willpower*, Dr. Alex initially states that the reason so many people buy motivational books year after year is that our attempts to visualize positive goals are ruined by painful negative images from our past–from our subconscious, of course! If our conscious mind and our subconscious are in conflict, guess which one wins out! But then most of his book is about dealing with those negative images so that they don't prevent our positive goals from working successfully. It involves inviting God's Light and Love into the negative image on our Heart screen.

I just had to get the permission of Dr. Alex's publishers to include a summary of this main message in my new book, *Yes You Can–With God's Help! Second Edition*. And I considered it 'the final piece of the jigsaw puzzle' for my book. But I had to test his suggestion myself. What if it didn't really work?

Being brutally honest

I'm 'a man born before my time'! (Ha!) I was born two-and-a-half months premature. And there were no humidicribs in 1943. My birth weight was 2 pounds 11 ounces (1.3 kg), and I was 14 inches (35 cm) long. I was in the hospital for three months after 'Mum' came home!

My grandfather told Mum that she could have a child's grave that he had, for me. When she started to cry, his reaction was, "Well, face facts, woman! He couldn't possibly survive!" I still have my baby's bonnet that fits only a small orange. But then I had a congenital hernia which strangulated at 12 months! ... (I am now almost 6 feet tall, and the proud father of three grown-up children and five beautiful granddaughters.)

Mum had a very strong personality; there was only one way to do anything–*her* way! When she disapproved of something I did wrong, she never smacked me or yelled. She would just look at me with that annoyed look on her face. And as a toddler I'd get a knot in my chest that lasted, on and off, for most of my life. I felt that nothing I did was ever good enough for her.

I was a happy-go-lucky child, until the focus of attention was on me. And the pressure was on me to perform well academically like my three older brothers, who were close together, whereas I was in some ways like an only child, coming eight years after my third brother. (At least my brothers were always really kind to me, and never bossed 'little Dennie' around.)

Even at university I took an extra year to get my Bachelor of Arts degree and Diploma in Education, coming after one of my brothers who, like me, had trained as a high school Languages teacher, and had gained First Class Honours in Latin and a couple of special university awards! I failed Latin in First Year!

Even as a teacher for 25 years, I had some problems with some larger classes, preferring smaller, more informal French classes. (A former colleague, a good mate–I'm their daughter's godfather–described me recently as someone who he had seen as being nervous but who still went ahead and 'did it anyway'.)

After eight years I chose to accept an opportunity for thirty teachers to train as Reading teachers, working with small groups of early-high school students, mainly boys, with specific reading and related problems. I could empathize with their lack of confidence and witnessed some outstanding improvements which even carried over to their schoolwork generally, because I introduced them to goal visualization. I *loved* working with them!

Have you tried goal visualization?

I had begun reading about visual imagery towards the end of my university studies. I was interested in anything that would help me to overcome the anxiety and lack of confidence I felt. I prepared for my speech at my 21st Birthday celebration, which was held at an up-market reception place. Having visualized myself standing up and delivering my speech, I was more confident in my delivery. Then later in the night–without the assistance of any alcohol–I was able to respond to a challenge to get up on the stage and sing a couple of songs. Some people commented later that they'd been surprised at how confident I was at that time. But my new-found confidence was short-lived. As Dr. Alex explains in his book, fears from my childhood emerged from my subconscious to pull me down again.

Several years later, as a married man with three very bright children, who were all to become incredibly talented adults, I decided to join Toastmasters to try to improve my confidence in public speaking. After working my way through several categories, I decided to prepare for the forthcoming heats of the Speech Contest. I visualized myself standing up and giving a well-prepared speech. Well, I won that particular heat with a speech that my main competitor–an older, much more experienced speaker–labelled "a bloody-good speech" to me! (That's a very Aussie expression.) But for the finals a short time later, I was back to delivering a very lack-lustre speech. Around that time, a very smart friend of mine was honest enough to comment one day, "Beneath that bright exterior there's a sad little boy!"

Emotional healings that last

As Dr. Alex explains in his book *Beyond Willpower*, if we visualize ourselves inviting God's Light and Love into that painful scene regularly, and often enough, its painful effects become gradually less and less, until it has little or no influence on our positive affirmations. BUT I've experienced *instant* healing with several of my visualizations! So have several of my friends. My favorite place for visualizing my negative memories is in a beautiful little Indigenous church, at a quiet time with few people around.

An early painful memory was of my first day of school in Kindergarten at age 5, my first day of 'untying Mum's apron-strings.' I have no memory of the classroom on that day, just of a boy named Peter. I was 'scared stiff', but was wanting to be friendly, so I walked over to him in the playground and said, "G'day!" "Shut ya gob!" was his crude reply ('gob' is an unacceptable word for 'mouth'). He was obviously feeling anxious, too, and later we actually became good friends.

Well, three weeks after that day I ended up in hospital with acute nephritis, 'a terminal kidney disease', and was recovering at home for the next twelve months! Some illnesses can be particularly 'psychosomatic' ('relating to the interaction of mind and body'), can't they? But since inviting God's Light and Love into that scene, I now feel relaxed when thinking about it. I see Jesus standing there beside us in the playground! And my kidneys are fine!

Another negative memory that I subjected to Dr. Alex's suggestion didn't actually happen in real life (!), but was a recurring nightmare. It occurred less often in later years, but still did so as recently as the week before I put his suggestion into practice! In my dream I was still a young French teacher in the late 1960s or early 70s. It was the first day of the new school year and classes were already under way, but I hadn't been given an initial timetable. So I was wandering around the school, not knowing where my French class was! And the school Principal wasn't far behind me. I was sure he would catch up with me and want to know why I wasn't already with my class. And that's when I would wake up, shuddering!

This fearful scene visualized on my Heart screen was immediately wiped away with a whiteboard eraser, up and down, then across and back, as if moved by an unseen hand, until the 'screen' I was visualizing with my eyes closed was completely white! ... No more teaching nightmares, even fifteen months later!!! And even when I think about it now, there's not the slightest discomfort!

The break-up of my twenty-year marriage many years ago is naturally another painful memory from my past. Because summer was not yet over, I used to drive out to the beach after work, lie on the sand and 'wallow in self-pity'! But when I visualized myself on my Heart screen recently, lying on the sand and feeling sorry for myself, the image that replaced it was Jesus and me walking hand-in-hand along the beach, with me feeling peaceful and contented. And that's how that image has remained ever since.

Even the knot in my chest, which I've experienced on and off until recently, has been healed! As I sat in that little Indigenous church, visualizing God's Light and Love coming into me, it felt like a laser beam was coming into the middle of my chest. That's where the knot had been whenever I was nervous. It felt as though the laser burnt out the flesh affected by the knot. It even felt as though a tiny puff of smoke was coming from my chest! Well, ever since then I've no longer felt that knot in my chest. Sounds crazy, but that's what I experienced!

But of all the healings that I wish to share, the one that I find the most interesting and powerful is the memory of an occasion that occurred in my first year of high school as a 12-year-old in 1955. Our high school used to hold our annual prize-giving in the architecturally grand Sydney Town Hall, with its balcony on three sides, and the stage in front of a magnificent huge pipe organ. Such is the grandeur of the place, and I was pressured into singing a solo accompanied by a grand piano on stage, on the night that it would be filled with students, teachers and parents! I've already mentioned that I was a happy-go-lucky child–until the focus of attention was on me!

Well, I did sing a solo there–apparently–but I had blocked out any visual memory of that traumatic event for sixty (60) years! That is, until I decided to apply Dr. Alex's suggestion to that scene. But because I couldn't actually visualize it taking place, I simply imagined that empty stage, which I had seen on so many other occasions.

When I invited God's Light and Love into that scene, I saw myself as a young boy–12-years-old–singing a song on that stage and holding Jesus' hand. That's when the feeling of dread left me! I knew that I had been healed of that painful memory. But I had no idea of the consequences of that healing.

A few weeks later, when I was doing some cooking and had nothing of any significance on my mind, what 'popped into my head' was the idea, "I think the first word of the song I sang in the Sydney Town Hall was 'Beautiful'!" Nothing more. But a week or so later, while I was driving close to home, and with nothing else on my mind but concentrating on my driving, I began singing, at the top of my voice, "Beautiful dreamer, wake unto me, Starlight and dewdrops are waiting for thee ... " And I proceeded to sing both verses of Stephen Foster's classic composition, word-perfect! After

60 years of no conscious memory of it!!! Now that's what I really call 'an emotional healing'!

Fantastic! Thank you, Dr. Alex, for bringing this message to us! And thank you, God, for revealing it to him!

As you have no doubt realized from my story, I now feel so much more peaceful and contented with my life! And it feels wonderful! Oh, I know what you're thinking! You're thinking, "Some of my memories are much more painful than yours!" But I can vouch for the fact that any agonizing memory from the distant, or even more recent, past can be healed, or at least minimized so that it is no longer strong enough to sabotage your positive goals. All you have to do is bring it regularly to your inner screen, with your eyes closed, and invite God's Light and Love into that painful scene, as Dr. Alex recommends. And after maybe a number of weeks, or even sooner, you'll find that it's hardly noticeable, or has even disappeared completely! And then you're free to visualize your positive goals successfully!

Go on! Give it a try! You'll be glad you did! You, too, can succeed, be happy and contented, and find peace and joy in *your* life!

About The Author

Denis Franklin is a qualified Christian counselor and a retired schoolteacher with extensive personal experience in goal-setting with God's help! He is Australian, enjoying life in the tropical city of Darwin, and he thanks God for his good health. He has five beautiful granddaughters.

He is the author of the motivational/spiritual book *Yes You Can–With God's Help!* Second Edition, the first edition having been published in 1991. The Second Edition includes a summary of the main message of Dr. Alex Loyd's *Beyond Willpower*, about the healing of painful memories from the past.

Denis has experienced first-hand the liberating effects of the healing of so many of the painful memories from his past. He encourages you to free yourself from your negative memories, with God's help, so that you can be free to visualize your positive goals successfully.

He can be contacted on: denis_franklin@bigpond.com.

CHAPTER 14

A PATH TO THE HEART: HOW I FOUND MY WAY BACK

Michele Whitteker

I never planned to be approaching middle-age, stripped of my worldly possession, and starting over. Yet here I was. I was returning to my birthplace, driving an old, beat up 1996 Subaru. I was feeling rather beat up myself. I began to seriously question who was I really? I was no longer the free-spirited Canadian living a charmed life in the wild beauty of New Mexico. Nor was I the successful Pilates instructor or entrepreneurial real estate owner. Who I thought I was had eroded.

On top of all this my mother was dying. A phone call confirmed that her bladder cancer had returned. Truthfully, my mom was full of cancer. Although I was her only daughter we were never really close. Time healed our differences so now we had a wonderful bond. I was seduced by New Mexico's beauty and laid back lifestyle for 13 years.

Due to certain ill-fated choices, sadly, the affair had to come to an end.

One such choice drained me on every level. I purchased a run-down house with a friend as an investment. We wrote up a contract based on a favorable and predictable market. Once the contract was signed I was filled with a sense of dread. Perhaps, you know what I mean by this gut feeling. The real estate lawyer confirmed what I knew intuitively. He said get out of this as soon as possible. My worst suspicions came to fruition. I walked away from the house with nothing.

Losing the house devastated me so even after a few more years I was still at a really low point emotionally. I couldn't forgive myself or my business partner. I felt ashamed and angry. My home-based Pilates studio was gone. I continued to teach but I felt like I was just going through the motions. Even when I thought things couldn't get any worse I made another bad decision.

Needing to move I rented a house with a man while ignoring flashing neon signs of his dysfunctional nature. In the haze of addiction, his stories didn't warrant my concerns even though he spoke of violence connected to organized crime and issues with authority. After our first argument, disturbing behaviors surfaced. He was verbally abusive then stopped speaking to me. When he told me I was extremely messed up, it was like a punch in the stomach. I believed him. Then rage surfaced which I expressed mainly by punching and screaming into pillows.

Eventually calming down, I knew I had to get out. While he was away on vacation, I went into high gear preparing my escape. Back in Canada it would take several more years before I could shift from being a victim to feeling empowered. These experiences of struggle I see differently now. They were necessary in my journey towards inner peace and self-acceptance.

Where it began

How does a librarian's assistant from Vancouver, British Columbia find herself living in Santa Fe, New Mexico? It all started with a phone call. I met a woman who had a friend in Santa Fe that did sessions and gave courses. I was looking for direction in my life. Could she help me with a career choice? Never once during the call did that come up. After the session I stood on my balcony breathing in the crisp, salty ocean air. The sun was setting in the hazy pink sky. I felt more alive than I had in a long time. I began travelling to Santa Fe regularly to take her courses.

These courses awakened in me a need to connect with others who were seekers. I was looking for people who wanted more meaning, clarity and healing in their lives. During her courses, small groups would sit together using an information tool called muscle testing. Muscles show signs of weakness or strength based on the truth of a statement. We used the testing to clear traumas from our DNA. These courses had a New Age feel yet would draw people from all walks of life. My new spiritual mentor would sit teaching for hours about spiritual principles. Eager students would take extensive notes as the wisdom flowed out of her like a cascading waterfall, relentless and intense. We would look to each other nodding our heads. I had finally found my tribe! When it came to making decisions, I often turned to her wisdom for answers. She asked me why not move to Santa Fe? In a flash, I had my answer. I was coming.

Ignoring my Intuition

During my time in Santa Fe, the real estate market was buzzing with excitement. I had an emotional impulse to buy myself. A house would fill a void in my life. It was a project I needed. I had recently split from my partner who offered me a lifestyle of financial ease which I had never experienced before. Now I was on my own. The house offered a new start. It was an anchor to my instability. It was the solution to my financial needs. The only technicality was I couldn't get a mortgage. I wasn't going to let that stop me so I had to find a business partner.

My emotional needs would override any sound business judgments and intuitive knowing. The result was a rather bizarre business partnership. The one person who might be interested was already buying and selling successfully. I knew her from my spiritual group. I remember walking away from her studio once vowing never to do business with this woman again. I ignored that valuable piece of information. I pushed forward trying to negotiate some kind of contract. When anxiety and uncertainty surfaced I rationalized. I was just being emotional.

In desperation I finally had a notarized contract which was fatally one-sided. She was willing to do one, and only one thing, get a mortgage in her name. I would be responsible for all the rest. I would live in the house paying all the expenses: the mortgage, renovations, landscaping and repairs. Eventually we would sell at a profit. I would recoup the down payment and my expenses. We would split the rest. At least, this was in theory. It seems that everyone but me saw that my partner had everything to gain but nothing to lose. By the time it sank in I had already signed the contract. It would appear I signed in blood as the house would leech the very life out of me.

Losing Perspective

Soon enough that anchor became an albatross. I worked tirelessly for over two years to try to make a wrong choice right. During this time I went down a dark tunnel of bitterness. You may have also made choices in your own life you later regretted. By taking responsibility we take the high road learning spiritual lessons from our decisions. I did the opposite. I took the low road complaining about how unfair it was. Something on an unconscious level was taking over. I felt out of control. I began to numb myself with alcohol and drugs. When the mortgage increased, because my debt load was so high, I could no longer afford to live there. The only thing now was to try to sell the house and end this torture.

It would not come to pass. The market had crashed. There was little interest in the house at the price I needed to sell it for. I felt so drained I couldn't problem solve. My business partner would have no part in my situation. She had no obligation to. My goal of creating money through real estate lay flat as a deflated balloon. I had to rebuild my life and my self-esteem. I felt defeated.

Clarity Amidst Chaos

Hiking connected me to the beauty of New Mexico that drew me here originally. Naturally, I would be interested in finding a hiking partner, enter Mike. We met at a trailhead.

Feeling euphoric from the fresh mountain air and the smell of sage brush I immediately warmed up to him. He made me laugh. He taught his little dog a funny trick. She would jump up to his thighs and into his arms. After he left to start his hike, I took a moment. Should I leave him my number? I left it under his windshield wiper. He wanted to get together that same evening. I declined but we made a plan to go on a hike. Hiking was a beautiful start to a relationship that would eventually lead to more chaos in my life.

Aside from hiking, Mike and I shared a common habit of escaping our pain by using recreational drugs. Long into the night Mike would talk incessantly about his interests and his past. He was captivating, so funny and intelligent! I would learn that in California, where the real estate market hit home owners hard, Mike had once owned a house. Tearfully he shared how much he loved his house. Eventually he would have to walk away from it. It was a tale I could relate to.

He seemed to have confidence I didn't possess. He offered a sense of safety when I felt vulnerable. He said he was a lost breed of men. These men open doors for women and protect them. I must have been projecting this need to be protected. He saw me as a "perfect" match. There was also the fact that I cooked and cleaned. It would be convenient for us to find a place together. After a few months I started to wake up to the situation I put myself in.

I finally started to see the role I was playing and rebelled. I stopped having dinner with him on his work schedule. Instead I ate alone at my dinner hour. He'd eat junk food in front of the television. He'd leave his late night mess for me to clean up in the morning. A rather insignificant argument escalated into an emotional volcanic eruption. I criticized Mike for not helping out before a guest arrived. It became clear neither of us could communicate on a mature adult level. While he shut-down completely, I gained perspective on the situation. There were things I did that were messed up. This didn't mean I was messed up. I tried to apologize for my part. He said nothing. The situation was now feeling crazy and unsafe. I had to make a decision. What was I going to do now?

Just as things were falling apart with Mike, my mom's illness had taken a turn for the worse. She started reaching out. That was not my mom's way so she clearly needed me. I knew her hour glass was running low yet how low I wasn't quite sure. What I did know was I wanted to spend as much time with her as possible. I called my spiritual teacher. I said, my heart is telling me it is time to go. She said, then that's what you need to do. Despite all the chaos around me that decision filled my heart with a sense of peace.

The Winds of Change

Knowing I had made my choice from love got me through the weeks ahead. I worked fervently to weed through 13 years of my life. I remember the piles. Everything from office supplies and business material to kitchen supplies and Pilates equipment filled the living room. I got it down to a few shipping boxes and a car load. In a few days' time I would cross the US border into Canada and connect with my family again. I was showing up for my mom.

Like many of us who care for our elderly parents, we find ourselves in a role reversal. I became the caregiver instead of the other way around. Patiently I helped her transition from her own room in a small house with minimal care to a nursing home. Suddenly, every little thing she owned became so important to her. This was her way of staying in control. To her, going into a nursing home was the beginning of the end.

Just as she predicted, she slowly began to slip away. I would kiss her lips lightly when I left but soon there was no life left in them. She held on miraculously night after night as my family sat in turn to be by her side. She went in a moment when only the staff were present. Her skin was like tissue when her heart finally stopped beating. She was out of pain and free. In that way it was a beautiful thing. Being with her as she was dying erased all our differences. All that was left was the love. I would miss her friendship so much. She had such an incredible way of listening. Whatever mistakes I made seemed to be washed clean with her unconditional love. Now, I would have to find that same love in myself.

Deeper Healing

Loving myself was truly the heart of the matter. My self-worth was so low I was constantly giving away my power. In the case of the house I gave my power away to my partner. I ignored my intuition and all the signs that were telling me something doesn't feel right. Lacking confidence in my ability to make decisions, I let others make them for me. It was Mike who wanted to move in together. I looked to him to take care of me. He was my "knight in shining armor." Since these decisions were made from a disempowered place, I was constantly feeling like a victim.

Playing the victim fed the angry, victimized child in me which was the root of my self-sabotaging choices. I was never able to articulate the betrayal of childhood sexual abuse. I couldn't express my deep sense of loss when my dad retreated into depression. So I stored them. When these memories triggered, anger and rage surfaced clouding my ability to see the situation clearly. My emotions were of a betrayed child. My reactions came from her. To change my patterns of self-sabotage I needed to bypass my brain. I needed to go straight to the heart of this wounded child.

I couldn't deny the pain I was in any more. So I found ways to let it surface so I could start to heal myself. I began an in-depth women's empowerment coaching program that was a safe place to go deeper into childhood trauma. I didn't want to numb out anymore. I let this wounded self–express herself through letters. Through writing, the emotions began to be revealed. Then another healing gift emerged from an unlikely place.

Finding Answers

My spiritual mentor was given some books from a mutual friend who was dying from cancer. On the top of the pile was *The Healing Code*. Our dear friend was unable to heal his own wounded self. He left this world full of anger. Yet, he left us with a chance to heal ours. While addressing low self-worth I knew I had found something with tremendous power. My body was shaking and I began to sob from such a deep place. I was touching on deep cellular memories. So began a journey towards loving myself unconditionally. I was able to love even the wounded, scared, immature and angry parts I previously denied. No doubt you have experienced the healing power of love. Through love we can find it in our hearts to forgive. Through forgiveness we can heal ourselves.

Lightening the Load

I had to forgive myself for all the mistakes I made so I could finally embrace where I was in my life. I had to forgive all the parties involved in my victim story. I didn't want to be that victim anymore. I wanted to be free of those emotions which were weighing me down. I wanted to tell a new story. I wanted this story to be uplifting and positive. I want it to help others to accept and love themselves more deeply. If your story is no longer serving you then it might be time to write a new story too.

Towards the light

Perhaps like me you have struggled in your life. Things didn't turn out as planned. The butterfly, in its struggle to push itself out of the cocoon, pumps a fluid into its wings enabling it to fly. If we change our perspective, we can see our struggles as a cocoon phase in our lives. I always said I was on a spiritual path. What I learned is divine intervention ensures we stay on it. The hard times I went through helped me to witness patterns of self-sabotage and self-hatred. Those experiences were full of lessons that would help me change. I couldn't deny I had problems. I couldn't continue to blame others and play the victim. Our mistakes can serve in our transformation. They allow us to expand who we think we are. So perhaps one day we can step into a better version of ourselves, truer to our heart. The darkest of times can serve to open us up to greater freedom. We emerge changed just like the butterfly.

About The Author

Michele has been sharing the power and benefits of Pilates for years.

Now she is combining her passion for health and healing with empowerment coaching for women. She lives in Guelph, Ontario.

michelewhitteker@live.com

www.michelewhitteker.com

CHAPTER 15

RELEASE THE CHAINS THAT BIND YOU
Tracy Abbott

Sitting on the plane, I was exhausted. I felt like I hadn't slept in days. My mind was racing with thoughts. I am such a bad mom! I hate leaving my children. I should be grateful to have this job and make the money that I do. My chest pounded as I struggled to catch my breath. What was happening to me? Maybe it was the car ride to the airport that did me in.

It must have been the song on the car radio. *I know I am not strong enough to be everything I am supposed to be.* I always thought I had to be strong enough, that I had no choice. Instead I felt shattered. I found myself sobbing with no ability to stop. "I have to snap out of this. I have customer meetings in three different cities this week and I can't miss my flight. Come on Trace, get your game face back on." The next thing I knew I was 10 exits past the airport with no idea where I was. I was really scared as I realized I had blacked out with no recollection of driving on the freeway. I looked for some familiar landmark, but there was none. I pulled off to the side of the road and struggled to catch my breath. I shook my head, rubbed my eyes and rolled down all the windows. I felt like a lost little girl, and I prayed to God to help me. Eyes puffy and make up smeared, I somehow found my way back to the airport and my flight.

I replayed the event over and over in my head. Traveling away from my family for work was nothing new. I was always struggling to manage my faith, my 20-year marriage, parenting and on top of that one of the most stressful careers in a male dominated industry in corporate America. I was always doubting, second guessing and trying to find that "perfect" balance. Nothing was making sense. Was I finally losing control? Did I ever even have control? Why did I black out? My fear was escalating. Something deep inside was telling me this wasn't just about leaving for another business trip. I felt like I was exploding into a million pieces inside. I told myself, "If I let myself cry I don't think I will be able to stop. How will I be able to function, let alone work?" Crying was a sign of weakness, a sign of being emotional and that simply wasn't allowed in the business world.

What I could not know at that moment was that giving up control wouldn't ruin me. It would allow real truths about my past to surface. I would be able to see how I was using the same survival skills I learned as a child to survive in my career.

That early morning car ride was the beginning of a new journey for me, a journey that involved seeking the truth in my life which in turn would lead to new found freedoms. I had spent years "doing" what I believed I had to do for the good of my family, but in the end, it was at the expense of my family and my health. I hope that sharing my story will encourage you to be courageous and open to the truth and healing that can be present in your life so you and your loved ones might find health and happiness early in life.

The Crash

I was aggressive. I was tough. I had relationships. I would only do it for a year. That is why I took the job 16 years ago. The company I chose was known for its brutal sales tactics, its unethical behavior and its lack of women employees. I looked at it as a challenge and a means to an end. The earning potential would shorten the time I would have to work and being a new mom of a 12-month old, it seemed like the right thing to do. Once on board, I was coached, "Don't make a mistake or show weakness, one mistake is all they need." It became clear very quickly there was not a lot of support for women managers, and I realized I was on my own. This was the motivation I needed to prove my worth. Being in sales was about driving revenue, something I knew how to do. My career success took off but so did the rumors. "She gets the business because she sleeps with the customer." In a male-dominated environment, it was quite commonplace that successful women got accused of sleeping their way to the top. Are you someone who has had to experience this? Did it make your blood boil like it did mine? I used my anger as more motivation to prove them all wrong.

My one year turned into many. I am sure you are wondering why on earth I stuck it out. Well, I had built a great team and I was loyal to them. We had a lot of fun and were good at what we did. I just chose to ignore the adversity, jealousy and aggressive attacks against me. I turned a blind eye to what I witnessed in front of me: blatant disrespect and the degradation of women.

As crazy as it may sound, I believed I was lucky. Yep, you heard me correctly. With my tenure growing, I figured I must be doing something right as women didn't survive in this company. I was making a lot of money, had great insurance, loved working with my clients and my team and I had survived so many ugly organizational changes and layoffs. While my close friends and family members were losing jobs, why wouldn't I consider myself fortunate? While it was probably not a healthy choice, once again I was justifying why I needed to stay in my negative work environment. Have you ever chosen to stay in negativity instead of looking for another alternative?

As the toxicity in my workplace grew, so did my determination to continue to survive. One thing our team knew how to do was laugh our way through challenges and this helped tremendously. I also knew I had to be smarter than my peers and act like a man. I even read a book called *Self-Made Man* about a woman who disguised herself and spent time in different environments to understand men better. I learned so much and used it to my advantage at work. I saw that I was capable and that being "on" at all times was working. I had developed several career mentors that taught me valuable survival techniques and strategies for winning the battles. The downside was it was exhausting. It was taking its toll. I had nothing left for my husband and children when I got home from work. If you are a mom, I am sure you can relate to the tank being empty at the end of the day. The anxiety in the house grew. I attempted to control everything at home to offset the chaos and toxicity at work. Adding fuel to the fire my 12-year-old daughter said to me "Mom, I don't ever want to have a job like yours. You are miserable." I felt like someone had punched me in the stomach. So much for trying to keep things under control. I was creating chaos at home not managing it.

Nothing seemed to make me feel better. I was convinced that if I just prayed harder, did more yoga and worked out more, things would certainly improve. That couldn't have been further from the truth. I had so much stress in my body that the workouts I did started having an adverse effect. I couldn't get through a run without my muscles tightening, and I would have to stop. I became riddled with illness and recovering was getting harder each time. I approached being sick like I did everything else. I believed I just needed to get through it. I constantly wondered what was wrong with me. Why was I getting so sick all of the time? Friends, family and doctors all told me "You need to slow down, and you need to change your environment." I reacted the same way every time "I can't! I don't have any other options!" The truth was I was frozen with fear. I had never proactively made a change in my life. I let circumstances dictate change. That way if things went wrong, I didn't have to take ownership.

Many, if not most people, would have given up long before I did. Because I felt fortunate to have a job, I didn't think I had a choice but to stay. It never occurred to me there was a different path. It wasn't until that car ride to the airport that I started to realize I was coming apart at the seams and that I wasn't going to be able to keep up the pace any longer.

Truth Unveiled

"You need to read the book *The Healing Code*." This was the directive from my doctor. He said it might help me in getting to the root of my stress and resulting illnesses. He knew my job was unhealthy for me. He had been telling me this for several years. There was the constant traveling, sometimes at a moment's notice and many times across the globe. I was so committed to building client loyalty I would extend my trips to close a deal or solve a significant client issue. I got so used to doing this I was unaware of the significant drain it was on me and my family. My doctor never had a good answer when I asked "How am I supposed to find a healthy alternative that provides the level of financial security we need?" It never occurred to me that my view of financial security could be skewed. As a result, I wasn't chomping at the bit to take the suggestion seriously. However, I was so desperate to understand what was happening to me that I put my pride aside and bought the book. I was surprised to find that I couldn't put the book down. It all made so much sense. Root causes for emotional and physical pain could be found by releasing the stress the body was carrying. It could be a past hurt or a memory, one that I was aware of or even those I didn't remember. The chronic neck and back pain, the weak immune system, the headaches, anxiety–something was triggering these symptoms, and this book said it had the answers. "Wow, if I just did what the book said, I could transform my thoughts. I could be free from this pain that had no identity and maybe even identify the source."

I was motivated to make this work. The deeper I went, the more unsettled I got. I was frustrated. I wanted to get better and was willing to put the time in. Yet, the work stress continued to increase and the anxiety at home continued to take over. While the book gave me a greater understanding of what was happening to me and what my triggers were, I still felt out of control. I was managing this new healing protocol like I managed everything else in my life. It was a task with an end goal. This end goal was removing all of this pain. I didn't know what that felt like, but I knew that nothing around me was changing so I figured I must be doing something wrong. Little did I know that I was trying to address healing my issues with my mind and my own understanding. I was not letting God take the lead. How often do you attempt to control things before you even have a chance to think? It was my modus operandi.

One night one of the topics in the monthly healing session (given by the author of *The Healing Code*) was dealing with unhealthy memories, conscious or not. All of a sudden, I found myself sobbing like a five-year-old little girl. And this little girl was me. Her chest was pounding and she was overwhelmed with fear. I had no idea what was happening. I felt vulnerable and exposed. I had a feeling something big was occurring and I wanted to run and hide. Instead, I saw Jesus in front of me holding a curly blond haired, blue eyed little girl in his arms. She was sobbing into His chest and He was telling her she was safe and her Daddy couldn't hurt her anymore. I, as the adult, stood there witnessing this and the truth roared in like a tidal wave sweeping over me. I fell to the ground covering my mouth with my hands to muffle the screams. The truth was revealed. I had been sexually abused at the hands of my father.

I felt my throat closing in. How can this be? This makes no sense. I loved my Daddy, he loved me. We had been so close my whole life. Events of my past flashed before me. His attempt to kiss me when I was 23. It was disgusting, yet I dismissed it as one of his drunken episodes. The shower in Palm Springs. I had replayed that in my head over the years, but since I didn't remember anything that happened in the shower, I believed nothing happened. Why is this memory all of a sudden burning a hole inside of me? I felt like throwing up. Sweat was forming on my forehead. I knew then there was no turning back. The ugly truth of my abuse was here to stay.

Desperation

I was alone in my grief, unable to speak the words out loud. Hearing them would make this all real. I had a secret inside of me that I had kept even from myself. Now what do I do? All those years I had asked God what my cross to bear would be? Would he take one of my children? Would I end up with a terminal illness? Here it was right in front of me. I had been sexually abused by the one I trusted the most and never knew it. Why did this just come out now? I was 47 years old!! Anger seethed through my veins thinking about the life I could have had, the life he took from me. The loneliness, the illnesses and the inability to have a normal relationship with anyone–and now I knew why! I felt like someone hit the scramble button on my life and all of my memories of events and people were in a big pile in front of me surrounded by chaos. Nothing was what it appeared to be. My mind wouldn't stop reeling. How am I going to function, keeping this secret with me, while I try to figure out what to do? I had spent years hiding my pain from everyone, and now that I knew the source, I didn't know if I could continue the facade. I had been a master at recreating myself on a daily if not hourly basis, but now it seemed impossible. I needed time, but there wasn't any. Things at work had taken a turn for the worse, and my husband was growing impatient with the outbursts that occurred daily. I knew I had to tell him, but the thought of it made me feel sick inside. So, I avoided it. I prayed hard every day for help, yet I knew it was my definition of help. I wanted all the pain to go away and didn't want to do the work needed. I was still trying to control the circumstances.

I started to look into counselors who specialized in sexual abuse. "Did I really have to do a google search?" I certainly couldn't ask my friends or family about it. I found a place that did extensive psychological testing. I thought to myself, "Perfect. They are going to find that all of this isn't true and that my mind is playing tricks on me." Unfortunately that wasn't the case. I was diagnosed with Post Traumatic Stress Disorder (PTSD). What? This was something that war veterans experience, not wives and mothers. My ratings on anxiety and depression came back so high they were shocked. "These numbers indicate severe issues and yet you are high functioning. We normally suggest an in-patient approach with these results but believe we can start with the outpatient program." I found myself floating above everything in the room. I was disengaging at a rapid rate. I remember leaving there in a daze and don't remember driving home. High functioning? Did he really say that? I didn't even see myself able to do the simplest of tasks because the person I had been seemed to have vanished.

I was all alone in this and knew I needed to finally tell my husband. In my heart I knew he would support me. What was I afraid of? Was it voicing this horrible truth out loud to someone I love and fearing disbelief? Was it that he would see me as the broken helpless little girl that I was and leave me? This was the man I had been married to for 20 years– and I was afraid to speak? Have you ever been afraid to talk to someone near and dear to you? It shocked me how afraid I was. I prayed for the courage to take the first step in speaking the truth out loud, and God prevailed. I sobbed so hard I couldn't even get the words out. I could see the fear in his eyes as he waited to hear what I had to say. As the words came out, I saw his pain. He held me for a long time and reassured me everything would be okay. My body finally stopped shaking, and I felt safe for the first time. At that moment, I felt a glimmer of hope that we would survive this together.

Fortunately or unfortunately, things were escalating at work, so what better time to distract me from this awful pain. It seemed better than digging into the ugliness of the abuse. I was being pressured to do unethical things, but my usual tactic of waiting things out and hoping for the best wasn't working. I had run out of time. I was going to be pushed out the door for not participating in unethical behavior. I leveraged my internal relationships, and they confirmed these realities. I was furious! This was so wrong! How could they get away with this?

I talked the situation over with my mentors, my career coach, my husband and our lawyer. I decided to fight for what was right and deal with the consequences, whatever they ended up being. But in order to minimize the impact on me and my family, I needed a plan, one that ideally included another job and protection within my existing environment. I was petrified as this meant reaching out and asking for help. I was not one to ever ask for help. I didn't want to appear weak. But on the other hand I was always willing to help anyone at any time, never for one minute seeing them as weak. Do you perceive someone who asks for help as weak? Most likely not. Once again, I had a distorted perception of what a basic human need looked like.

I asked someone internally for a job so I knew I had a place to land. He was so supportive and offered to do whatever was needed to help. I then called a top executive and asked for his support with my situation. He was amazing and talked me through how he planned to protect me. It required keeping things under wraps and operating business as usual. I thought, "How convenient. I happen to be very good at that." I couldn't believe these guys really wanted to help me. My distorted view of relationships and my mistrust of everyone blocked my ability to see the support that was right in front of me. Maybe you can apply my new revelation to a situation in your own life.

I thought I could manage this work situation now that I had air cover. I forgot to take into consideration the emotional hurricane that was going on in my personal life with the abuse and trying to manage my family. This was typical in my world. I always underestimated situations and then wasted so much energy being angry and frustrated that things weren't different.

Acceptance

I couldn't control the flashbacks. The harder I tried to control them the fiercer my subconscious worked at getting the memories to the surface. In the beginning I had wanted to know everything so I could prove to myself I wasn't crazy. After the first flashback, I didn't want to know anything more ever again! It wreaked havoc on my mind and body. I sat in a hotel room begging God to take the pain away. I sat at my kitchen table screaming "No more! I can't take it."

One day I was taking my kids home from school, and I realized when I reached the house that I had no recollection of driving them home. My heart started racing, and I was paralyzed with fear. I had read about these blackouts in the material I had received about PTSD. I was putting my children in danger. I sobbed for hours and finally pulled out the Rosary and prayed to our Blessed Mother Mary for her intercession. I needed to surrender my will to the Lord and allow him to help me. It had taken hours for me to start praying for help. If only I had thought of doing that earlier! Have you done something similar and then found yourself asking the question "Man, why didn't I think of doing that sooner? I could have saved anguish and time!" Ahhh we are so human!

I met with my doctor and he became very serious. "Tracy, it is time to take a leave of absence from your work and take this PTSD stuff seriously." I left his office shaking. I realized I had not been focused on getting better. I had been focused on shuffling the chaos that was happening all around me in hopes it would all go away. I knew this was the right decision but what would I tell everyone? Inside, my anxiety soared. I had to come up with a story, a believable story. I had to hide the truth from everyone. It was bad enough that I had to take a leave of absence - but because of my past? For the first time I was able to give my anxiety to God. I realized I didn't have to come up with a story. I could choose what I communicated and to whom. It was my decision and what a freeing experience it was.

It was done. I was officially on leave, and I was in a position I had never been before–vulnerable by choice. I had to trust the process and those around me to help me. Could I do it? I had it in my mind that I had 90 days to get completely better. When my counselor informed me that the time would be spent dealing with symptoms versus getting into the abuse work, I was not happy. As she educated me on the severity of the symptoms, it became clear. I needed to focus on being able to function on a day to day basis before I took on addressing the pain of the abuse. I realized this whole healing thing was going to take a whole lot more than 90 days.

God's Turn

During my leave of absence, I realized I needed to restart my relationship with God. I had always thought I had a strong faith but, as with everything else, I realized it was a relationship that I controlled. It was on my terms. I signed up for a five day silent retreat. It was the best thing I could have ever done. It provided the time necessary to remove all of the clutter and noise from my brain. I had nowhere to run but to the Lord.

He was there as he had always been with his arms outreached. I cried with no shame and surrendered to his plan. His path was so clear. He wanted me to be free from the pain of the abuse and finally become the child He created me to be. For the first time in my life, I truly felt His presence and protection. The vision of Jesus holding me in his arms returned, but this time instead of fear, I felt peace. I realized I had the courage to face these new realities as long as I had Him. I felt hope.

Revelations

As my healing began, awareness grew all around me. All of the skills I had learned as an abuse survivor were how I managed every aspect of my life. I used disassociation as a means of survival. I existed on the outside of situations observing the events in my life as if they were not my own. I learned this is a very common survival technique used by abuse victims as the pain is too much for a child to handle and separating from the actual event was the only way to survive. My career fueled my need to be someone else and operate with no emotion, rule by facts and stay focused on an end goal all of which I learned as a child. I succeeded because I became someone else–a confident, attractive, motivated woman. I chose to ignore the relentless degrading and disrespecting of women. After all, it was what I was used to. My job was to build successful teams and long term customer relationships. I was able to master this while living in isolation on the inside. I look back now and think, "How was this even possible?"

I also realized I carried a huge disdain for injustice. I tried to change my work environment by taking on being in charge of a committee that was focused on retaining women. I saw this as a way to drive change, a change that was so desperately needed. I didn't realize until later that I was looking for the justice that never came my way as a child.

The awareness of the impact my abuse has had on my family has been the most painful to face. They suffered the most from my isolation, especially my husband. I had been in my own little boat for so long and so desperately wanted my husband in it with me. Yet I was the one who kept him at a safe distance from me leaving him treading water next to the boat. Imagine how tired he was. I always thought it was he that didn't want to be with me when in fact it was my inability to trust that kept him out. Consequently, I understood that rowing on my own left me going in circles, heading nowhere and totally exhausted. We were quite a pair.

Hope

As I faced the pain and turned it over to God, my emotional pain became lighter. The art therapy I did opened my eyes to my subconscious and I began to get to know the real me. I was a broken, angry, devastated little girl who needed to heal. Over time, I began to shed the anchors and bricks that were filled with fear, hatred and silence. I gave them up to Jesus and his Mother Mary. As a result I experienced freedom from within me for the first time and hope became a reality. With Jesus by my side, I was finally able to make decisions and choices regarding my career that were good for the whole family. My personal life with my husband and children calmed down considerably as I learned to simplify my life and rely on the Holy Spirit to guide me on a daily basis. The word "simplify" has become my new go to word. We have all heard that less is more! I now try daily to implement this in my life.

Experiences are a mix of suffering and joy. Mine have been no different. Truths of many kinds were unveiled: awful truths, beautiful truths, awesome truths: "My Daddy hurt me." "My mom didn't protect me." "I am a good mom." "My husband loves me just the way I am." "My colleagues care about me and want to see me succeed." The freedom that came from facing these truths enabled me to make healthier decisions across all areas of my life.

I learned to surround myself with those who were also seeking the truth in their lives. I allowed (without consciously realizing it) a support group to develop around me. I began to speak the truth no matter how hard it was. While the healing is far from over, there are days I have the confidence necessary to face my trauma head on. This in and of itself gives me peace, something I never thought would be possible.

My counselor tells me on an ongoing basis, "This is a life-long process."

My consistent response is, "But I don't want it to be!!" I still get angry about what happened to me, and I still want it to go away. However, as the pain lessens and I experience more peace, I accept this truth more willingly.

Free at Last

We have all heard that out of something bad comes something good. Have you seen this ring true in your life? Have you seen joy come out of pain? I never really understood this until I experienced it first-hand. My speaking openly about my sexual abuse has encouraged a few people in my life to take that first step in speaking the truth in their own lives. My pain and my trauma gave hope to someone else and it brought me so much joy. It is my hope that through sharing this story with you that you too will have the courage to take your first step, a step to whatever truth you may need to face. When we are wounded by abuse or any significant trauma it can seem virtually impossible to recover. Abuse is capable not only of destroying the human body but also the mind and spirit. But we don't have to let it destroy us. I am living proof. At this time I am both emotionally and physically healthier than I was, but by no means am I completely healed. That will just take time. I experience more real joy than I have in the past, and I am more confident in my abilities to make better decisions. I finally quit my job, and instead of letting financial worry drive my decision, I am listening to my heart. The more I listen the more I am willing to wait for the job that is right for the emotional and physical well-being for me and my family. Yes, my husband and I have to make changes in our lives to accommodate our new choices, but I see now why it is worth it.

There have and will continue to be many a day that my anxiety skyrockets, and I get angry about the cards I was dealt. I also continue to question why it took so long for the abuse to be revealed. Oh how my life would have been so much easier had I dealt with this 30 years earlier (or so I think). I may never get the answer I am looking for, but my faith tells me to trust in God's plan, not in my own understanding.

I hope you find the courage to act and give yourself the gift of freedom sooner rather than later. Do your best not to wait until you are 47 or older. Your rewards will be enjoyed so much longer. If you are open to healing, it will come. I promise. The truth really does set you free!

I can do all things through Christ who gives me strength.

About The Author

Tracy Abbott resides in Dallas, Texas with her husband and 3 children. She has spent the last 25 years in the IT industry in sales and business development.

Tracy enjoys traveling with her family and spending time on the beach. She is high spirited, passionate about her Catholic faith and believes laughter can get you through anything.

ptabbott@sbcglobal.net

CHAPTER 16

THE GEMS OF THE FORGOTTEN
Vivienne Spanopoulos

Burning Alive

For someone who loved life, I struggled to comprehend how I had come to dread every day. I was living with the reality of a debilitating skin disease that was so horrific I resembled a leper, diseased and disfigured. My stamina had steadily been worn down as I battled this worsening condition for the past seven years. At 27, the normally smooth, protective barrier of my skin had turned into a flaming, irritated and infected shell, burning away any hope I had of ever having a normal life again. Even sleep was no escape. Raw, oozing and painful wounds would stick to the sheets and every turn of my body and face would tear my flesh away. Imprisoned in my own skin it now felt like a torture chamber. As the experts one by one threw their hands up in despair, I knew two things: I'm alone; and I'm determined to overcome this illness.

Who would've thought that the answer would come in the form of an ordinary man and that after four 90-minute sessions I would be cured? Chris was a practitioner of Neuro Linguistic Programming (NLP) which is a talking therapy and a very effective tool for reprogramming subconscious memories. He explained that "conflict at the level of identity will often create illness" and my two identities, Australian and Greek, were found to be at odds with each other. While others wrestled with the miraculous nature of this healing, I was absorbing one thing: I could *change my past...*

The Early Years

Torrents of abuse regularly spewed from my father's mouth. The hairs on my arms would stand up, my stomach would clench and I'd try to look away as his tall solid form moved toward me, yelling abuse mixed with obscenities over and over. I would often seek refuge with my mother, an extremely kind and wise woman or my older sister with whom I found comfort, laughter and a sense of safety. But my father's moods dominated. Growing up in our house was like walking through a minefield. I never knew how to please him, and I was desperate to because he terrified me.

But what made our relationship complex was that I could see he loved me. He was a devout man, Greek Orthodox, and always striving to provide the best for his family. And later I came to know that he'd suffered tremendously himself in his early years. His love got twisted amongst the demons that he wrestled with. Instead of praise, he criticized. Instead of support, he undermined. Instead of care, he neglected me. And instead of love, he filled me with fear.

"I have prayed for your recovery," he told me, at the height of my illness. "I have asked God to strike me down if he must, but to make you well." A month after my recovery, my father had a debilitating stroke that left him paralysed down his right side and fighting for his life.

Fragments of Memory

"Bubby come here and sit on my lap," my father said. He called me bubby as an affectionate way of saying I was the baby of the family, the youngest. I never liked that name...

"Nobody loves you like your father and mother, remember that" he continued.

"You can't trust anybody. There are no friends you understand? You and your sister have each other. Never fight with your sister. Promise me ok?"

"Yes Dad. Of course," I answered.

My father had a constant stream of advice, rambling lectures, monologues and abuse. He was a man who liked to dominate every situation and where he couldn't, he left.

"I have never made a mistake in my life!" He always said. His stories were full of his heroics and the blatant stupidity of whoever else figured. "No one knows what I know," he would say. "I'm an Achilles!" His image of himself was so inflated and unreal, that I could never depend on anything he said. Yet his will seemed limitless and his perception periodically razor-sharp. In those instances, he appeared to know what could not be known by normal means. His instability and sharp mind were impossible to keep up with. But all that was nothing compared to his moods.

His erratic outbursts meant that so many relationships were severed. This fractured our extended family–a huge part of Greek family life. And put in jeopardy every connection we had.

If Music be the Food of Love...

The only leeway my father gave us was in our pursuit of music. Mum had received a small inheritance and she funded our learning of the piano and violin. Having learnt the piano herself at her boarding school in Tamworth in Australia, I remember my mother made every effort to support us learning music. I believe she saw it as a gift she'd lost when her family all moved back to Greece, though I'm not sure she realized how crucial it was for keeping us sane!

So Anthea and I played both the violin and the piano. Music was my refuge and my passion. Many times I would sit at the piano, my mind and heart a jumble of pain and suffering. I'd sit and simply play and play. Afterwards, I'd leave the piano changed, a little healed, somehow helped. Music was also an escape ticket for me. More than once I'd say I had a rehearsal and go somewhere else just to be out of the house.

Family Life Shattered

That was not the excuse however, when one night I returned home late. This night was not unlike many evenings before so I was totally unprepared for what followed. I walked in via the side entrance to the kitchen and there he was. Disheveled, toothless and raging, he approached me. He yelled abuse at me and started to kick me and hit me. "You whore! Where have you been? You have been out with a man haven't you? You are a disgrace! You bloody, fucking whore!" I froze. For all the times I'd stood strong and argued with him, I was suddenly disarmed. He'd never hit me before. His rage escalated and while the abuse poured out, he grabbed my hair with both fists and banged my head against the wall behind me repeatedly. I don't remember whether I turned to protect myself or whether he spun me around, but then I was being kicked violently in the back of my thighs. As my internal world was collapsing, I stared at the cold, white wall, immobilized at every level. Surprisingly I stood, rather than falling to the floor. It seemed I had no choice but to stay there and tolerate his rage. When it was spent, I retreated to my room, my body bruised, my spirit rocked and my heart shattered.

Some decisions are formed from your gut, from necessity, and have a steely, unequivocal, unshakeable form to them. At 18 I did the unthinkable in a Greek family and moved out of home. I was immature, had no idea how to look after myself and had no job. Without concern for practical matters like money or the future, I moved in with three guys who were university friends and started a new life. My father said, "You'll be back. You can't survive without us!" But as was often the case, my father was wrong.

Survive I did, but I also struggled, a lot. Lost and wounded I became rebellious about most things for the next few years. I started to have disdain and disrespect for people and things. I was hugely resentful of how I'd been treated but it came out in random and mostly self-destructive ways. My smoking habit escalated to 35 a day. At university I became a student representative and fought for causes I believed in. I do remember one day sitting in a room full of women at a feminist meeting. Out of 30 of us, they had all been sexually abused ... I was shocked!

In the midst of my deepest confusion and feelings of being lost, I wandered into a Spiritualist Church and there I began meditation classes. I was to spend nine years attending classes there and also giving much of my free time to their fund raising. The teachers and friends there became a new family for me, largely because opening myself to a spiritual way of life was like coming home for me. Meditation resonated so deeply in me that it was to steer my course to the present day.

Behind the Scenes

Growing up, I watched my father drink every few hours and for such a disciplined man, it seemed incongruous to have this flaw in his character. The extent of his dependence was masked for many years, since in Greek culture it's typical to drink wine with your meals, but especially because I never once saw him drunk.

He explained to me that once when he was 15, he got extremely drunk and nearly drowned in the river in his village in Greece. Someone rescued him, and he vowed to himself to never get drunk again. He fulfilled that vow. Yet alcohol dependent he was, though he would never ever admit that.

Late in his life when he was hospitalized, he pleaded with me to bring him a bottle of pills. I had only known he took sleeping pills, nothing else. "Please Bubby, can you bring me a bottle of Clonazepam?" His invincible façade was crumbling.

So I went home, and there in the kitchen cupboard were four *opened* bottles of Clonazepam, an anti-anxiety pill, plus four types of sleeping pills, three or four opened bottles of anti-depressants and Prozac. Achilles was being brought to his knees.

"Vivienne, it would be perfectly reasonable to cut ties with your father. You understand he has not treated you properly don't you?"

"I'm Greek," I replied. "That would be like cutting my own arm off." My gut told me that no matter how my parents behaved my family was a part of me. Years later I would see a spiritual link: that resolving these relationships would heal me. At the time, I only knew what I felt, that I cannot just run away from my family and my history, as much as I wanted to.

The Yoga Connection

Once I'd recovered from my severe skin disease, I found I had a new lease on life. I re-entered the workforce and started back at the gym. There I discovered yoga. I gradually fell in love with it, completed a teacher training program, and started to teach part-time.

Where meditation brought me home, yoga brought me to life! I loved working with my body. That part of me, that had fallen apart not long ago, was now rebuilding and feeling stronger and freer by the day. I now had two solid practices that would accompany me wherever I went and would become my guides through any difficulties ahead.

I have to confess that I wasn't a 'model yogi.' You'll have an easier time if you're thin (read "skinny"), long-limbed and flexible. Here I was short, strong but kind of stiff, a little overweight, with slightly crooked legs that never quite appeared straight. This was not an auspicious beginning, but I had no idea I was genetically unsuitable! So I pursued yoga with great enthusiasm, joy and commitment. And I was rewarded with a renewed sense of health, vitality and youthfulness. Yoga delivers to every participant the one thing I needed to begin to truly heal–*awareness!* I didn't know it then, but the goal of yoga is self-realisation.

I already had intuition. I think living in constant fear hones your senses. I already sensed many things before they happened. I already had advice and strategies for problem-solving. My mother had filled me with tons of everyday wisdom that worked. I was a very practical, organized person. I was responsible, committed and hard-working. What I seriously lacked was insight into myself. That was about to change.

Asia Beckons, Mother Falters

"Well why do you want to go to this Hong Kong anyway?" Shouted Dad.

"Papou" My 10-year old niece addressed her Grandfather using the Greek word. "Sizzy' (the name my sister's children coined for me) is talking about going to Singapore, not Hong Kong. She has got a good job there and is excited to go.

She'll come back and visit us all. I think you should let her go."

Even though I was 40, in my father's eyes he was in charge, though we both knew reality was otherwise. His desire to control everyone's life was insatiable, and in some instances he was still victorious. But I was finally leaving Australia and going to start a life in Singapore teaching Yoga, knowing nobody there, but once again not concerned about the details. At some level, I knew I had to go far, far away.

Also, in 2003, my mother was diagnosed with dementia. This was devastating to me as my mother and I had always remained extremely close. I helped her as much as I could, and she, even in her desperate need, was selfless. She said, "I always told you, if ever I get sick, don't stay home and look after me. Put me in a nursing home, but make it a good one! And come and visit every week with a carton of cigarettes and a bottle of whisky! If I'm on my way out, I may as well party!"

My mother had held our family together. She had been the strong, behind-the-scenes force that had managed all the family difficulties. Perhaps the strain had taken its toll. She had also been caring for my father for the last 12 years since his stroke. So while he could walk, he was largely housebound and his right arm useless. Now their roles were switching and over the next few years he would become her caregiver. I had always thought I would care for my mother if she got ill. It was a strong desire I had stemming from how much I loved her. In her time of need, my father asked me to come home from Singapore and stay with them and help my mother. I couldn't face living in the same house as both of them, so with a heavy heart and a feeling of defeat, I declined and Mum went into care.

My years in Singapore began to heal so many parts of me that had suffered back home. The kind, softer way of the people here started to melt some of my hardness, my guardedness. I was blessed to be immersed in an Asian culture, which taught me many things: courtesy, kindness, respect, acceptance, non-linear thinking, how to go with the flow, and tolerance.

Living in Singapore also healed so much of my relationship with my father. He grew to respect and accept me as I became truly independent of his approval and inwardly secure in my choices. I considered this transcendence of a life of fear and the healing of our relationship the most important thing I'd done to date.

Increasingly, yoga was waking me up! It was showing me who I was as a person. I always saw myself as a social, happy person and ready to laugh. But as I took my work more seriously, my work persona became hard and stern. I hadn't realized it but two things were happening.

My separation from a more outgoing and social culture back in Australia had cut me off from an important outlet of expression that had made me laugh and feel connected. And of course my anger had started to rise more and more to the surface. Where previously it had appeared on my skin, red, angry and demanding attention, now it was coming out of my mouth, and I was at a loss of how to deal with it.

Through regular yoga, I was beginning to become more sensitive, more attuned to myself and others and more insightful. The process is very beguiling initially. For the first 10-15 years of my yoga practice, I found increasing levels of peace and contentment in myself and my life. From 15 years onwards, the challenges deepened. It didn't seem to matter that my relationship with my father had healed. This anger had not yet expressed itself and was seething inside like a caged beast. Those parts of me that had never been healed–the rage, the resentment, the deep pain and suffering from an abusive childhood–now stepped forward. Losing my cool and getting angry and frustrated was bad. Dealing with my guilt over that, knowing how much damage is inflicted through anger was unbearable. As the cycle of anger and abuse tried to continue, I resolved that it would end here. From experience I know that if I set my intention, then solutions come. And then I go to work for as long as it takes. This was going to take all my strength.

The Planets Start to Align

Despite having two stable relationships in my twenties, since I recovered from my illness, I'd always struggled to make a relationship work. In January 2014, I started giving twice weekly therapy sessions to Paul, a previous yoga student. Almost three years prior, Paul had a terrible cycling accident and became quadriplegic.

After surgery and much therapy, Paul could walk again. Johnny Walker had decided to sponsor Paul and his friend Gregory (an ex-world record holder in Paralympic swimming) to do a high altitude trek in the Himalayas. Paul asked if I'd join their expedition to Ladakh, in far northern India along the Tibetan Plateau. I agreed to go as his therapist, and so in June we headed off to tackle the challenge together.

The trek was an incredible experience. Paul and Gregory succeeded in completing the trek, though not without considerable difficulty at times. Our local guide Rigzin, a Tibetan Buddhist born in Ladakh, was a high altitude mountain guide. His specialty was taking groups up 6,000 m (19,500 ft.) peaks. The most well-known peak Stok Kangri (6,150 m) he'd summited 54 times. Rigzin had quite broken English, a joyful smile and a gentle presence. His answer whenever he was asked how much further we had to walk was "20 minutes." Gregory grew to love that answer because he said, "Twenty minutes always sounds achievable, and by the time you realise its going to be longer, you don't care anymore."

After the trek, Rigzin and I stayed in touch. This man from one of the most remote areas of the planet, whose culture was about as different from mine as you could imagine, who was 20 years my junior, became my boyfriend. As with everything else, life had brought me just who I needed for the road ahead. Rigzin was open-hearted, caring and gentle. He was easy-going, supremely adaptable yet extremely strong. Together we would navigate the road ahead and help to heal each other.

Weeks after our relationship blossomed, I got a phone call from my sister. "Hurry home. Dad is gravely ill." So I packed my bags and flew home and drove directly to hospital. My father was unresponsive. Every breath was only possible with him gasping deeply for air, despite the oxygen mask. Two days later I visited him on my own and told him he should die with a clear heart and mind, that all is forgiven and we all did the best we could. That night he passed away around 11:00 p.m. He died exactly a week before his 90th birthday.

Life Tools

At my most difficult moments, I've learnt to seek guidance and solace in prayer, meditation or yoga. As a young girl, I turned to music and would play the piano or violin. After an hour or so, my mood had shifted and I felt ok again. Then I experienced yoga and its transformative effect on me. I know that when we move our bodies, whatever state we're in starts to change. Often now, when I'm overcome, I walk. If I just continue to walk, then my state of mind changes. I found walking is a reliable and powerful anti-depressant.

I know that when I meditate daily, I'm more likely to experience a more peaceful daily rhythm. And the pain from my past finds its way into my awareness, in a timely way. As I'm ready, I recognize and accept it, and healing begins. In my case I had a lot of buried memories that I'd forgotten. And I suppose to most people they'd be content to leave them buried. But the truth is I was still broken in ways and in some areas feeling unfulfilled. Mary Oliver puts it beautifully in a line from one of her poems: *"Are you breathing just a little and calling it a Life?"*[3]

What I discovered was that those fragments of memories held not only the pain of the past, but some strength, some gift, some treasure that was part of me. I came to realise that as I uncovered another fractured part of myself, there

---

[3] Mary Oliver - Have You Ever Tried to Enter the Long Black Branches.

alongside the pain was an ability, a way of being in the world, a creativity or connection that I needed and without it, I wasn't quite whole. These fragments held my ability to love.

I discovered that my journey with yoga and meditation would guide me towards wholeness. When I began my first classes, slightly awkward and quite unaware, I didn't realise that these practices would be such powerful tools for self-transformation and self-healing, that one of the features of this process was my increasing tendency to draw towards me the right solutions, the right people, the right experiences for my growth. There is nothing random about this process and over the years the depth and beauty of it increases. What I was also stunned to realise was that it didn't matter that I wasn't the most acrobatically gifted practitioner out there.

The yoga world is crowned with some amazing demonstrations of extreme postures, and I always admire those who have that. I myself am nothing outstanding in that regard. My practice is solid, and I'm diligent, but there's no dazzling display. The point is, the gift of yoga, as I know it, is bestowed on me regardless. From my experience, it's the dedication to regular practice that matters. Yoga doesn't single out the physically gifted. But the emotionally committed receive ongoing guidance and a deep connection to divine support in all the myriad of ways that presents itself. Some mundane - others magical!

This process taught me to trust life, and this unleashed my creativity, excitement, confidence, patience (well sometimes), and peace. At the same time, I was gaining the ability to hear truth and non-truths wherever they were presented.

My gut sense would react with experiences and people. The sound of truth had a resonance and clarity to it, and falsehood seemed to clash and stop short. Of course, this perception wasn't constant. In situations that were intense or charged I was more likely to lose my clarity of understanding. The ramifications of this were huge.

In a time when the truth seems elusive, when people everywhere are wondering who or what they can trust, what is dependable and reliable, I found my way. I found that the only thing that is solid and ultimately real is my connection with the magic and beauty of life and with a spiritual outlook. What do you rely upon? What is it that is your north star, that guides and supports your passageway through life? In the last 10-15 years, I've rarely made any of the larger decisions regarding my life changes.

Where I have moments of indecision, this indicates it is not the time to act, but to wait. Otherwise, the signposts in life are abundantly clear even when the pathway I choose seems crazy to others. There is a deep comfort and solace in letting life guide me. And though I've been led through some extremely difficult experiences, I understand that my mission is self-healing. And nothing less fulfills me anymore. Having started, I can only continue. But more than that the high points are full, rich and heartfelt. Authentic love gathers around me more and more, and I know I am blessed.

Mum and Dad

What I learned from my mother was that everyone responds to kindness. And the power of her love and kindness held me together when I could have easily fallen apart. I also learned that to be kind is not enough. Despite my mother's deepest wishes to extricate us all from the tyranny of my father, she wasn't strong enough to do that. I know she did all she could, and I am at peace with that.

From my father I learned to rise to a challenge and to persist, despite all odds, towards that which you know inside is right for you. I learned that there can be a hundred voices shouting against yours, or even one loud and frightening voice overshadowing your own timid knowing. My father made it easy to realise that I could not possibly follow his guidance, no matter that he loved me, no matter that he terrified me and despite all my vulnerability. I was privileged to experience the absolute appropriateness of my own inner knowing.

Unmasked

A few years before my father died, I visited him in hospital. He hadn't drunk any alcohol since he'd been admitted a month earlier. He also didn't ask for any more pills. He appeared different somehow, but at first I couldn't put my finger on it.

This man who'd always been so demanding, so forceful, so self-centered said to me after I'd been there for 15 minutes, "You're only here a few weeks in Sydney. Why don't you go and visit your friends. I'm ok. I'm at peace, and I'm comfortable. Go and enjoy yourself."

This man who had no friends, who was probably lonely, who had always pressed me to be with him, had flipped. Without alcohol and pills, I was meeting my real father for the first time. And he was who I always hoped he could be: kind, thoughtful and caring.

I believe we are all struggling to present our true selves to the world. I struggle against my anger at my past, even now when all that is over and Dad is dead and buried. What are we raging at? When will the anger be satiated? Some are fighting fear that keeps them in dead marriages, boring jobs or crippling life roles. Some are fighting the pain of the past that doesn't let them realise their dreams, or the fear of the future that makes people settle. Some fight addiction that keeps them trapped and others are a slave to desires that rule their behavior but cause so much pain.

We are most of us fighting against something. My hope for you is that you find a way to transcend the fear and pain that we become ruled by. Let's allow our true selves to shine.

About The Author

Vivienne's 30 years' of teaching experience began as a meditation teacher in Sydney, Australia and brought her to Asia and the US in her quest to investigate health and healing. After many years as Principal Teacher at the well-known COMO Shambhala Yoga Studio in Singapore, she now runs Yoga Alliance certified teacher-training programs in Asia as well as retreats and workshops in Asia and Europe.

Vivienne is also a skilled bodyworker utilizing a meridian-based therapy that manipulates fascia which she studied in Boston. Her clients see her for issues ranging from pain and restricted movement, to post-surgical complications, disease states such as multiple sclerosis and more complex cases like paralysis due to stroke or spinal cord injuries.

In addition, Vivienne has a Bachelor of Arts degree in Psychology & Philosophy from the University of Sydney and a Diploma of Remedial Massage from NatureCare College of Natural Therapies. She has studied NLP, Bodytalk and applied anatomy.

Vivienne knows the practices of Yoga, Meditation & Meridian-Based Stretching are able to provide deep healing and transformation. She is as interested in advancing the mind as the body, in raising awareness as cultivating peace, and in offering all clients access to their own guiding sense. Many clients attain not only a clear resolution to their problem but find themselves adopting long-term strategies for healthy lifestyle practices.

viv@stretchsolutions.org

CHAPTER 17

HOPE IS WAITING: MY STORY
Richard Bajkowski

I will never forget the day my mother died. She had been agonizing in the hospital for a week and her belly, grossly expanded from the disease, made her look six months pregnant.

She died from a form of liver disease known as primary biliary cirrhosis. Working in the medical field, I know what suffering those three words bring, and I hate them.

While at work I called her doctor's office. The doctor's partner, who excelled at having a horrific bedside manner was put on the phone. "Yeah, she's going to die," he nonchalantly stated. I was livid for being so coldly slapped out of my denial. For the first time in my career I left work without telling anyone.

Numb and disoriented from the inevitable, I sped to my parents' house and shared the news with my father and brother. I gently relayed to them what the doctor had said about Mom's dire condition and explained how vital it was that we bring her home for her final days. Being the youngest child and accustomed to not having my opinion respected in my immediate family, I was prepared for the impending resistance.

Dad, panic stricken and distraught shouted, "No! There has to be more they can do!" My brother quickly agreed with him. I was afraid that there was a very real possibility of my mom dying alone in a hospital bed and I let my medical training kick in. In my field we are trained to block out our emotions to focus on the tasks at hand. I calmly stated to them: "I strongly suggest bringing her home." They relented.

When someone is terminally ill and near the end, they sometimes go through a period of disorientation and come out of it just before they die. After a week of not being able to respond, Mom was sitting up in bed, weakly attentive. "You're coming home, Mom." I told her.

Wanting not to be a bother, and at the same time so badly yearning to come home, she weakly replied, "Oh no, honey."

"Yes, Mom, you are." My response toppled her protest.

"I have the best family," she strained to vocalize.

Having my mom back after not being able to interact with her was a short-lived comfort, as she began to throw up blood. After the staff cleaned her up, I got ready for the long, five-minute drive in the ambulance to her home.

The medical team settled her in a makeshift bedroom in the dining room. She saw her grandkids and even had a bite of vanilla ice cream. Growing up, I remember seeing my parents kiss once. That night, my dad kissed her on the forehead, and an hour later she was gone.

Yet hope was waiting.

My brother had always been Mom's favorite, the smart one, while I was the less desirable funny, athletic one. For most of my life I'd competed with him for her affection and approval. He seemed to get everything handed to him, and I was out in the cold fending for myself. Against the dark backdrop of my thoughts, I replayed the memory of a report card day when I was nine.

I brought home stellar grades, only to end up crying in the bathroom when Mom ignored my achievement and rewarded my brother. She bought a shiny new coin set of his birth year, printed with "1961—A Wonderful Year." My consolation prize was her saying, "Your report card is good, too," through the bathroom door. My heart was destroyed. And now in this moment, my mind vacillated between sorrow at losing her and memories that made me feel cheated.

Christmas came soon after my Mom died. In my Dad's living room, under the tree that held the same ornaments I had seen all my life, we celebrated numbly, putting on happy faces for the kids. Mom was highly organized and bought presents for us months in advance, and as we handed them out, all I could think was how scared I was to open the last present she had for me. If I opened it, that would be it. She'd be gone. I can't remember receiving any genuine affection from my mother. I can't remember her ever saying she loved me. Yet I still didn't want to let her go. I suppose I was holding out hope for an "I love you" to be in the box.

In controlled agony, I unwrapped the last Christmas present I would ever get from her. Would my heart be trampled on by her again even in death like it was when I was nine? Something inside must have told her what to do for me months before she passed on. I pulled off the last piece of wrapping paper and opened the box. Inside was a shiny coin set from my birth year, and on it was "1965 — A Wonderful Year," just like the one my brother got well over thirty years before. I cried uncontrollably. Hope arrived and an amazing journey began.

One of my favorite books is *Man's Search for Meaning*, by Victor Frankel. It's the account of his horrific fight for survival in a Nazi prison camp. Of the many incredible things Mr. Frankel did to bring hope to himself in the living nightmare of the Holocaust, there's one that affected my life greatly. Though he was certain his wife had been put to death by the Nazis, he would imagine himself going on dates with her. He imagined the restaurants and enjoying their favorite foods, having conversations with her and laughing together. He made everything so real. Even in death, the love of his life saved his life. He was in hell but hell was not in him. The same is true of you. Hope and love are in you!

It's understandable if that doesn't feel true yet. Life is a process. My own process took me from crying with joy at opening my Mom's gift to an internal scream of, "Yeah, a lot of good it does me now!" That's what happens when the light of love hits bitterness. My darkness was exposed, if only to me. If you relate to feeling like this, know it's okay. We can be patient with each other as we work through it all.

We're all different, each with unique stories, but the part of the process I find we all must face is forgiveness. Forgiveness is the only thing that could deal with the bitterness that had built up for so long. When I was able to let go of these feelings, memories returned — good ones, fun ones, silly ones, not just the ones that reinforced my pain.

I remembered my Mom had an amazing sense of humor. She was the one who taught me how to play "Pull the Finger." I'm laughing as I write this. I know it's juvenile, but if you don't know that game, imagine eating a bunch of beans and waiting. Just before you are about to pass gas, you ask someone to pull your finger and let it go. I'm a kid at heart and if growing up means I have to give up this memory, I don't want to. Maybe you're not amused or maybe like me you are cracking up. Either is fine. We don't have to agree on what's funny, but laughter is healing for everyone.

Choosing to be grateful for the renewed memories of her humor unlocked more memories of how wonderful she was in other ways. She taught me not to take myself so seriously. She was generous. She was not just smart but brilliant. And I know now she was proud of her kids, including me. The thing I love most about my Mom is that she loved all her family fiercely, with all of our dysfunction, emotional warts and all. She had 10 other siblings and a multitude of nieces and nephews.

I still hurt and am bitter at times, but these feelings lessened in strength and frequency, so much so, that I can usually laugh at them pretty quickly. I'm certainly not perfect, but good enough and becoming better.

If you'll open yourself up to hope by forgiving, hope will open you up to love. If you are open to love, love will be victorious over death. Just like Victor Frankel's wife, Mom still makes me laugh. She still plays pull my finger, gives me more hugs than when she was alive, and I know she is proud of the person she has helped me become.

You may say I never let her go. That's fine—I don't want to. My Mom still lives in my heart, because there's more than enough room now. Had I let bitterness take over, it would have killed my heart, along with any connection to her. So I thank God I get to have positive memories of her with me, and carry that joy into my own family.

As my wife and I grow in loving our kids, we read a lot of parenting articles, and I'm learning not to drive myself crazy with all the advice. But one article that stuck out to me was about a parent who raised six kids who went to college, all completely on scholarships.

One of the things he did with his children was to buy them the car of their choice. One catch—the car had to be from a junkyard, and they had to rebuild it by themselves with the help of the internet and a car manual. Knowing full well that his kids were going to make mistakes, he supplied unlimited money for parts and tools. You can imagine the mistakes they made. One kid put motor oil in the radiator! Eventually the kids had the coolest cars in town with no less than 350 horsepower.

What if we could generously forgive people, and ourselves, for mistakes, offenses and misunderstandings ahead of time, knowing we all make them? What if we could live unoffended and unguarded? What if we weren't afraid to fail at loving, but were inspired not to? I'm not saying our lives are like a junk car, but what if we were less afraid to make mistakes while learning to build our lives, just like those kids learned to build their dream cars? We can! Hope is waiting to show us the way to our dream life.

In my life, forgiveness has led to hope, peace, and real love. In my mind, I think of it as "fore–giving," choosing to live in forgiveness before there's even an offense. A word of wisdom, however. Though all people need to be forgiven, some need not be in your life for a time, so you can heal.

Forgiveness can rebuild a relationship, but it's primarily to free the one who's been wounded. For years I replayed offenses in my mind over and over. Maybe you do, too. Stopping to forgive that person one more time has helped me more than I can say. I know in real life we all get hurt. Forgiveness doesn't make your life happily ever after, but I know from experience it opens the door to genuine joy.

When I was in college I was introduced to the books of Leo Buscaglia. Leo was a crazy (in a courageously good way) professor who understood hope, forgiveness, and love. When a student committed suicide he wanted to do something about human disconnection, and started a class at his university called Love 1A. He based it on the thought love is so big that he had as much to learn as anyone in his class. He didn't teach it; he facilitated it. I devoured every book he wrote, and dreamed of someday being in his class. He made love feel like a beautiful, irresistible adventure. He was right! Love is big, alive and real. It is manly, womanly, childlike, and it's for everyone, including you. It's time to believe that for yourself.

In the 1991 Peter Pan remake, *Hook*, Peter returns to Neverland all grown up. Swept up in the demands of adulthood and the problems that come with it, he's lost his childlike wonder, and consequently, his ability to fly.

The dreaded Captain Hook has stolen Peter's children in an attempt to destroy his nemesis. Peter's only way to get them back is to relearn how to fly by getting in touch with his happy thought.

Many of us, like Peter, have lost our happy thought. Somewhere, among the painful trials of life, we lost it. Like Peter, we need to learn how to fight for our greatest treasures by getting in touch with our happy thought and, as in the film, that may take some time.

Part of the Alcoholics Anonymous steps include surrendering yourself, and your problems, to a higher power. I came to know that higher power as God. He was, and is, essential to my healing. I understand even mentioning God can be a source of pain to those who have been hurt by people who've misrepresented Him.

I believe God loves you enough to understand this and doesn't mind being called a higher power, universe, or source of creation. Twelve–step programs have helped millions of people overcome the debilitating tragedy of addiction and can help give you hope in any situation simply because *you are God's happy thought.*

I don't know your pain or situation. Maybe I can't understand your level of heartache and disappointment. Perhaps you can't understand it either. However, I know there is hope. We are living in exciting times right now in which God is healing and loving His creation like never before. Hope is coming alive.

With the information age there have been huge advances in psychology. I don't have all the answers, but based on my experiences, I would like to share some programs/resources that have helped me heal. Anthony Robbins, Alex Lloyd's *The Healing Code, Theophostic Ministry* by Ed Smith, and *Sozo* from Bethel Church have been dear to my heart in helping me on my journey. These were instrumental in assisting me in finding my own happy thoughts.

Things hoped for are sometimes meant to be shared so that we can encourage each other and enable hope to grow. Even though we haven't met, I'm hoping you'll join me in hoping together. I hope for ruined relationships healed and love restored. I hope for physical healings. I hope for dreams coming to fruition and passion for life reignited. I hope that you find your happy thought. Dare to hope, because I know that hope is waiting!

About The Author

Richard Bajkowski is originally from the East Coast and currently resides in Northern California. He is married to his wife of 14 years and together they have two funny and creative children who are the light of his life.

By day, Rich works as an ultrasound technologist and enjoys sharing the news of a baby's gender with excited parents.

His passion in life is seeing people healed, living in authentic freedom and becoming who they were truly meant to be.

Rich likes getting to the heart of a matter and comes alive when people are set free of pain and can enjoy the life that was given to them.

He can be reached at richardbajkowski@outlook.com

CHAPTER 18

MORE THAN WE EXPECTED

The Womacks – Bobbie and Larry

Preparations

Bobbie Womack

I begin on November 7, 2013. We'd been in the Philippines for twenty-seven years, and had been watching this storm for a week as it drew closer gaining intensity. We did as much preparation as we could–cutting large limbs out of our mahogany trees close to the house, taping up and boarding windows, trying to make sure everything was secure. We told the students of our Bible school to evacuate for the first time ever.

Our property was so near the ocean you could stand at our gate and throw a rock into the sea. That's on the school side, the south side of the property. The north side of the property is our residence. Our neighbor across the road has a sea wall and a concrete house. We have a twelve-foot high concrete block perimeter wall around our entire property. Seems safe enough

We'd gone through lots of typhoons before. As we watched online, we could see the storm progress through category three, category four, and finally it become a category five. In all 27 years we lived in the Philippines, we never saw anything worse than a category one or two here in Leyte. Our building had become a place of refuge for the fishing village down the road from us. They would come and hunker down in our big concrete three-story school building. But this time we said, "You guys are going to have to evacuate to the local elementary school." We also had two staff families living on the property who had to be evacuated as well. One of our staff, Arnold, volunteered to stay behind and watch the property in case a wall was breached.

My husband, Larry, stayed behind at our house, while I went to a friend's house the night before the storm was to hit. It was further inland, in town, but only a half a block from the bay.

November 6th, two days before the storm was due to hit was spent in making preparations, boarding up windows, moving vehicles behind the wall. We tried to make everything safe and secure. We were thinking that we'd be safe behind the wall, so much so that three other missionary families put their vehicles on our property for safe keeping. We had motorcycles with sidecars that we used for ministry in the feeding program back there too.

When I left Thursday night the 7th, the ocean was flat and calm. It was a beautiful night. As I passed through the fishing village people were milling about. Their little fishing boats were pulled off the beach and in between their houses for safekeeping. People were gathered in clusters discussing the approaching storm. Nobody was evacuating, even though there had been evacuation notices because of the storm surge that was predicted. In our area we'd never really had a storm surge, so we didn't realize the potential devastation one could cause. We found out later.

When I woke up at 5:00 a.m. the next morning, there was already lots of wind. The typhoon was coming and there was no escaping it. I was able to make one last phone call while the cell phone connection was still working. I called Larry and said, "How's everything?" He said, "It's really getting windy." By 5:30 a.m. the power was off. The electric company turns the power off purposely when storms come, because they knew poles would be down, and they don't want people electrocuted. Now, I'll let Larry tell his side of the story.

Protection

Larry Womack

To start, I'd like you to know that the presence of God is very real. In Hebrews 13:5, *He will never leave us or forsake us.*

At the time, I had been reading a chapter of Proverbs every day during my quiet time. It just happened to be Proverbs 8 that day. Like Bobbie said when she called the power was still on. It was getting windy out of the north, and I thought the storm might have been going south of us. Not long after we had talked the power went off, and the wind started coming directly from the east, from the ocean. It grew stronger and stronger causing a large limb to split from the trunk of one of our mahogany trees and crash down.

I was in the house and noticed that our ceiling fans were not going around, but were bouncing up and down with the ceiling because of the strong wind. I put on a motorcycle helmet to have some head protection in case it fell, then I stood in our bedroom doorway and just watched it. Due to such hard blowing rain I could hardly see anything out the front living room windows.

On the west side of our home we had a sliding door, rattling so much you could hear it breaking. I went over to the door to open it, to save it from breaking apart, but when I opened the door, clear water streamed in around my feet. That was about 6:00 a.m. Before long the water turned a sandy brown, like ocean water, and came rushing in faster. It was ankle deep in just a moment. This has never happened before. Now the wind was stronger than ever.

I walked back to the bedroom doorway. In just a short time the water inside was knee deep. They mentioned before that there was going to be a storm surge, but we didn't know how high.

The water kept getting deeper. Things were happening so quickly that I can't explain what I was thinking. I started back toward the kitchen for some reason. We had a wooden bookcase that divided the living room and the dining room, and as I started back toward the kitchen, it floated up and crashed backwards in the water scattering its contents. Then the refrigerator came floating through the kitchen door - laying on its back. I turned around, went back to the bedroom doorway. By that time the water was waist deep. I looked out the living room window and saw a brand new Mitsubishi that belonged to our friend who was in Manila at the time, floating by with the emergency flashers on. That's when I thought, "Goodness! This is going to be bad!" It felt so unreal that I could hardly comprehend it.

I went into the bedroom. Our bed was made of rattan, and the mattress was rubberized foam. It was floating on the surface of the water, above my waist now. I guess now I'm just thinking survival mode. The bed was floating. I got up on the bed.

It was going up pretty quickly. I looked out our bedroom window, which was seven feet tall, and I couldn't see any sky, only water. Our house was under water. Inside, the water level was going up rapidly toward our ceiling, which was made of four-by-eight sheets of plywood. I'm thinking, "What am I going to do? How am I going to get above it?" I'm thinking I'm going to be trapped.

At just the right moment, as I'm bending down because the bed had risen up to the ceiling, one of the plywood sheets blew out right in front of me and opened a way into the attic. I pulled myself up. The roof was coming off on one side of the house. The wind, they said later, was sustained at 195 miles an hour with gusts up to 240. (A category 5 starts at 156 miles an hour). There is no category 6, but we heard experts say days later, "If there were a 'cat' 6, Typhoon Haiyan, is it." You could actually hear gusts above the screaming wind. I started crying out for help and couldn't hear myself scream, the wind was so loud.

I pulled myself up into the attic where a beam goes the length of the house from east to west and is about twelve inches wide. It sat on top of the concrete block wall and was the main support for our home.

This is how I can say that I know God is real and that He is always with us. In the midst of the screaming wind I heard a voice in my heart, a clear, practical, and commanding voice. It said, "Sit here till I tell you to move."

That is exactly what I did. I sat down on the beam against a concrete post with my back toward the ocean. The entire right side of the ceiling had blown away by this time. I was sitting between our bedroom and the storage room where I had gotten the motorcycle helmet. At this time our property and the inside of our house was filling up like a swimming pool. I saw my son's boogie board floating on the other side of the storage room.

It wasn't rushing water, just rising really fast. I saw that boogie board, and I thought to myself, "I would like to have that." I had no more thought it than the boogie board came floating across the room to where I could just bend over and easily pick it up. Psalm 139:2 *He understands my thought from afar.* I was thinking that if the wall fell down I'd at least have something to hold on to.

The roof was ripping apart and letting the wind through. I used the boogie board as a shield against the pelting rain and salt water hitting my face and arms. It felt like needles driving into my skin. Now all the walls parallel to the sea were breaking apart allowing the ocean to rush in. On both sides of my wall the water was like raging rivers passing through.

It kept going through my mind that the weather forecast said the storm would make landfall at 9:00 a.m. My watch showed around 7:00 a.m. I was losing all hope. The storm hadn't even landed yet–there was no way to survive this.

Then I remembered Proverbs, chapter 8. I guess I began to talk to the sea. It talks about wisdom's role in creation. It says wisdom was there when God made the barriers for the sea, and it cannot transgress His command. I was telling the water, *God made a boundary for you, and you cannot transgress it*. I'd just read that Proverb, but I'm wondering to myself where the boundary was.

I was pretty sure this was my last day, and I started crying out to God and praying for Bobbie. I prayed also for our staff, Arnold, who was in his apartment on the school side of the property. Then I began to pray for our two grown children here in the States, that God would give them peace when they would hear what happened to me. As time went by and I prepared myself to meet the Lord, the most sincere prayer I had was, "See you in a little while."

All of a sudden, in the midst of the worst storm on earth, peace fell on me and on that place. Peace beyond understanding fell in my heart. I set there and just really worshiped and prayed. The presence of God was as so real! I felt such peace that I even gave thanks to God for the storm.

After a time I looked down on both sides and realized all I could see was water rushing through. There was nothing in our home, no walls left standing. All I could do was give thanks for God's presence. That was all that mattered.

As the morning progressed, the water stopped rising. That brought some relief. But the wall I was sitting on rocked back and forth with each wave.

Finally, the ocean began going down. I regained some hope of survival. It was a good time, in a way. By 10:30 a.m. the water had already receded from the house. There was nothing left inside, no furniture, pictures or walls. The water took everything with it. What it left were large chunks of concrete walls and blocks and a coconut tree. I recognized part of our neighbor's wall laying in our living room, a concrete section that weighed hundreds of pounds. His house was completely destroyed, nothing left but a slab of concrete.

As the storm was passing, the winds were shifting from east to south, so I changed positions on the wall to face north. There was no roofing on the north side. I was sitting there and looking down our road into a different world. Psalms 46 describes it. *God is our refuge and strength, a very present help in time of trouble. Even though the earth should change ...* The entire landscape was so different that I didn't recognize anything. It had gone from beautiful, lush tropical green to just brown, grey and broken.

The ocean was dirty brown, not clear anymore, and not a leaf left on a tree, what few trees were left. Around 11:00 a.m. I was sitting there watching some young guys walk down our road. I'm thinking, "Where did they come from? How did they survive to do that?" Then I hear a guy down below me call, "Brother Larry." It was a former student of ours, with Arnold, and three other guys who were former and current students!

Surprised, I looked at them and said, "What are you doing here?" I had thought only Arnold stayed behind, but here they were! God really preserved their lives. They had retreated to the stair well on the second floor of the three-story school building, which still stands to this day, the only one of several buildings on the property to survive.

In between the school building and the beam on top of the wall where I'd sat inside our house, nothing was left of the property. It was all gone. God protected those two places where we took refuge.

I felt peace to get up and move then, so I went around the column I had been leaning on. On the back side of that column, just behind where I'd been sitting, was a little plastic ointment container, no more than an inch tall. I recognized it right away. It was Bobbie's salve that the doctor had given her for a rash on her hand. I thought it so odd that it had somehow survived all that wind, rain, and water when everything else was gone. I picked it up and stuck it in my pocket.

Then I climbed on down and hugged those guys. After an experience like that, you wonder if anybody is going to be alive anymore.

Reality Sets In

We looked around, not really knowing what to do. There's absolutely nothing in our house. Being a guy, I wanted to go see my tool room. It was all cement, but only two walls remained, and it was full of sand. I did see an old electric drill and a couple of little sockets but all else was gone.

Our neighbors on the west side had built a native house of bamboo and palm leaves right beside our wall. Now that twelve-foot high wall around our property was completely destroyed. This man's house was actually attached to the back side of our property. He would have been perfectly safe from a typhoon any other time, but not this time due to the storm surge. As I looked around there, I saw a big crack in the downed wall. Inside, I saw the body of a girl. I turned around to motion to Arnold when I saw the girl's brother standing next to him. He and his cousin had held on to that floating Mitsubishi, saving themselves. I motioned Arnold to come over, and the brother came with him. We were looking into that crack and he began to weep. It was his fourteen year-old sister. When they came and dug out under the wall the next day, we learned that he had lost his mother, his father, his sister, and two younger brothers.

I guess that's when reality set in about the day.

I said, "Arnold, I want to go find Bobbie." Arnold said he wanted to go with me because his family was on the other side of town. He had about eight miles to walk. I had about three. The four students also walked with us. So we set out down that road. If I hadn't been there for over twenty years I wouldn't have even known where I was. There were no landmarks anymore. Even the cement structures had been blown apart and washed inland.

That family that owned the Mitsubishi lived about a quarter mile down the road from us on the beach. There is nothing left of their house at all except the cement foundation and a concrete bathtub. During the storm—we learned later—their helper had stayed behind to watch the house. She was told repeatedly to leave, but was so loyal to the missionaries that she felt an obligation to stay there and protect their belongings. She didn't survive. Come to find out later, her son, daughter-in-law, and grandchild also stayed in that house. As far as we know their bodies were never found.

We continued on. All the properties down the road were gone. As we went farther we saw our Filipino friend, Fred. He and one of his neighbors were coming up the left side of the road. They were helping a guy, with a nasty-looking broken leg that was bleeding profusely, hoping to find medical help.

We talked with him a minute before we saw Art, whom we've known for twenty-plus years. He and his wife were going around their home, but it was gone. I thought, "How did these people make it?" But they made it.

They were looking around, picking up things like a plate, a spoon. We talked, and he told me about everything he lost. He said, "I lost my driver's license," and I said, "Oh yeah. I did too." He said, "We lost our passport," and I thought, "Yeah, me too." Then in that same tone of voice, he said, "I can't find my son." Just as matter of fact, not frantic at all. It took me aback. I felt so sorry for them. We knew his son. He has twin boys, nineteen or twenty years old. One of them was at a safe place. But this one had stayed behind with his parents.

We found out the next day, his son came walking back later that afternoon. He had been swept inland for about a mile and had a big gash on his leg. I can imagine the reunion between them. Just next door to them was one of our staff members, Dante Lingo and his wife, Delor. They were walking around, weeping and searching. I walked over to Dante and gave him a hug. He said, "Brother Larry, we have found the body of Daniel," their oldest son of twelve years, "and Carlo," seven years old. "But we cannot find Diane," their little girl, five years old. They had four children. One survived. They found Diane later that day in a stand of broken down bamboo.

We continued down the road, seeing what was left of our neighborhood - just piles of debris, wood, bamboo, metal, nails, dead dogs and pigs–and people. At the end of our road we climbed over about a twelve-foot high pile of debris in the middle of the road just before Carl's and Susie's house.

Seeing Carl and Susie Miller, Southern Baptist Missionaries, was a joyful moment. When we climbed over the debris pile, and I saw their home was intact and they were well. Their house had been flooded nearly up to the ceiling. It was a great reunion to see that they all survived. The four students ended up staying up with Carl and Susie to help clean up. It took days to get all that stuff cleaned up. Then, Arnold and I continued our trek through all that debris for another two-and-a-half miles.

There was a lot of water pooled in the lower areas of the road. We went by the Coca-Cola plant and the outdoor bodega where they stored their cokes. The walls had been breached and Cokes were everywhere. I saw people picking up and carrying away cases of Cokes. I thought, "That's their drinking water for tomorrow." In some places, the water was knee deep and very murky. We ended up stepping on some of those Coke bottles. I helped a lady get through the debris.

We finally got to the main road that leads into town, and toward the bay near where Bobbie was staying. There were hardly any structures left on the bayside, they were all washed over onto the main road and beyond.

All along the bay for about a mile, there had been these little bamboo houses with nipa palm leaf roofs, they had been on stilts over the water in rows four or five houses deep. Every single one was gone, only a few posts remained. All that debris was strewn across the road and neighborhoods. And sad to say, there were many bodies in that debris.

We passed Bethany hospital, a large hospital. The bottom level was completely washed out, no medical care left there. I wondered how many patients didn't make it.

I was beginning to lose heart at seeing all the destruction, and I was concerned about Bobbie's safety. As we were walking through the debris in the road, I stuck my hand down in my pocket and touched the forgotten container of ointment. I pulled it out and looked at it. It was like the Lord spoke to me and said, "Your wife is okay because you have her medicine." All of a sudden I had hope again. I was starting to realize how hard the next few days would be, but I knew God would take care of us.

We had to climb over lots of debris to make the turn going onto the street where Bobbie was staying. There is a school house across the street that had been used for evacuation.

These schools are mostly single level with many classrooms where lots of people could evacuate in the case of a typhoon. The surge had flooded the school and all those people had to hold on to the rafters to save their lives. The debris around the school buildings was up to the eaves of the roof, eight to ten feet high in places.

We crossed that pile of debris and there in the street was Sarah Cha, the woman Bobbie had gone to stay with. We hugged, which was odd, because you don't typically hug Korean ladies.

We were so happy. I was as excited as a little kid as I asked, "Is Bobbie here? Is Bobbie here?" She said, "Come with me." We walked, crawled, and climbed over the debris to get into her house, which was full of black, smelly mud. I finally got to the stairs with Sarah running ahead of me, saying, "Bobbie! Bobbie! Guess who's here." It was about 2:00 in the afternoon as we clung to each other and wept together. I couldn't have hoped for a more wonderful reunion! Through it all I had not gotten one scratch on my body, just a bruise on my left arm where I held on to a wall stud.

Provisions
Bobbie Womack
The next four days were amazing to see how God provided what we needed. A few dry matches were found in Sarah's house where five of us stayed for the next 4 days. The gas stove that had been under water worked so we could cook rice for our supper that first night. A hand pump still worked and after many pumps clear water begins to flow. A 55-gallon plastic drum with barnacles on it had floated in right beside the pump. How convenient.

The next morning, we were able to find Larry a shirt and ball cap in the debris before heading back to our house in the hot sun to see if we could find anything like canned food or an article of clothing. We did find a few cans inside a sand filled cabinet. One of Larry's tee shirts was wrapped around barbed wire beside a pair of my capris. We didn't find much else, but we were happy to have that. When we walked back to Sarah's house, many of our Filipino friends gave us cans of sardines, corned beef, rice, Raman noodles and two bottles of Coke, all of which had been "harvested" from the destroyed warehouses. Supper: sardines with our rice!

Early Sunday morning Sarah and Larry walked to City Hall after hearing four computers and generators had been set up so survivors could contact family letting them know they were alive. Our daughter saw Sarah's post on Facebook, the names of those we knew were alive. It just so happened it was a few hours before her birthday when she saw her parents were alive. She still says that was the best birthday gift ever. The remainder of the day was spent cleaning up broken glass and black mud out of the house. We were thinking we were going to be there a while. We saw the first helicopters, both media and military, surveying the damage of Tacloban City.

Monday our drinking water is almost gone. Finding a large kettle, we filled it with water from the pump. Plenty of fire wood lay all around. Larry started a fire, and we placed the kettle on it. While waiting for it to boil, we began looking around the property in a storage area. Standing on a once flooded car, Larry looks over a chain-link fence covered by a tarp and finds 16 one gallon jugs of purified water! And many one liter bottles! God continues to provide! We also find a pedicab and are able to get it out with some help.

The tires were low so we couldn't ride on it. We were headed back to the Millers' house so we pushed the pedicab asking others if they knew of an air pump. We were told to look over there, over here, but nothing panned out. We continued to walk when a motorcycle zoomed past dropping an air pump right at our feet! Smiling I said, "God, I know that's You." The driver of the motorcycle stopped and the passenger jumped off and ran back to retrieve his pump, but first he was gracious and filled our tires.

Monday afternoon we heard planes arriving at the airport. Once there we were told by a stranger to go see the American guy at the control tower. We had no idea who this person was but we went looking. I almost cried when we found this American guy ... U.S. Special Forces! He informed us of incoming cargo-laden C-130s that were arriving and would take evacuees back to Manila. Needing to return the pedicab and retrieve our few belongings, there was no way we could travel the seven miles back by foot in time to catch the first flight out, so we opted to leave Tuesday. We stayed with the Millers who lived just a mile from the airport.

Tuesday, November 12th, before dawn we began our walk to the now crowded airport. Philippine Military controlled the crowd as the C-130 landed early afternoon. The U. S. Special Forces guy helped 50 of us through the crowd onto the tarmac and onto the revved-up plane, entering through the rear cargo door. An hour and a half later we land in Manila.

December 8th, one month to the day Typhoon Haiyan hit, we landed at the airport in Lexington, Kentucky, to a wonderful family reunion.

Reflecting

After losing every material thing and almost life, people see more clearly what is most important to them. For us it is not possessions and stuff, but an even closer walk with our Heavenly Father who proved repeatedly His care and concern for His children in dire straits. An attitude change developed, a positive change of being more caring about others. More patient. More loving and praying for others. I cannot answer the question Why. Why it happened. Why so many died. All we can say is, "What now, Lord, what will You have me do?" And walk forward with confidence knowing God is taking care of us.

About The Authors

Larry and Bobbie Womack arrived in the Philippines August 16, 1986 thinking to be there for one year to do follow up Bible studies from an evangelistic meeting held in Tacloban City, Leyte. During that year of teaching many Filipinos the Word of God, they both sensed the Lord leading them to stay, which they did. They began a free three-month discipleship Bible school in their home in June of 1988. By 1990 the Bible school was relocated into a larger building to house the 20 to 25 students and grew into a five months study.

During the 1990's they began ministering to two indigenous groups, the Manobo and Mamanua, traveling to the mountains to share God's Word with them. Their chief and her family attended the Bible school as well as many of their youth and young adults.

November of 1993 they began their first feeding program, feeding the neighboring fishing village children. Seeing the sicknesses of these children, a medical ministry began to care for their illnesses as well as teaching the mothers health and hygiene.

They also raised two children in the Philippines, Lydia who is now married living in Kentucky, and Luke who is a city fireman in Tennessee.

Larry and Bobbie were on their 27th year of living in the Philippines, 25th year of teaching, and on their 50th group of students when Typhoon Haiyan arrived November 8 2013, destroying everything and washing it all away but the school building. Today the school building has been repaired and classes resumed.

Today Larry and Bobbie live in Mt. Vernon, Kentucky on 84 acres of hills, hollows, and trees.

Larry is a handyman and ministers in the local church when called upon. Bobbie works part time at an assisted living facility and volunteers at the local pregnancy center.

CHAPTER 19

BE FORGIVEN: LOVE AND APPRECIATE YOUR TRUE SELF

Gail Marie Goodin

Money, assets, investments, a home, corporate career in Maine, all are gone. I am a different unique person living in a different new part of the country. Nothing is the same, especially me, inside and outside.

I have survived five diagnoses of life-threatening diseases, including cancers and dealt with intense skin issues. Preceding all of this, I heard doctors say each time: "It will take a spiritual miracle for you to heal." I also heard: "Surgery is needed within the week or you will become an invalid for life. What would you have done? What might you have felt?

I have always known miracles, dreams, and desires can come true. If they did not, many times I would have given up when they did not manifest. I felt the failure, jealous envy, shame and guilt. Is there a place within you that relates?

A judge lived within me. It destroyed compassion and hope for me. I decided I was spiritually unforgiven, not good enough to receive. This started in the third grade. I became that identity. Do you have a painful identity that is a lie when you cannot make something happen?

"You are dripping shame," said one awesome spiritual mentor after listening to me. That statement startled the truth awake to lies within me of a false identity. Such a gift it turned out to be. Have you, through love, caused an awakening within you of denied pain? I suddenly realized! This is not my plan! What do I want to create? It is not this! I could not trust in forgiveness.

Generational and projected guilt, shame and inferiority lived as feelings in my body. I compared myself with others in my perception of failed achievements. This drove me even harder to be good enough to be forgiven. I never forgave myself. This can become an addiction and did. Have you ever endured this suffering?

As I became willing to feel, I was told by a doctor that the body is a map of the unconscious mind. It cannot be deceived. Where there had been numbness, now feelings of discomfort began. I would hold my breath because of the fear. Do you ever forget to breathe?

Trauma, abuse and attacks all caused neurological symptoms and illnesses. In the resulting fear and stress I did not feel safe or secure. Poverty consciousness arose from my many losses. Negative memories created an inner concealed Post Traumatic Stress Disorder unrealized by me. Have you ever felt such feelings ?

I judged myself. Unconsciously I faked being strong, fooling even myself of my learned helpless, hopeless, hurt, and sense of unworthiness. Survival rather than thriving became my game in the outer world! Have you ever put the outer life and world ahead of your inner peace?

Unconsciously I was being run by inner pain that I had repressed. I had no idea about what was going on. I thought my mind's thoughts were true. I would find out how much deep pain I had experienced that made me sick continuously. What might run you? Outer world values and circumstances had always determined my worth and success No matter how much heartfelt good I did, I was never enough.

The Good News is that you, like me, will get to know truth! The one captivated by an identity of fear and unforgiveness now knows who she truly is. You will experience hearing the Good News of all that is possible.

Suddenly, I heard him begin to describe "burnout." I felt the shock of disbelief. Everything he was describing was me! I had all those symptoms. How could this be? I had believed in this life of completion of goals. What else was there?

I heard the voice in my mind exclaiming "I have only been at this job for a year and a half. I always stay with corporations ten years." All of this money, income, benefits, home, relationships, saving, and assets, are more than I have ever earned or had. I am there with all the goals I have ever thought I needed. Does any of this cause a reaction within you?

As the speaker finished, I remember walking over to the table. In disbelief I really signed up for his New Year's retreat in Hawaii. The brochure said the purpose was to actualize awareness of one's own inner core of truth. Second was to firmly plant truth on a strong foundation of service and fulfillment. What does that mean?

Childhood dreams do come true! Another surprise a few months later, even before Hawaii, I was in a bus on a Colorado mountain road. The little cow girl in me who dreamed of riding her horse in the West had suddenly actualized.

Little did I know how connected it was to the retreat in Hawaii! Sheer drop off! I could feel the canyon below as my stomach reacted to my thoughts. What if the bus gets too close to the edge and falls off the road!

Opening my heart to whom I was created to be, confused my corporate outer life brain! Share in the co-creation of a new world of love and wisdom as spiritual Oneness? Join with others as a community? New questions and experiences described in the brochure were excitingly foreign. Or were they just plain terrifying. Is this familiar at all for you?

Tears of vulnerability just flowed for one whole week I was in this community. I received new life. Participation with loving, caring, highly inspired people clarified the cause of my burnout. Have you ever had an experience of remembering who you really are?

This experience let me know the importance of connecting deeply with others. I recognized it as one solution to rising world problems. They also shared cutting edge solutions in health, government, education, food, water and more including cures for cancer. Is there any response now raised within you?

What was I hearing? I could not continue living in my ignorance. I had no idea how important all this knowledge would come to be for me! Does any of this cause a reaction within you? I woke up deeply and suddenly. The focus on self-care as love and appreciation for who we truly are as people and environments became real. Now responsibly true. What is your experience of this?

Suddenly I knew my destiny was to be a contributing part of this wisdom. I saw that my false trust in outer circumstances that I could see or control was in denial. New commitments began in love and forgiveness! Does any of this stir you?

Oneness within one's true self and of each other was always the intention from the moment of our creation. This outcome for all called me forth as a knowing of the true focus of the upcoming time on planet Earth. Is any of this true for you?

"In six weeks you will leave all you have ever known. You will travel across this country. You will connect with many of these and other wise people. This is an inner journey. You will come to know the truth of who you are in service to the divine within you."

Those were the words I heard as I sat in my seat on the flight home from the retreat in Colorado. Shocking but true, I knew. Have you experienced a calling of self-love and appreciation that includes forgiveness of all you have ever known who lived? I had no idea this was an intervention. I had no idea I was separate from myself. What spiritual path? I only knew I was never good enough to be forgiven by God.

Somehow I was guilty of something that had me feel unforgiven since age six. It was like an addiction for me. Go to confession, make something up, feel okay and belong for a little while. Since sixth grade, this was my way of being. Do you relate in any way?

Exactly six weeks later I drove out of the driveway in my light blue Subaru Brat mini truck. Inside this truck was my large Lab/Saint Bernard dog, the possessions I had kept, as well as the thought, "What have I done?"

I headed west again to our first of many destined connections. Last stop I thought would be Hawaii in December to join the retreat led by the minister who woke up my burnout! Little did I know, my traveling would not stop for years! What parts of you might show up in challenging new circumstances?

Learning began immediately and continuously and spiraled me way outside the box. Reconnections very quickly became awakenings of new connections in all areas of life.

Is change a friend for you?

Cutting edge people globally involved stimulated my identity. My actions responded way beyond my expectations from their support. Courageously with wisdom I was prepared for major transformation.

Two Nobel Prize winners offered me complimentary trainings. They saw my commitment and fear. First the founder of Accelerated Learning taught me my dominant learning style in how I learn. Amazed, I was released from my painful identity of being stupid.

The hidden rage flowed through me in my two-week experience of his brilliance. Deep grief from not recognizing my learner style touched and healed my heart and identity. I now use this for myself and clients. Forgiveness is always needed to heal the loss of the true self.

Another Nobel Prize winner awakened me to the effects of inner and outer energies as life force. The necessity of energy to be able to flow and connect within myself for health and well-being challenged me as one who often holds her breath in fear. Do you give your body, mind, emotions, and spirit regular and deep breaths?

Muscle testing was a mandatory "yes" to my healing. Amazing, brilliant, cutting edge, internationally known teachers were my next support and gift. This scientifically, medically recognized tool would contribute to my being alive. Would you have been open to this?

That was my beginning of years and years of training in service in determining what was true and what lie lived in my unconscious mind. Do you recognize your calling within that leads you to unexpected results?

Cutting edge learners that became internationally known mentors saved my life. Now I am one desiring to support others as I was supported and prepared for life changes. I learned if I am not growing I am dying. Do you trust change? My experience is that a messenger is always sent before I need the message. As you will see, so it was when I experienced this first out of the box test.

The doctor came up to me, looked at me, put his hand around the front of my throat and said: "You need to get to a doctor quick!" My mind and mouth said: "Do I have cancer? My dad is dying of throat cancer in Florida." What might you have done or felt?

His look at me did not say "no." He just walked away as the doctor chosen to do a routine exam for my upgraded position at the hospital. In terror, new place, new job, two days until Christmas, my daughter is arriving tomorrow, no answer from the yellow page calls. I called back for help. The nurse's angry words brought the doctor to the phone.

I heard him say "I was just trying to scare you; you have a week." Then he gave me a doctor's name. A week later, after listening to the new doctor affirm the need for immediate thyroid surgery, the new wiser me refused.

All my connections and new learning knew the symptom is not the root cause. I refused knowing I had work to do to live. I asked the gentle doctor to muscle test me. In shock but willing to see my body show stress or truth he did.

God always was in charge in the perfect support I would need, despite what I thought I needed. The muscle test indicated a strong inner response to refusing surgery while opening to the root cause through action. How do you actualize Truth in extreme circumstances?

My return check-up a year later proved the truth of my choice and healing. As is true of this one, all the spontaneous healings of the six I did experience have been medically, scientifically, and spiritually proven. When something greater has you on a path, can you trust the creator of the path?

I felt a very strange feeling as I put the key into the ignition. My ear felt like rubber with no inner connection. Then the terrifying numbness continued down the right side of my body to my foot, during the two blocks drive home.

The ambulance and my friend arrived at the same time I made it home. "Too healthy to have had a stroke is what I heard, but we need to make certain." The attendants agreed to let my friend drive me if I would go directly to the hospital.

Being lifted into the car was a new experience as was waiting in the emergency room all day for an opening for an MRI. We made good use of the time and my training exploring for beliefs, emotions, and traumas all day.

There was no fear only the wisdom and determination to find the root cause of this sudden symptom. The MRI report read by the doctor was forwarded to a neurologist for immediate spinal surgery within the week. "Your spine is closing up," said the doctor as we parted.

However, by the time we left the hospital, the full feeling had returned on my right side. I was full of gratitude for that and that my friend had stayed with me all day long. It was my first experience of that support; I had been alone in all other healing except for a practitioner. Loving support is the greatest healer! Would you agree?

I woke up the next morning, sat up on the side of the bed. Numbness started. I heard myself say: "If this is going to happen, I am not going to be able to go anywhere or do anything." It was as if I shifted an old inner negative decision as a result of the previous day's experiences. My friend told me what to do from his prayer. I did. Would you?

The moment I did what he said, I had a miracle as a memory. The cord at birth had been wrapped around my head from my forehead to the base of my neck in a circle.

Immediately the feeling on my right side returned, has never left since; it has been at least ten years. I have never seen the MRI. That huge shift in consciousness brought a miracle into existence. I healed. The MRI still showed the cause of the symptom. The symptom could permanently leave. We had addressed the root cause. I sense my belief in being stupid and all that surrounded that belief as a lie was the root cause.

What do you believe about your mind?

The neurologist's office called the next day to say they refused to see or treat me. I had been asked if I had insurance. I had to say no, also to the $300 cash they required. The report is still in their office for about ten years now. Research has proven the lack of forgiveness to be one of the major causes of disease, returning symptoms, and ongoing lack of health. Much of my unforgiven issues were stored in my unconscious mind as forgotten repressed memories. Did you know that about you?

"Gail, do you have cancer?" he asked. I said, "No." His reply was that all my symptoms were of cancer. He told me to sit in silence, to look, to see. I reluctantly did, I saw, and I did admit I had cancer. One more time, a symptom!

He wanted to put me in the hospital. I refused to continue the vicious circle of be well, get sick, work hard to pay the costs, get sick, be well, go back to work doubly hard to pay the bills.

Bottom line, he agreed to put me on a healing cleanse. I went home and was to return the next morning to pick up the cleanse and begin it for a month. Unexpected as this was, I felt a huge fear come over me.

Exhausted, I went to bed, woke up, felt terrible, phone rang, friend telling me about a God-gifted healer who had passed. She said he worked from the other side with God and his gifts that had healed thousands. She knew how ill I was. I fell asleep, woke with a jolt, and heard a voice in my head say: "Your bone cancer is going to be healed; it will be painful."

I fell asleep again, woke up in horrendous pain, as if all the bones in my shoulders and spine were on fire, burning up. I passed out, woke up hours later in sopping sweat, sheets, and clothes. My healing was confirmed by the doctor the next day on all levels.

He gave me a stronger cleanse that would take about three weeks to get the toxic residue out of my body. This was true including ten pounds of release from all parts of my body. Tears of gratitude still come as I share this with you. How was this for you to experience reading? This was my last diagnosis and need of cancer healing. People noticed immediately the difference in my spirituality. Spontaneous healings have needed to happen for me or I would not be here. More tears of deep gratitude as I share.

There is a true identity within us as a unique expression of the divine love of God. This is our origin that gives us infinite potential and possibility of healing experiences and a way of being that unites us all in Oneness.

My acceptance of my true identity was the only way I could release all the lies of guilt, shame, failure and judgment. This was my only true connection to divine unconditional love that could heal me and my past false identities and beliefs.

I am alive. There was a time I did not want to be. I was about ten years old when this happened. My mother attempted suicide. I believed she was dead. As the ambulance attendants rolled the stretcher through the room, my father held a notebook in front of me. With deep emotion, he pointed his finger at me and asked why I did not tell him. I froze. I had never seen it before.

He then left, taking my younger sister with him. I was all alone. I walked outside. I climbed my favorite pine tree, up and up, like always to see. My pet calf was usually out there with the cows I loved.

I saw nothing but the buzzing electric wire in front of me. I reached out with my right hand to grasp it; my guilt and sorrow were so deep. I should have been there. I had not been taking care of her, like always, when she was so sad. It was my fault. I reached out.

A Presence came. I did not grasp the wire. Something got me down out of the tree. At the same time, unknown to me, my mother chose to live, proven spiritually by church officials as an angelic intervention. This was my first spiritual miracle. Have you experienced miracles that deeply touch you?

The trauma was so great I "forgot" all memory. The guilt and responsibility for others' lives became a way of life for me in fifth grade. I carried the desire to no longer live hidden way down deeply in my unconscious. Autoimmune disease began. How is it for you to hear other's traumatic experiences?

In my low self-esteem another trauma followed. I was kidnapped by two men, fought fiercely so was dumped out on a dirt road. I still do not know how I got home. Trauma upon trauma, abuse, attacks, all became stored way down within. Do you believe these can create symptoms of disease?

These things then attached to emotions, images, and beliefs were a big part of the root cause of all the life threatening illnesses. The last of the memories that needed conscious healing were storing a desire to die, an unworthiness to live. I have learned that two things are necessary for being authentically alive. One is to be living in forgiveness and allow love, joy, peace and truth to be the dominant inner self-love presence.

For me this has meant healing my relationship with God as a complete surrender of all that keeps me separate from self, others, and especially my divine connection with all the gifts that benefit the highest for all.

The second is the commitment to love and appreciate myself and others as a unique expression of the divine love of God. This includes the extraordinary gifts I have, as do others, and to receive these and give them. Because human love is always conditional in some way, knowing I am forgiven allows divine love to flow to me and through me. This then allows me to be God's love and share God's love, the greatest gift of all to and for all.

This then creates all the miracles of my, and our, deepest desires within reflected back from the outer world. My greatest lesson in all of this was letting go of giving power to outer world circumstances for my identity and desires. What is your greatest learning?

At one time, the outer world was what I called life. I had no relationship with the truth that life is inside me as a divine gift of Love. I learned that a focus on life out there for solutions was fear and stress in action. Do you experience letting go as a surrender that gives inner peace?

We have the power to heal. Once we increase our love through forgiveness everything starting with our cells in our body, mind, and spirit return to truth as forgiveness, freedom, wisdom, and finally the ultimate innocence of programmed beliefs, emotions, and actions controlling our lives with lies. I learned that this forgiveness must include complete acceptance and inner peace or there is more to forgive. Peace is my inner guide. What is your experience of peace?

People came before me with the God given wisdom I needed to heal into wholeness within. Then the outer body healed. My prayer is that I may be the same for others as a messenger of true contribution for the highest in Oneness for all concerned.

My greatest desire since childhood is to be a difference that makes a difference. A doctor once gave me a surprise check. It was a large check and he said: "I know you will never put up, shut up, or stop helping people!" This is true; he knew me well.

During the first month of my journey I was walking on a beach feeling the waves come over my feet. I looked down and saw a small grey amazing rock. It had a number of holes clear through it. In awe I picked it up and turned it over and over. Just like me I thought, empty within. Holes from lack of forgiveness, loss of identity, and ignorance of truth. I accepted this rock as a challenge and an opportunity to heal.

Today I know myself as healed, wise, and forgiven. I accept the gift of my true identity as a unique expression of the divine love of God. My simplified focus is being an empowered contributor in the evolving new world of peace.

What do you Know?

About The Author

Gail Marie Goodin has dedicated her life in service of empowering people and organizations with the goal of creating oneness on the planet. She has served as a mentor in areas of education, government, and volunteer organizations for over 26 years.

Gail's achievements are a result of service at the local, state, national and international levels, including: invitations to White House briefings, a leader of a ten million member volunteer organization, featured in a Fortune 500 magazine for outstanding volunteer service, and Outstanding Young Woman of the Year in the State of Maine

Gail Marie also participated in a government project that addressed the healing and stewardship for lands of mass burial grounds in Russia, received mentorship from two Nobel Prize winners and was invited to co-author this book.

Gail Marie experiences inner joy, compassion and fulfillment when she mentors individuals and groups in Self Care. Her unique approach is transformative to her clients.

Gail loves to mentor people willing to commit to living the identity, infinite potential and vision of the Absolute Authentic Partnership (AAP).

The AAP has been endorsed by a number of leaders in

energy medicine, spirituality, and accelerated learning, as a tool to empower self-care and gifts of life force.

Please contact Gail at the email below for more information or visit her website for a better understanding of the services she offers, all directed to give her clients results in greater love, joy, peace and well-being.

website: gailmariegoodin.wordpress.com
email: pathofjoy.innerjourney@gmail.com

68356111R00184

Made in the USA
Charleston, SC
12 March 2017